Deleuze Studies
Volume 9 Number 3 2015

Deleuze. Guattari.Schizoanalysis. Education.

Edited by Greg Thompson and David Savat

Edinburgh University Press

This publication is available as a book (ISBN: 9781474406581) or as a single issue or part of a subscription to *Deleuze Studies*, Volume 9 (ISSN: 1750-2241). Please visit www.euppublishing.com/journal/dls for more information.

Subscription rates for 2016

Four issues per year, published in February, May, August and November

		Tier	UK	EUR	RoW	N. America
Institutions	Print& online	1	£143.00	£157.60	£166.80	$283.50
		2	£178.50	£193.10	£202.30	$344.00
		3	£223.00	£237.60	£246.80	$419.50
		4	£267.50	£282.10	£291.30	$495.00
		5	£303.50	£318.10	£327.30	$556.50
	Online	1	£121.50	£121.50	£121.50	$206.50
		2	£152.00	£152.00	£152.00	$258.50
		3	£189.50	£189.50	£189.50	$322.00
		4	£228.00	£228.00	£228.00	$387.50
		5	£258.00	£258.00	£258.00	$438.50
	Additional print volumes		£120.50	£135.00	£144.00	$245.00
	Single issues		£45.50	£51.50	£54.00	$92.00
Individuals	Print		£42.00	£56.50	£66.00	$112.00
	Online		£42.00	£42.00	£42.00	$71.50
	Print & online		£53.00	£67.50	£77.00	$131.00
	Back issues/single copies		£11.50	£15.00	£17.50	$30.00
	Student Print		£25.00	£39.50	£49.00	$83.50
	Student Online		£25.00	£25.00	£25.00	$42.50
	Student Print & Online		£32.00	£46.50	£56.00	$95.00

How to order

Subscriptions can be accepted for complete volumes only. Print prices include packing and airmail for subscribers outside the UK. Volumes back to the year 2000 (where applicable) are included in online prices. Print back volumes will be charged at the current volume subscription rate.

All orders must be accompanied by the correct payment. You can pay by cheque in Pound Sterling or US Dollars, bank transfer, Direct Debit or Credit/Debit Card. The individual rate applies only when a subscription is paid for with a personal cheque, credit card or bank transfer.

To order using the online subscription form, please visit www.euppublishing.com/page/dls/subscribe

Alternatively you may place your order by telephone on +44 (0)131 650 4196, fax on +44 (0)131 662 3286 or email to journals@eup.ed.ac.uk using your Visa or Mastercard credit card. Don't forget to include the expiry date of your card, the security number (three digits on the reverse of the card) and the address that the card is registered to.

Please make your cheque payable to Edinburgh University Press Ltd. Sterling cheques must be drawn on a UK bank account.

If you would like to pay by bank transfer or Direct Debit, contact us at journals@eup.ed.ac.uk and we will provide instructions.

Contents

Articles

Education and the Relation to the Outside: A Little Real
Reality   273
David Savat and Greg Thompson

The Dictionaries in Which We Learn to Think   301
Tim Flanagan

Classroom Video Data and the Time-Image: An-Archiving the
Student Body   318
Elizabeth de Freitas

Slave to the Rhythm: The Problem of Creative Pedagogy and
the Teaching of Creativity   337
Francis Russell

Saints, Jesters and Nomads: The Anomalous Pedagogies of
Lacan, Žižek, ... Deleuze and Guattari   356
jan jagodzinski

Forum on Schizoanalysis

Assemblage Theory and Its Discontents   382
Ian Buchanan

Schizo-Feminist Educational Research Cartographies   393
Jessica Ringrose

Producing the NAPLAN Machine: A Schizoanalytic
Cartography   410
Greg Thompson and Ian Cook

A Strange Craving to be Motivated: Schizoanalysis,
Human Capital and Education   424
Sam Sellar

Fucking Teachers   437
P. Taylor Webb

Notes on Contributors   452

Education and the Relation to the Outside: A Little Real Reality

David Savat   University of Western Australia and
Greg Thompson   Murdoch University

Abstract

One of the more dominant themes around the use of Deleuze and Guattari's work, including in this special issue, is a focus on the radical transformation that educational institutions are undergoing, and which applies to administrator, student and educator alike. This is a transformation that finds its expression through teaching analytics, transformative teaching, massive open online courses (MOOCs) and updateable performance metrics alike. These techniques and practices, as an expression of control society, constitute the new sorts of machines that frame and inhabit our educational institutions. As Deleuze and Guattari's work posits, on some level these are precisely the machines that many people in their day-to-day work as educators, students and administrators assemble and maintain, that is, desire. The meta-model of schizoanalysis is ideally placed to analyse this profound shift that is occurring in society, felt closely in the so-called knowledge sector where a brave new world of continuous education and motivation is instituting itself.

Keywords: Deleuze, Guattari, schizoanalysis, education, control society, surveillance

Deleuze Studies 9.3 (2015): 273–300
DOI: 10.3366/dls.2015.0188
© Edinburgh University Press
www.euppublishing.com/journal/dls

What does schizoanalysis ask? Nothing more than a bit of a *relation to the outside*, a little real reality.

Deleuze and Guattari 1983: 334

Capitalist society can endure many manifestations of interest, but not one manifestation of desire [...], even at the kindergarten level.

1983: 379

One of the aims of *Deleuze. Guattari. Schizoanalysis. Education.* is to focus on the radical reconfiguration that education is undergoing, impacting educator, administrator, institution and 'sector' alike. More to the point, it is the responses to that process of reconfiguration – this newly emerging assemblage – that are a key focal point in this issue. Essential to these responses, we propose, is Deleuze and Guattari's method of schizonalysis, which offers a way to not only understand the rules of this new game, but also, hopefully, some escape from the promise of a brave new world of continuous education and motivation. A brave new world of digitised courses, impersonal and corporate expertise, updateable performance metrics, massive open online courses (MOOCs), learning analytics, transformative teaching and learning, online high-stakes testing in the name of transforming and augmenting human capital, overlays the corporeal practices of institutional surveillance, examination and categorical sorting. A brave new world, importantly, where people's continuous education is instituted less, or not simply, through disciplinary practices, and increasingly through a constant and continuous sampling and profiling of not simply performance but their activity, measured against the profiled activity of a 'like' age group, person or institution. This continuous education, including the sampling that accompanies it, we are all informed through various information and marketing campaigns, is in our best interest. An interest that is driven and governed by an ever-increasing corporatisation and monetisation of 'the knowledge sector', as well as an interest that is sustained through an ever-increasing and continuous debt.

Education, of course, is an important *leitmotif* in the work of Deleuze and Guattari. This special issue of *Deleuze Studies* attends to education in a number of ways, from theoretical pieces to applied pieces. What is common to the pieces in this issue is the engagement with the conceptual and analytic tools provided by way of Deleuze and Guattari's work, which are used to trouble education orthodoxies, to think beyond those coded or institutionalised practices, enunciations and performances, paranoia and complexes, that infiltrate, pervade, inculcate and increasingly constitute the education surface. The papers selected in this special issue come from the *Deleuze. Guattari.*

Schizoanalysis. Education. conference held in Perth in 2013, which aimed to bring together education researchers and theorists interested in the work of Gilles Deleuze and Felix Guattari. This was a timely gathering as the use of Deleuze and Guattari's work is becoming more and more prevalent, perhaps due to the particular conditions that trouble education so much.

That said, we note that the engagement of the field of education with the work of Deleuze and Guattari is relatively recent, compared with many of their post-1960s French contemporaries, such as Bourdieu and Foucault. Over the past two decades an emerging body of work has grappled with the somewhat daunting task of applying Deleuzian concepts to education assemblages. Of particular note were the early contributions of Elizabeth St Pierre and Inna Semetsky to considerations of a nomadic research approach (St Pierre 1997), subjectivity (St Pierre 2004), becoming (Semetsky 2006) and semiotics respectively (Semetsky 1999).

The connection between Deleuze and the classroom is well known. There is a multiple-becoming of Deleuze as student, Deleuze as teacher and Deleuze as professor. When Deleuze worked as a teacher at Amiens High School from 1948–52, we are informed that he 'adopted an idiosyncratic teaching style – addressing the most concrete problems facing his students – sports, flirting, animals – with humour' which extended to playing the saw when he tired of teaching (Dosse 2011: 101). Deleuze, of course, also taught in his university career, where his classes were unusual for the context. As Stengers recalled:

> Even when teaching, Deleuze would never answer a question, enter into a discussion or explain himself. He would listen and smile. Maybe what you would feel as an answer would come later, but in an indirect way and as an event. You would never know what kind of part, if any, your question or suggestion had played in what you received as an answer. Here, for the first time, I felt as if I was addressed, as if something that matters had to be conveyed to me – not to me as a person but as somebody who would have to go on living in this world for some time ... Deleuze loved the Nietzschean image of the arrow thrown as far as possible, without knowing who will pick it up, who will become a relayer. (Stengers 2006)

At Vincennes from 1970, Deleuze was inserted into a radical university, where open discussions rather than lectures were the norm, multidisciplinary approaches replaced traditional courses, and experimental teaching was demanded by the students. Accounts of Deleuze's teaching seem almost impossibly positive, he was exemplary. His classes were always packed and overflowing so that it was hard for Deleuze to get in the door (Dosse 2011: 356). Deleuze's practice as teacher was both a portrait of the strategic 'humble assistant' opposed to the established orthodoxy of the authoritarian master as much as it was a true mastership of the emitting of signs (Bogue 2013: 22). Of note is what Dosse called the 'international diaspora fascinated by Deleuze as his classes were full of foreign students from all over the world' (2011: 360). Deleuze's pedagogy, and his understanding of what it means to learn, is taken up by Flanagan (2015) in this issue in the context of language learning. This pedagogical thrust is extended by Russell (2015) who asks whether creativity and innovation may be conceived as pedagogies of difference at all.

Guattari, on the other hand, is often described more as an activist than as an academic. That said, his approach to activism must be seen as pedagogic as much as transveral, in that he saw that intellectual work needed to move beyond the academic, and become 'public', so as to shake up the disciplined approaches to knowledge he saw in universities, government organisations and institutions. In this, he was particularly interested in working with professionals with institutional affiliations, such as psychiatrists, anthropologists, teachers and psychologists (Dosse 2011: 76). Indeed, Guattari's work at La Borde may be seen as a group pedagogy, concerned as it was with the promotion of 'human relations that do not automatically fall into roles or stereotypes but open onto fundamental relations of a metaphysical kind that bring out the most radical and basic alienations of madness or neurosis' (quoted in Massumi's introduction to Deleuze and Guattari 2005: x). Guattari's group pedagogy is further evidenced by the creation of the Federation of Institutional Study Groups and Research (FGERI) in 1965. FGERI was successful in winning government research grants and published their own journal. In this issue, Jagodzinski's (2015) paper looks at Deleuze and Guattari's 'public' pedagogy counterposed to the pedagogies of Lacan and Žižek.

However, apart from a general interest value, it has not been Deleuze and Guattari's practice as teachers and pedagogues that fascinates education researchers. Rather, it is the conceptual and theoretical tools that Deleuze and Guattari's work provide, and especially their potential to make some sense of what it means to live a life in a capitalised, paranoiac education world and what may be possible beyond, or what a politics of affirmation might look like, that interests people. Perhaps, as St Pierre argues, it is because 'we need new concepts in order to think and live education differently' (2004: 285), as:

> we are indeed in crisis at the beginning of the twenty-first century as the educational philosophy privileged by the federal government imposes on all

who care deeply about education 'flimsy concepts' that are 'too regular, petrified, and reduced to a framework ... the most universal concepts, those presented as eternal forms or values [that] are the most skeletal and least interesting'. (St Pierre 2004: 286)

So, rather than stressing biographical accounts, the focus is on the importance of the concepts and the use that is made of the processes and practices of formal education that formed a powerful lens through which Deleuze and Guattari worked through their conceptual work.

Certain concepts have been 'put to work' in educational theory, from explorations of concepts of affect (Cole 2011; Sellar 2014), the event (de Freitas 2013), rhizomes and nomadic thought, to specific education assemblages, such as the literacy machine (Masny and Cole 2012), the curriculum machine (Wallin 2010), the teaching machine (Mercieca 2012), the testing machine (Thompson and Cook 2012, 2014), the policy machine (Webb and Gulson 2012), and the research machine (Coleman and Ringrose 2013). There has also been work that focuses on specific subjects, often arts (Allan 2014), science (Gough 2006) and mathematics (Gangle 2013) as sites of multiplicity. As well, there is widespread use of Deleuze and Guattari to understand specific segments of education, such as early childhood education (Sumsion 2014). The field is already so profuse, trying to limit it to a few key references is obviously a failed enterprise, already it 'flees on all sides' to such an extent that we must leave out more than we can include. However, this proliferation itself is interesting, why is it that Deleuze and Guattari resonate so strongly, and why at this time?

Of course, the proliferation of these concepts, and the glee with which they may be purloined, is not without its challenges. In terms of the uptake of Deleuze and Guattari's concepts in education, Wallin (2012) has diagnosed 'two major symptoms pertaining to the reception of Deleuzian thought in educational philosophy and curriculum theorizing'. Firstly, there has been a depoliticisation of Deleuze, 'increasingly apparent through the systematic reduction of such inherently political formations as the rhizome, the fold, smooth space, and nomadology into vogue theoretical slogans' (Wallin 2012: 148), a point that Buchanan also stressed with the use of the concept of the rhizome in other areas, including thinking about the Internet (2009). Importantly, for Wallin (2012: 148) 'the development of Deleuzian concepts for education have not been rendered dangerous enough, falling back into the kinds of personal exploration, perpetual semiosis, and postmodern relativism eschewed by Deleuze'. The second symptom that Wallin identifies is the 'dubious "disappearance" of Deleuze's collaborator, Felix Guattari' because 'it is in engagement with the revolutionary politics of Guattari that we might begin to cultivate a sense for what remains most dangerous in the collective Deleuzeguattari desiring-machine' (Wallin 2012: 148). On this point see also the special issue of *Deleuze Studies* (Genosko 2012) on Felix Guattari as well as *The Guattari Effect* (Alliez and Goffey 2011). To this we would add that the ethic of critique of individualism that is at the heart of their project is rarely embraced, as is the charge to seek a politics, and an education, of affirmation rather than simulacra and repetition.

The importance of institutional education, as a machine of coding and encoding that functions as repetition and simulacra, is for Deleuze and Guattari emphasised in *A Thousand Plateaus* as an 'abstract machine acting not at all as a signifier but as a kind of diagram (a single abstract machine for the prison and the school and the barracks and the hospital and the factory ...)' (Deleuze and Guattari 2005: 67). Institutional education is stratified through a double pincer movement, an 'unstable equilibrium' such that there are always 'two distinct formalizations in reciprocal presupposition and constituting a double-pincer... We are never signifier or signified. We are stratified' (Deleuze and Guattari 2005: 67). Partly this stratification proceeds through language through those order-words of the schoolmistress for whom each 'order always and already concerns prior orders'.

> The compulsory education machine does not communicate information; it imposes upon the child semiotic coordinates ... we must define an abominable faculty consisting in emitting, receiving, and transmitting order-words. Language is made not to be believed but to be obeyed, and to compel obedience. (Deleuze and Guattari 2005: 76)

Not only is institutional education central to processes of stratification, it is central to segmentation, as power operates through:

> a straight line or a number of straight lines, of which each segment represents an episode or 'proceeding': as soon as we finish one proceeding we begin another, forever proceduring or procedured, in the family, in school, in the army, on the job. School tells us, 'You're not at home anymore'... these figures of segmentarity, the binary, circular, and linear, are bound up with one another, even cross over into each other, changing according to the point of view. (Deleuze and Guattari 2005: 209)

The school is a power centre or foci which is 'molecular and exercises its power on a micrological fabric in which it exists only as diffuse, dispersed, geared down, miniaturized, perpetually displaced, acting

by fine segmentation, working in detail and in the details of detail'
(Deleuze and Guattari 2005: 224). de Freitas' (2015) paper is a powerful
musing on how technology such as videoed lesson research reinserts this
molecular and micrological fabric through specific conceptualisations of
the student body.

Of particular interest in this regard is that education, its processes,
practices and abstract machines are changing. In Deleuze's short essay
'Postscript on the Societies of Control' he argues that disciplinary forms
of power that have sustained the school are giving way to a new,
frightful, social, institutional and subjective power exemplified by modulation. For Deleuze 'disciplinary society was what we already no longer
were, what we had ceased to be' (Deleuze 1992: 3). Deleuze described
this as a society of control typified by a mode of power that is 'short-term
and of rapid rates of turnover, but also continuous and without limit'
in comparison to 'long duration, infinite and discontinuous' disciplinary
modes of governance and self-governance (Deleuze 1992: 6).

In societies and their institutions dominated by disciplinary and
thermodynamic power, moulds such as physically immobile enclosures
and institutions 'cast' individuals. However, in societies of control
power is modulatory; 'a self-deforming cast that will continuously
change from one moment to the other, or like a sieve whose mesh
will transmute from point to point' (Deleuze 1992: 4). In disciplinary
societies, power is contained within the institution, and operates in
part through the construction of clearly defined spaces specific to which
are particular functions – shifting place means starting again within the
relations of power. In societies of control, power does not operate
through enclosure, meaning that one is always subject, that there is
no starting again as a consequence of shifting space. Sellar (2015)
argues that human capital theory, particularly as it pertains to education
through organisation such as the OECD, is emblematic of this transition.
The limitless postponement that characterises modulating power means
that the subject is never finished with the technologies of power, to the
extent that in some respects no subject is created at all (Savat 2013).
Stated differently, disciplinary power creates a student as a defined
form, while modulation creates an entirely formless student, essential
for continuous education, and the combined result being dividuality
(Savat 2013). In such a context the school student never starts again
and will always be constituted by the various forms of measurement
enacted at schools. Thus, control is of a new modality and ethic of
power.

Critical for the disciplinary society are the 'environments of enclosure' such as prisons, schools, hospitals and families that work 'to concentrate; to distribute in space; to order in time; to compose a productive force within the dimension of space-time whose effect will be greater than the sum of its component forces' (Deleuze 1992: 3). Lazzarato (2006: 173) argues that environments of enclosure 'fix forces and their relations into precise forms by according them a reproductive function' that has the effect of confining the *outside* or 'the virtual, the power of metamorphosis, becoming' (175). The purpose of the disciplinary school is to neutralise difference and the power of variation to make individuals, and masses, governable and self-governing as a direct effect of what is actualised through enclosure. Control societies are characterised by technologies and dispositifs of 'acting at a distance' that deliver 'corresponding processes of subjectivation and subjection' including the formation of new publics that take place less in *space* than in *time* (Lazzarato 2006: 180). 'The capture, control and regulation of action at a distance of one mind on another takes place through the modulation of flows of desires and beliefs and through the forces (memory and attention) that make these flows circulate' (Lazzarato 2006: 185).

However, while Deleuze's essay on control has taken on an important role for education research, particularly in the areas of education policy (Watson 2010), testing (Thompson and Cook 2012), accountability (Webb 2011) and teacher/principal subjectivity (Ball 2000), it is fair to say that it has often been understood as an extension of discipline, and read through a Foucaultean lens, rather than understanding that Deleuze is outlining a radically different modality of power that journeys far beyond articulations of the liberal–humanist subject and/or capitalist individual. Indeed, Foucault too in his later work recognised a profound shift was under way. In essence, and a key focus of the collection of papers in this special issue, it concerns what is to be done when those historical machines and modes of subjectification become affected through different, and digital, corporate and computerised/cybernetic machines (Deleuze 1995: 175). If, as Deleuze suggests, control operates through 'continual monitoring', the challenge is 'to create vacuoles of non-communication, circuit breakers so that we can elude control' (Deleuze 1995: 175). If Foucault gave us the methods of archaeology and genealogy, Deleuze and Guattari gave us schizoanalysis as a new weapon for both eluding control without falling back onto an image of the institutions of 'harshest confinement as part of a wonderful happy past' (Deleuze 1995: 175).

Schizoanalysis for Education

Deleuze and Guattari offer a variety of definitions of the term schizoanalysis. Indeed, Deleuze expressed a view not long after the publication of *Anti-Oedipus* that they 'renounced the use of the term' (2004b: 278), along with other terms such as 'desiring-machine'. As he explained: 'We don't know very well what they mean, we no longer believe in the words.' Of course, he also qualified as part of that explanation that they did not care all that much for the meaning of words, as they are 'totally interchangeable'. The frustration that this might generate on the part of a reader is in part what Deleuze and Guattari perhaps wanted to produce. That should not surprise us though, and as Hughes (2012) explains, Deleuze's work has a rigorous conceptual structure that enables words to change meaning across and within texts. As many have pointed out, this suggests, as Deleuze and Guattari themselves do, that we need to focus less on what the term schizoanalysis means, and more on what it does, especially in terms of how it functions in relation to other concepts.

Guattari (1998) notes that from the outset his own project, which he 'loosely' termed schizoanalysis, 'was never conceived as a self-enclosed field', and was both 'humbler in its aims and broader in its scope' than, for example, psychoanalysis. He also saw it as already existing in a variety of situations and forms, and emphasised that it 'has the potential for becoming a discipline for reading other systems of modelisation' (433). However, he also stressed that it should not function as a general model 'but as an instrument for deciphering systems of modelisation in various other fields or, to put it somewhat differently, as a meta-model' (433). As he defined it, albeit provisionally, schizoanalysis is '*the analysis of the incidence of assemblages of enunciation among semiotic and subjective productions within a given, problematic context*' (Guattari 1998: 433) (original emphasis). Ringrose (2015) in this issue puts schizoanalysis 'to work' within a feminist project which desires to push back and through binaries and dualisms through attention to the psyche-subjectivity.

Some of Deleuze's own texts are instances of a schizoanalysis, broadly constituting a 'transcendental and materialist analysis' that explores a 'transcendental consciousness' and that takes various formulations across his body of work (Hughes 2008, 2012). In particular what Deleuze and Guattari stress is central to their analyses, and what Deleuze (2004a) explains was Guattari's early intuition, is the idea that 'the unconscious is directly related to a whole social field, both economic and political, rather than the mythical and familial grid traditionally employed by psychoanalysis' (194). Schizoanalysis is focused on the manner in which the unconscious is situated in any given social field, as well as how this social field structures thought and action in particular sorts of ways. In this respect schizoanalysis partly defines itself very much against psychoanalysis, and Freud and others, in terms of how the relationship between the unconscious and the social field is conceptualised. In particular they take issue with Freud's metaphor of the guard that sits between the conscious and the unconscious, and the manner that Freud and others theorise repression (Bell 2012: 136). Deleuze and Guattari propose a reversal of Freud's schema of the unconscious as '[t]he unconscious does not apply pressure to consciousness; rather, consciousness applies pressure and strait-jackets the unconscious, to prevent its escape' (1983: 338).

It is precisely on this point that Deleuze and Guattari (1983) identify the first task of schizoanalysis, which is that it 'goes by way of destruction' (311). What schizoanalysis aims for is not interpretation of ideas and beliefs, not working through issues (Buchanan 2008: 117), in the manner that psychoanalysis does. Instead what it aims for is the destruction, 'with all its strength', of 'beliefs and representations' (314). In particular, of course, schizoanalysis, certainly in *Anti-Oedipus*, takes to task the beliefs that are built up, or rather held up, by psychoanalysis, and in particular Freud's approach to the unconscious and its relation to the conscious, that is, the social (Buchanan 2008). Notably they stress that 'it is not psychoanalysis that makes us believe' but rather that 'these demands come from elsewhere and from deeper down' (Deleuze and Guattari 1983: 314). Psychoanalysis is instead blamed for 'causing beliefs to survive even after repudiation; causing those who no longer believe in anything to continue believing; reconstituting a private territory for them, a private Urstaat, a private capital (dreams as capital, said Freud)' (314). One of the principal and first key tasks of schizoanalysis, then, is deterritorialisation.

Destruction, disengaging the deterritorialised flows of desire, our impulses and drives (Smith 2007: 71), while critical to schizoanalysis, is not in itself sufficient. What is equally critical is the prevention of what they term a reterritorialisation of those impulses and drives subsequent to their deterritorialisation. How, after all, 'would they keep from forming for themselves yet another ... territory' (Deleuze and Guattar 1983: 315)? As they state:

> [w]e are all little dogs, we need circuits, and we need to be taken for walks. Even those best able to disconnect, to unplug themselves, enter

into connections of desiring-machines that re-form little earths ... there is no deterritorialisation of the flows of schizophrenic desire that is not accompanied by global or local reterritorialisations, reterritorialisations that always reconstitute shores of representation. (315–16)

It is precisely for this reason that schizoanalysis consists of a second, and positive, task.

This positive task 'consists of discovering in a subject the nature, the formation, or the functioning of [their] desiring-machines', that is, the unconscious and the partial objects that constitute it (Deleuze and Guattari 1983: 322). In short, they indicate that in effect a diagram is to be constructed. Thompson and Cook (2015), in this issue, use the diagram in mapping the ways that testing machines operate in classrooms through the desiring-production of the teacher. This brings to mind the role of the schizoanalyst as a mechanic because 'schizoanalysis is solely functional' (Deleuze and Guattari 1983: 322). Vital is that the types of questions that are asked here are of the type 'how does it work?', 'what does it do?', and that questions such as 'what does it mean?' are avoided. Indeed, typically the latter question is an indication that a reterritorialisation is possibly at work (Buchanan 2008: 121). Schizoanalysis, Deleuze and Guattari explain, is not about whether something resembles something else, those 'shores of representation', such as a concept or person. Instead, schizoanalysis 'should deal solely (except in its negative task) with the machinic arrangements grasped in the context of their molecular dispersion' (1983: 323). It is the task of the schizoanalyst to discover 'what a subject's desiring-machines are, how they work, with what syntheses, what bursts of energy in the machine, what constituent misfires, with what flows, what chains, and what becomings in each case' (338). As Buchanan puts it, 'rather than asking us to get to know our inner self, [Deleuze and Guattari] require us to know how that inner self was constituted' (2008: 121).

Here it is important to stress that the three tasks of the schizoanalyst be undertaken at the same time, as well as continuously. As Deleuze and Guattari explain, the destructive task is 'in no way separable from [schizoanalysis's] positive tasks – all these tasks are necessarily undertaken at the same time' (1983: 322). Schizoanalysis, both as method and process, is about the ongoing and continual process of questioning and destroying beliefs and values, that is reterritorialisations, as well as about the ongoing and continual process of understanding how we produced those particular beliefs and values in the first place.

The third task of schizoanalysis, which is also positive, is more complex, and consists of four theses. The first thesis, they explain, is that every investment is both molar and social, that is, desiring-machines are social. Desiring-machines do not 'exist outside the social machines that they form on a large scale; and no social machines without the desiring-machines that inhabit them on a small scale' (1983: 340). Desiring-machines, that is, the unconscious (Hughes 2008: 17), and the multiplicities they constitute are inseparable from the social machines or social aggregates, and 'constitute one and the same process of production' (Deleuze and Guattari 1983: 340). This is a point they continuously stress in their work, including in their later *A Thousand Plateaus*. This also explains why Deleuze and Guattari, often to the point of frustration for some, frequently switch their own terminology regarding the molar and the molecular, as well as the interior and the exterior. One key reason they themselves offer is that what they are trying to come to terms with is a constant variation or oscillation, sometimes describing the molar and molecular 'as the paranoiac, signifying, and structured lines of integration', and at other times as 'the schizophrenic, machinic, and dispersed lines of escape' (1983: 340). In short, sometimes, they make clear, we are dealing with reterritorialisations, and sometimes with deterritorialisations. Their explanation for this is simple: 'The answer is that everywhere there exist the molecular and the molar' (1983: 340).

The second thesis is that we need to distinguish between desire and interest. As they explain, we need to distinguish in social investments between 'the unconscious libidinal investment of group or desire, and the preconscious investment of class or interest' (1983: 343). The latter they associate with larger social goals, such as the formation of class, pointing out that 'those who have an interest ... are always of a smaller number than those whose interest ... "is had" or represented' (1983: 344). On this point they explain that the concept of ideology is of no use, because what it hides are 'the real problems, which are always of an organisational nature' (1983: 344). In particular they take issue with the distinction that the concept of ideology necessarily draws between what is objective and subjective. As they point out 'everything is objective or subjective, as one wishes' (1983: 345).

Instead what Deleuze and Guattari emphasise is that we recognise that our impulses and drives are part of the infrastructure, and not something that somehow exists outside of it. Instead of relying on some distinction of the objective and the subjective, they instead propose that:

the distinction to be made passes into the economic infrastructure itself and into its investments. Libidinal economy is no less objective than political economy, and the political no less subjective than the libidinal, even though the two correspond to two modes of different investments of the same reality as social reality. (Deleuze and Guattari 1983: 345)

Libidinal investment, they state, does not 'bear upon social means and ends, but upon the full body as socius, the formation of sovereignty, or the form of power for itself, devoid of meaning and purpose, since the meanings and the purposes derive from it, and not the contrary' (1983: 345), which is why the concept of ideology is inadequate to the task. Again this highlights one of the key principles of schizoanalysis: that 'desire is always constitutive of a social field ... desire belongs to the infrastructure, not to ideology: desire is in production as social production, just as production is in desire as desiring-production' (1983: 348).

What Deleuze and Guattari aim to provide here is an explanation for why even the most excluded members of society:

invest with passion the system that opposes them, and where they always *find* an interest, since it is here that they search for and measure it. Interest always comes after. Antiproduction effuses in the system: antiproduction is loved for itself, as is the way in which desire represses itself in the great capitalist aggregate. Repressing desire, not only for others but in oneself, being the cop for others and for oneself – that is what arouses, and it is not ideology, it is economy ... A violence without purpose, a joy, *a pure joy in feeling oneself a wheel in the machine*, traversed by flows, broken by schizzes. Placing oneself in a position where one is thus traversed, broken, fucked by the socius, looking for the right place where, according to the aims and the interests assigned to us, one feels something moving that has neither an interest nor a purpose. A sort of art for art's sake in the libido, a taste for a job well done, each one his own place, the banker, the cop, the soldier, the technocrat, the bureaucrat, and why not the worker, the trade-unionist. Desire is agape. (Deleuze and Guattari 1983: 346–7, emphasis added)

Again, the important point in schizoanalysis here is the recognition that our impulses and drives always constitute a social field – are always arranged by (our) social formations, including in the sense that we desire our own repression. If that is the case then we ought, importantly, not to distinguish between a political economy and a libidinal economy. As Smith (2007: 71) explains, for Marx, for example, our thought, that is, our impulses and drives, our desire and desiring-machines, are determined by class or class consciousness, that is, the political economy, while Freud holds a view that we are somehow determined by unconscious desires, that is, a libidinal economy that typically stems from familial conflicts. Instead Deleuze and Guattari propose that desire, our drives and impulses, our desiring-machines, the unconscious, is part of the very infrastructure, that is, the economy. As Deleuze states, 'there is only one economy, not two; and desire or libido is just the subjectivity of political economy' (2004a: 195). It is also in this context that we can recognise that our 'interests' are not the same as our 'desire'. Rather, our 'interests' are codificiations of desire, that is, desire that has been captured, which, as many have pointed out (e.g. Smith 2007; Buchanan 2008), marketing and advertising are exemplary of. It is also in this context that we can immediately recognise the importance of a schizoanalysis of education, given its somewhat unique position in capitalism as a social formation.

The third thesis that forms part of the third task of schizoanalysis is that libidinal investments of the social field have primacy over familial investments, that is, that the relation to the non-familial is always primary. Here Deleuze and Guattari posit that the Oedipus complex is in fact used as a 'sublime alibi' (1983: 356) by families, and argue that what is at stake here is, in fact, the family's relation to the outside: 'the mother reduced to housework, or to a difficult and uninteresting job on the outside; children whose future remains uncertain; the father who has had it with feeding all those mouths' (356). The economic situation, Deleuze and Guattari point out, 'the relation to the outside, is what the libido invests and counterinvests as sexual libido' (356). Yet this relation to the outside is precisely what the psychoanalyst does not engage with. Indeed, the relation to the outside is precisely what is prevented from entering the psychoanalyst's office, in effect situating psychoanalysis as 'a stupefying drug, where the strangest personal dependence allows the clients to forget, during the time spent in sessions on the couch, the economic dependencies that drive them there in the first place' (357). As Deleuze and Guattari state: 'We dream of entering their offices, opening the windows and saying, "It smells stuffy in here – some relation with the outside, if you please"' (357). In this they see the family as neither some microcosm, nor the psychoanalyst as solving any problems, but rather the family as producing neurotics, while the psychoanalyst is simply engaged in 'infinite maintenance, an infinite resignation', and in this way enables subjects to simply spread sickness to their offspring (361). The task of schizoanalysis here involves that of:

> tirelessly taking apart egos and the presuppositions; liberating the prepersonal singularities they enclose and repress; mobilising the flows they would be

capable of transmitting, receiving, or intercepting; establishing always further and more sharply the schizzes and the breaks well below conditions of identity; and assembling desiring-machines that countersect everyone and group everyone with others. For everyone is a little group (un groupuscule) and must live as such – or rather, like the Zen tea box broken in a hundred places, whose every crack is repaired with cement made of gold ... Schizoanalysis is so named because throughout its entire process of treatment it schizophrenises, instead of neuroticising like psychoanalysis. (362)

The fourth thesis of schizoanalysis is that there is a 'distinction between two poles of social libidinal investment: the paranoiac, reactionary, and fascicising pole, and the schizoid revolutionary pole' (1983: 366). The former is 'defined by subjugated groups', while the latter by 'subject-groups' (367). This means that the former are characterised by 'enslavement of production and desiring-machines to the gregarious aggregates that they constitute on a larger scale', by 'molar structured aggregates that crush singularities, select them, and regularise those that they retain in codes', and by 'lines of integration and territorialisation that arrest the flows' of desire, that is the impulses and drives that constitute the desiring-machines comprising the unconscious. The subject-groups, on the other hand, are characterised by 'inverse subordination and the overthrow of power', by 'molecular singularities of singularities that ... treat the large aggregates as so many useful materials for their own elaborations', and by 'lines of escape that follow the decoded and deterritorialised flows ... ' of desire (1983: 366–7).

Clearly though, as Deleuze and Guattari acknowledge, this characterisation is not without its problems, as the relationship between the two poles or types of investment, including their respective relationship with 'preconscious investments of interest' (1983: 367), is always open to question. 'Even the most overt fascism', they explain, 'speaks the language of goals, of law, order, and reason. Even the most insane capitalism speaks in the name of economic rationality' (1983: 367). In short, as with their distinction between the molar and the molecular, as indeed with a range of other concepts, things continuously shift. This too is another reason why schizoanalysis as both method and process needs to remain open and at the level of meta-model as Guattari stated.

In offering us a brief description of the three tasks that comprise the process and method of schizoanalysis Deleuze and Guattari very consciously avoid offering a model for us to follow (Buchanan 2008: 117). It is precisely Deleuze's approach to ethics, and the manner in which he distinguishes it from morality (Smith 2007), that immediately explains why they urge us to steer away from such a model:

> Deleuze approaches modes of existence, ethically speaking, not in terms of their will, or their conscious decision making power (as in Kant), nor in terms of their interests (as in Marx, for example), but rather in terms of their drives. For Deleuze, conscious will and preconscious interest are both subsequent to our unconscious drives, and it is at the level of the drives that we have to aim our ethical analysis. (Smith 2007: 68)

It is critical to recognise in this, following Nietzsche, that it is these impulses and drives that comprise desire:

> that interpret the world, that are perspectival – and not our egos, not our conscious opinions. It is not so much that I have a different perspective on the world than you; it is rather that each of us has multiple perspectives on the world because of the multiplicity of our drives – drives that are often contradictory among themselves. (Smith 2007: 69)

It is in precisely this manner that we constitute, or rather, are constituted as and by, multiplicities, that is, 'groupuscules'. The question that drives schizoanalysis is how the social formation, that is institutions, organise these multiplicities in some particular forms rather than other particular forms, and not necessarily in forms that are in our own 'interests', or more precisely, desire. In short, why do we desire our own repression?

It should be immediately clear then that schizoanalysis is at heart a political and ethical task, especially when at the conclusion of *Anti-Oedipus* Deleuze and Guattari state that schizoanalysis does not have a political programme. Any such programme, they explain, 'would be grotesque and disquieting at the same time' (1983: 380). Schizoanalysis speaks for no group or party, nor for the masses or, indeed, for itself. Their objective here is to try and be more humble in their aims for schizoanalysis, which, they state, is to create 'impressions'. Indeed, they claim that they 'like to speak in the name of an absolute incompetence' (1983: 380).

On this their explanation of why we should not mistake the figure of the schizo for that of the revolutionary hero is especially instructive – a notion that across their work they are quite critical of. Instead, they point out that they simply distinguish 'the schizophrenic as an entity from schizophrenia as a process' (1983: 379). The figure of the schizo is therefore treated by them as simply a tool, an instrument in schizoanalysis, and not the end all and be all. The schizo, in short, is not sufficient by itself. Indeed, those who valorise the schizo, and equate it with the revolutionary, simply turn it into an heroic figure, a reterritorialisation. Deleuze and Guattari's schizo is precisely the person 'who can no longer bear "all that": money, the stock market, the death forces, Nijinsky said – values, morals, homelands, religions and private certitudes?' (341). It is precisely this person, this desire, that Melville's character of Bartleby perhaps exemplifies best, especially in his emblematic statement 'I would prefer not to', a feeling that we suspect is not unfamiliar to those in educational institutions, especially in the context of the constant 'sampling' that Deleuze speaks of in his control societies essay, infused with an increased corporatisation across various sectors of the institution that is 'education' or 'the knowledge sector'.

For Deleuze and Guattari what is essential above all is a recognition that 'everything revolves around desiring-machines and the production of desire' (1983: 381). Schizoanalysis only asks what place any socius, that is, social formation, reserves for desiring-production:

> schizoanalysis makes no distinction in nature between political economy and libidinal economy. Schizoanalysis merely asks what are the machinic, social, and technical indices on a socius that open to desiring-machines, that enter into the parts, wheels, and motors of these machines, as much as they cause them to enter into their own parts, wheels, and motors. (1983: 381)

Above all, they continually impress upon us the need to look not at the individual tasks of schizoanalysis, its one negative and two positive tasks, but instead to consider them as a whole:

> the task of schizoanalysis is ultimately that of discovering for every case the nature of the libidinal investments of the social field, their possible internal conflicts, their relationships with the preconscious investments of the same field, their possible conflicts with these – in short, the entire interplay of the desiring-machines and the repression of desire. (1983: 382)

Schizoanalysis, then, is precisely a method, though why it needs to be validated as such by those of us working in the context of educational institutions is something that itself needs consideration. It may be that there is a more strategic or tactical element to this, especially in a context of people being brought to rely on seeking 'research funding' in an increasingly 'competitive market', that is, a market where there is increasingly less funding for research at all. A beautiful machine. Beautiful in the way that one might appreciate how well the machine works, even if only as an anxiety producing machine. Webb's (2015) contribution to this issue is to consider this beautiful, if terrifying, machine in the context of the teacher and the impact of policy reform. This is especially noticeable when the latest new teaching and learning 'innovations' are introduced to staff, which staff are sometimes encouraged, sometimes coercively and forcefully so, to apply to their teaching. This is typically met with comments ranging from 'ooh, that's a great idea', to 'ooh, that's horrible' – the latter being the phrase most frequently expressed by many of us working within educational institutions. 'Education' as a general institution is especially filled with exactly such machines, whether we consider these machines in their more disciplinary mode or their modulatory mode, regardless of whether we consider administrator, student, or teacher alike.

Regardless, schizoanalysis meets the variety of definitions as to what constitutes a 'method': a procedure, a way of doing something in accordance with a plan, a technique, and, indeed, more interestingly, an 'arrangement': 'The action or process of being arranged'; 'a plan or preparation for a future event'. As Buchanan (2015) notes in his contribution, unless there is some precision to a term such as 'assemblage', and, by extension, 'schizoanalysis', it ceases to have analytic power. Any machine only functions, produces a function or, indeed, a set of functions, and opens a particular 'universe of action' as Guattari termed it (as in the case of that universal machine 'the computer'), precisely because of the specific manner in which its components are arranged in relation to each other, including in relation to those components that form part of the social formation that (re)produces that machine (Savat 2009), that is, that interest or interests. Indeed, even the inclusion of a reference to our previously published work is a product of at least several of those anxiety-producing machines that comprise part of what constitutes education and research. Those of us in higher education are all told to do it: to 'form a little machine', so as to make our 'working' lives that little bit easier. To make us that little bit more 'competitive', in whichever way the system is gamified. Whether this be getting our colleagues to cite us – the cynicism (or not) of which the automated machines that comprise Google's 'H-Ranking' could not possibly recognise – or whether this be getting told that people in 'the Humanities' should cite themselves as author more on all of their PhD students' papers, 'just like in the Sciences'. In the Australian context, for example, some higher education institutions are informing their staff that books will no longer 'count', and at best will be treated as equivalent to journal articles – oh the joy. Of course, even as we see the introduction of machines that monitor and offer minute-by-minute updates of who cites whose work in what journal, literal minute-by-minute updates of what we publish, maybe it does not really matter. Such machines are precisely what many academics, for example, in some way invest themselves in, even if only to make life bearable. At what point do people state 'we would prefer not to'? Though within the capitalist socius these things are 'only academic' – after all, most of us have a debt to attend to. We are all, in our own little ways, fully implicated, have our interests, in the system. Even our politicians and governments continuously profess that they 'care' about the state of education, including, students, teachers and researchers. Who in the current context actually still recognises the cynicism in these statements? Unless they truly still believe in the slogans they create. Or is it simply a matter that everyone has given up (Buchanan 2014).

If *Anti-Oedipus* itself is an exemplar of a schizoanalysis (Hughes 2008) then perhaps schizoanalysis is best understood as a method, a meta-model, in the manner that it introduces 'desire into thought, into discourse, into action' (Foucault 1983). Here Foucault's preface to *Anti-Oedipus* offers some insight. As Foucault points out, fascism is precisely Deleuze and Guattari's major adversary. Not only historical fascism in its various reiterations. Not only the fascism we see from religious and other fanatics, but the fascism, in all its varieties, in our own heads. To use an earlier quoted phrase: 'a pure joy in feeling oneself a wheel in the machine' (1983: 346), whether it be as student, administrator or educator. In short, *Anti-Oedipis*, and schizoanalysis more generally, is a method for living a non-fascist life as Foucault states, and in that respect precisely also a process. Of course, while Foucault presents it as an 'art' of living counter to all forms of fascism, Deleuze and Guattari continually stress that the schizoanalyst is a mechanic – that we ought to become mechanics. That is, it is important to recognise here the confluence that Deleuze and Guattari continually emphasise across their work between art, science and philosophy. After all, at the core of schizoanalysis is Guattari's earlier notion of transversality (Deleuze 2004a), as part of a method that breaks connections and establishes new connections. In short, a method and process that continuously tries to open the windows to our fascisms, and helps us understand how those windows, those machines, are constructed in the first place.

This also makes clear why the focus in their method is less on why things work the way they are, and is consistently focused on explaining how things work. Again, the model they propose for schizoanalysis is that of the mechanic, holding Kafka up as one such mechanic (Deleuze and Guattari 1986). Kafka whose insights into the mechanics of modern institutions and the desires that comprise them, our desires, reminds us, as do our many administrators on a regular basis, including those in accounting, that:

'It is not necessary to accept everything as true, one must only accept it as necessary. '
'A melancholy conclusion', said K. 'It turns lying into a universal principle.'
(Kafka 2008:192)

The Perfect Storm – Education as Control

This leads to a key point of this essay – that education is undergoing radical reconfiguration and that the meta-method of schizoanalysis offers a way to productively understand not simply the rules of this new game, but also, as the quote from Deleuze and Guattari which begins this paper suggests, a means to relate to the outside. If the physical spaces of education are breaking down as Deleuze suggests, it is not necessarily a physical destruction. It is rather an opening, or indeed a smoothing, of the limits of what can be known about educational processes due to technical limitations. For example, the classroom is opening up, and this new relation to the outside is mediated by new technical possibilities. Education policy has become increasingly interested in leveraging these openings towards steering, or control, at a distance through technologies such as standardised testing. What is most obvious about this is the scale of the investment into the technologies of control. This is a corporate realm that, at least potentially, brings edu-businesses massive profits.

Analysing this reconfiguration requires, amongst other things, a broad sweep of the radical changes underway – both those proposed and barely imagined. Murphie (2014) describes a feature of this control through the notion of education becoming an auditland. Riffing off the book *Stasiland*, which portrays the German Democratic Republic (GDR) as a country based upon the proliferation of informers and the practices of informing, Murphie (2014: 2) argues that this needs to be understood through desire, as in Stasiland 'people very often became informers not only out of fear, but out of a desire for simple survival or perhaps even promotion'. The success of Stasiland was that it created the coordinates for informing as a sense-making practice, 'everyone had to go along with the Stasi one way or another precisely because they lived in what Funder calls Stasiland – an existential territory as much as a country' (Murphie 2014: 2). Auditland is the existential territory created by technics and cultures that 'use a flexible series of control procedures that differentially declare what is (un)acceptable' (Murphie 2014: 1):

> They therefore both energise and create shifting borders around what counts as performance, variably across multiple contexts. Audit also links the local

and global, the macro and micro, pragmatically, in what I suggest is a combination of instrumental and 'operational reason' (Massumi 2002: 110). Audit thus enables the creation and exchange of new forms of value. It enables new relations of production. Here I suggest that audit also enables the insertion of the micro-events of work or living, little fragments of time or nervous energy, into a global mnemotechnics – the external memory work done in the networks of global media (Stiegler 2003a). Across these contexts, I argue that audit's technics include a powerful use of the 'pseudo a priori' (Stiegler 2003a). This allows audit to variably repurpose the significance of events – in terms of what is (un)acceptable – before, during and after their occurrence. (Murphie 2014: 1–2)

Auditland operates through creating an existential territory of crisis, competition and digitised data. For example, in terms of this desiring-production, nations, systems, institutions and individuals are induced to compete through those technologies of audit. In a control society the datafication of life and practice as a strategy of endless governance has settled over education, bringing with it the language of efficiency, effectiveness, impact and lifelong learning.

And we could go on, but the point of linking schizoanalysis to the modulatory auditland that has been superposed on the disciplinary education is to return to destroying the desire to be audited and to audit, in place of considering what might be possible if the produced desire was understood. This precisely brings us to the madness, the delirium or insanity, of the educational institutions that we inhabit, and that turn increasingly insane in their very rationality. Indeed, it does not simply bring us to the delirium of the institutions that we inhabit, but to the very delirium that comprises our habits in a very real sense, and that is at the core of our social formation, that is, capitalism:

> Reason is always a region carved out of the irrational – it is not sheltered from the irrational at all, but traversed by it and only defined by a particular kind of relationship among irrational factors. Underneath all reason lies delirium and drift. Everything about capitalism is rational, except capital ... A stock market is a perfectly rational mechanism, you can understand it, learn how it works; capitalists know not to use it; and yet what a delirium, it's mad ... It's just like theology: everything about it is quite rational – if you accept sin, the immaculate conception, and the incarnation, which are themselves irrational elements. (Deleuze in Smith 2007: 75)

If there is any one concept or question that drove Deleuze's work, as well as separately Guattari's, it is precisely his interest in institutions (Hughes 2012: 115), understood in the broadest, that is social rather than governmental, sense of the term. Indeed, to a great extent institution is simply another word for Deleuze and Guattari's concept of the assemblage.

The question, then, is why *this* is the institution, the assemblage, that we desire? Why is this what we assemble in this particular moment? The processual aspect is important to remember here. 'Why *this* system and *this* form? A thousand others, which we find in other times and places, are possible' (Deleuze in Hughes 2012: 134). Of course, as Deleuze explains, while the institution may be a model of actions, a 'system of satisfaction' or 'system of means', this 'does not license us to conclude that the institution is *explained* by the drive' (1991: 47). Instead, 'what explains it is the reflection of the drive in the imagination' (48). That is, 'the satisfaction of drives is related, not to the drive itself, but rather to the reflective drive. This is the meaning of the institution' (49). It is this aspect in the process of the satisfaction of drives, that is, this specific aspect in the process of assembling, the specific manner by which that reflection, that reflective drive, and not the drive itself, operates, where interest codifies or captures desire. As Deleuze points out in relation to justice: 'We must understand that justice is not a reflection *on* interest, but rather a reflection *of* interest, a kind of twisting of the passion itself in the mind affected by it' (Deleuze 1991: 44). It is precisely that affection, that twisting of the passion, that is at the focal point of the method and model of schizoanalysis. That moment, that aspect of the process, is where codification and capture occur. This is precisely where the twisting of desire into interest occurs, and that is precisely why an understanding of the passive syntheses is so critical to Deleuze, and Deleuze and Guattari's work.

The question for us, of course, is why, when considering the shift to the brave new world of motivation and continuous education, that this is what we desire? More accurately, why and how do we assemble and arrange *these* particular components to construct *those particular* machines? What is it about the machine that Murphy identifies as 'audit culture' that we wake up in the morning for:

> In audit cultures, instrumental and operational reason work together to provide a powerful way of bringing control into relation with generative difference, and structure and hierarchy into relation with flexibility. Audit's obvious instrumental reason regulates in accordance with external forces. Its more subtle and often hidden operational reason adapts to situations from within. There is constant feedback between the two. The shifting nature of the (un)acceptable generates adaptive powers that combine instrumental and operational reason, macro and micro. This enables audit culture to install

multi-scalar, portable and adaptable regimes – both from above and in the midst of events. This creates a cultural tendency towards passive affects with regard to the 'system'. It enables systems to thus rework the parameters of the production of subjectivity. As such, audit meshes micro-events with global networks. (Murphie 2014: 16)

Importantly, we must stress the operation of capitalism, typically expressed through, and driven by, the monetisation of the knowledge sector and the corporatisation of educational institutions. This ranges across all aspects of education, whether it be using public funding to subsidise private educational institutions, or whether it be instituting so-called practices and methods of gamification. One example here is the introduction of workload models that monitor research and/or teaching outputs of individual staff, and that are used to establish a constantly modulating average of output that pits teachers and researchers alike against each other, rewarding those who produce above the average, and punishing those who fall below the average. In such a context while the 'ethical' colleague is induced to become-Bartleby – Bartleby in some respects as the figure of the spoilsport, and in direct opposition to the figure of the cheat as she still cares about winning and is still invested in the system (Huizinga 1955: 12) – this is always within a field where so many succumb to the joy of the machine even while they complain about that machine to their colleagues. So many of us experience, or more precisely desire, the joy of that very machine – 'phew, thank god I made it over the average, my teaching load won't increase', 'Poor Alice, she fell below the average, glad it's not me', 'Stupid George, sucker has to learn somehow.' In such a context all colleagues breathe a sigh of relief when a colleague who produces above the average output, is promoted a level or leaves the institution, thereby reducing the average of the level they just were moved out of, and thereby making life more bearable for those at that level. 'She was a nice person, but ...' Already in such a simple example we can see the insidious and dangerous manner in which discipline and modulation co-exist, feed and contest each other.

Why are these the precise machines that we assemble and work at maintaining and improving, even as it causes some so much agony, even as it fills some with ever more anxiety and neurosis – assuming there are those who still 'care' enough to be anxious and neurotic, still 'care' enough to refuse becoming-Bartleby – or more precisely, care so little to become-Bartleby (if some of our colleagues across the range of educational institutions are any measure)? Perhaps, more worrying still, those moments of agony, that pain and anger, those moments where we complain bitterly about 'the system', or whatever intricate new procedure is put in place, is precisely part of what we assemble the institution for: 'To confess, to whine, to complain, to commiserate, always demand a toll' (Henry Miller in Deleuze and Guattari 1983: 334). Why is this the machine that administrators, teachers, cleaners, parking officers, researchers, principals, students and vice-chancellors wake up, get dressed and continually head to the classrooms and other machines for, whether they be face-to-face, or, increasingly, online and available 24/7? What particular passions do we affect by way of this 'continuous education' machine? What particular desire constitutes itself and is in the process reconfigured by, and as, interest? What particular interest do our meetings, our classes and our systems actualise? What particular interest is it that twists desire in such a way to assemble precisely 'motivation and continuous education', continuous sampling, transformative teaching, human capital, and so on? More importantly, how do we find an existence, a life, despite those machines? If we could typify the collection of papers in this issue, we would suggest that they are engaged with exactly that, finding an existence, a life, within the continuous education machine.

These, then, are the new sorts of machines that frame and inhabit our educational institutions, and that are analysed in this issue, both negatively, as well as positively. These are the machines, more frightfully our machines, that apply to, or rather, produce a particular construct of the student, as well as that of administrator, teacher, school, university, college, and so on. These are the machines that are in the process of being instituted, and which, as Deleuze pointed out, have the characteristic of no longer breaking down. 'Breaking down' is precisely a characteristic or feature that belongs more to the mechanistic, industrial assemblages to which discipline is key. Instead, Deleuze argued that the concept of the virus belongs more to our new context. We would argue that schizoanalysis as meta-model and method suits precisely the latter schema.

1. Disrupt, by way of destruction and continuously so, the ongoing processual coding of desire – bump the record player as they state in *Anti-Oedipus*.
2. Understand how the machine works, that is, analyse precisely how interest inserts itself into the flow that is desire and recodes it.
3. Don't become a fascist in the process.

Or:

1. Disrupt the coding of desire.
2. Understand the coding process; that is, identify where and how the virus inserts itself into the coding and reproduces its own code – tease it out in all its intricacies.
3. Avoid as much as possible inserting new code.

Of course, whether the contributions in this issue are anti-viral or viral we would argue depends entirely on the assemblage in question. Deleuze and Guattari, by way of Henry Miller, suggest of course that schizoanalysis more generally is anti-viral: 'To sing doesn't cost you a penny. Not only does it cost nothing – you actually enrich others (instead of infecting them)' (1983: 334). Most, if not all of us, cause specific codes, specific trees, to grow in ourselves. Again, it is through assemblages that we live. Yet this is precisely what can produce sedimentation, somewhat like the production of sand colic in a horse. The removal of such sedimentation, as with sand colic, is necessarily ongoing and is precisely what the method of schizoanalysis can help alleviate. In short, schizoanalysis is simply 'a bit of a *relation to the outside*, a little real reality' (334). One important question is how we prevent sedimentation of continuous education and motivation, including the adoption of the discourse around, for example, transformative teaching, which at first seems compatible and in some ways exemplary of schizoanalysis, but needs to be analysed more closely for the interests it is an assemblage of and which it reproduces. After all, capitalist society, Deleuze and Guattari claim, cannot possibly sustain an expression of desire, even at the kindergarten level, which raises significant and problematic questions for those of us engaged in education.

References

Allan, Julie (2014) 'Inclusive Education and the Arts', *Cambridge Journal of Education*, 44: 4, pp. 511–23.

Alliez, Éric and Andrew Goffey (2011) *The Guattari Effect*, London: A&C Black.

Ball, Stephen (2000) 'Performativities and Fabrications in the Education Economy: Towards a Performative Society?', *Australian Educational Researcher*, 27: 2, pp. 1–23.

Bell, Jeffrey A. (2012) 'Modes of Violence: Deleuze, Whitehead, Butler and the Challenges of Dialogue' in *Butler on Whitehead: On the Occasion*, Lanham, MD: Lexington Books, pp.127–43.

Bogue, Ronald (2013) 'The Master Apprentice', in Inna Semetsky and Diana Masny (eds), *Deleuze and Education*, Edinburgh: Edinburgh University Press.

Buchanan, Ian (2008) *Deleuze and Guattari's Anti-Oedipus: A Reader's Guide*, London: Continuum.

Buchanan, Ian (2009) 'Deleuze and the Internet', in Mark Poster and David Savat, *Deleuze and New Technology*, Edinburgh: Edinbrugh University Press.

Buchanan, Ian (2014) 'Schizoanalysis and the Pedagogy of the Oppressed', in Matthew Carlin and Jason Wallin (eds), *Deleuze & Guattari, Politics and Education: For a People-Yet-to-Come*, London: Bloomsbury.

Buchanan, Ian (2015) 'Assemblage Theory and Its Discontents', *Deleuze Studies*, 9: 3, pp. 382–392.

Cole, David (2011) 'The Actions of Affect in Deleuze: Others Using Language and the Language That we Make...', *Educational Philosophy and Theory*, 43: 6, pp. 549–61.

Coleman, Rebecca and Jessica Ringrose (2013) *Deleuze and Research Methodologies*, Edinburgh: Edinburgh University Press.

de Freitas, Elizabeth (2013) 'The Mathematical Event: Mapping the Axiomatic and the Problematic in School Mathematics', *Studies in Philosophy and Education*, 32, pp. 581–99.

de Fretias, Elizabeth (2015) 'Classroom Video Data and the Time-Image: An-archiving the Student Body', *Deleuze Studies*, 9: 3, pp. 318–336.

Deleuze, Gilles [1953] (1991) *Empiricism and Subjectivity: An Essay on Hume's Theory of Human Nature*, trans. Constantin Boundas, New York: Columbia University Press.

Deleuze, Gilles (1992) 'Postscript on the Societies of Control', *October*, 59, 3–7.

Deleuze, Gilles (1995) 'Control and Becoming', in *Negotiations*, trans. Martin Joughin, New York: Columbia University Press, pp. 169–76.

Deleuze, Gilles (2004a) 'Three Group-Related Problems', in *Desert Islands and Other Texts: 1953–1974*, ed. Lapoujade David, trans. Michael Taormina, Los Angeles, CA: Semiotext(e), pp. 193–203.

Deleuze, Gilles (2004b) 'Five Propositions on Schizoanalysis', in *Desert Islands and Other Texts: 1953–1974*, ed. David Lapoujade, trans. Michael Taormina, Los Angeles, CA: Semiotext(e), pp. 274–80.

Deleuze, Gilles and Félix Guattari (1983) *Anti-Oedipus: Capitalism and Schizophrenia*, trans. Robert Hurley, Mark Seem and Helen R. Lane, Minneapolis, MN: University of Minnesota Press.

Deleuze, Gilles and Félix Guattari (1986) *Kafka: Toward a Minor Literature*, trans. Dana Polan, Minneapolis, MN: University of Minnesota Press.

Deleuze, Gilles and Félix Guattari (2005) *A Thousand Plateaus: Capitalism and Schizophrenia*, trans. Brian Massumi, Minneapolis, MN: The University of Minnesota Press.

Dosse, Francois (2011) *Gilles Deleuze and Félix Guattari: Intersecting Lives*, New York: Columbia University Press.

Flanagan, Tim (2015) 'The Dictionaries in Which We Learn to Think', *Deleuze Studies*, 9: 3, pp. 301–317.

Foucault, Michel (1983) 'Preface', in Gilles Deleuze and Félix Guattari, *Anti-Oedipus: Capitalism and Schizophrenia*, trans. Robert Hurley, Mark Seem and Helen R. Lane, Minneapolis, MN: University of Minnesota Press.

Gangle, Rocco (2013) 'From Brackets to Arrows: Sets, Categories and the Deleuzian Pedagogy of Mathematics', in Inna Semetsky and Diana Masny (eds), *Deleuze and Education*, Edinburgh: Edinburgh University Press, pp. 155–73.

Genosko, Gary (eds) (2012) 'Félix Guattari in the Age of Semiocapitalism', *Deleuze Studies*, 6: 2.

Gough, Noel (2006) 'Shaking the Tree, Making a Rhizome: Towards a Nomadic Geophilosophy of Science Education', *Educational Philosophy and Theory*, 38: 5, pp. 625–45.

Guattari, Félix (1998) 'Schizoanalysis', *The Yale Journal of Criticism*, 11: 2, pp. 433–9.

Hughes, Joe (2008) 'Schizoanalysis and the Phenomenology of Cinema', in Ian Buchanan and Patricia MacCormack (eds), *Deleuze and the Schizoanalysis of Cinema*, New York: Continuum, pp. 15–27.

Hughes, Joe (2012) *Philosophy after Deleuze: Deleuze and the Genesis of Representation*, New York: Bloomsbury.

Huizinga, Johan (1955) *Homo Ludens: A Study of the Play Element in Culture*, Boston: The Beacon.

Jagodzinski, Jan (2015) 'Saints, Jesters and Nomads: The Anomalous Pedagogies of Lacan, Žižek, . . . Deleuze and Guattari', *Deleuze Studies*, 9: 3, pp. 356–381.

Kafka, Franz (2008) *The Complete Novels of Kafka*, London: Vintage.

Lazzarato, Maurizio (2006) 'The Concepts of Life and Living in the Societies of Control', in Martin Fuglsang and Bent Meier Sorensen (eds), *Deleuze and the Social*, Edinburgh: Edinburgh University Press, pp. 171–90.

Masny, Diana and Cole, David (2012) *Mapping Multiple Literacies: An Introduction to Deleuzian Literacy Studies*, New York: Bloomsbury.

Mercieca, Duncan (2012) 'Becoming-Teachers: Desiring Students', *Educational Philosophy and Theory*, 44: S1, pp. 43–56.

Murphie, Andrew (2014) 'Auditland', *PORTAL Journal of Multidisciplinary International Studies*, 11: 2, pp. 1–41.

Ringrose, Jessica (2015) 'Schizo-Feminist Educational Research Cartographies', *Deleuze Studies*, 9: 3, pp. 393–409.

Russell, Francis (2015) 'Slave to the Rhythm: The Problem of Creative Pedagogy and the Teaching of Creativity', *Deleuze Studies*, 9: 3, pp. 337–355.

St Pierre, Elizabeth (1997) 'Circling the Text: Nomadic Writing Practices', *Qualitative Inquiry*, 3: 4, pp. 403–17.

St Pierre, Elizabeth (2004) 'Deleuzian Concepts for Education: The Subject Undone', *Educational Philosophy and Theory*, 36: 3, pp. 283–96.

Savat, David (2009) 'Deleuze's Objectile: From Discipline to Modulation', in Mark Poster and David Savat (eds), Deleuze and New Technology, Edinburgh: Edinburgh University Press.

Savat, David (2013) *Uncoding the Digital: Technology, Subjectivity and the Control Society*, Basingstoke: Palgrave MacMillan.

Sellar, Sam (2014) 'A feel for numbers: Affect, Data and Education policy', *Critical Studies in Education*, 56: 1, pp. 1–26, available at http://dx.doi.org/10.1080/17508487.2015.981198.

Sellar, Sam (2015) 'A Strange Craving to be Motivated: Schizoanalysis, Human Capital and Education', *Deleuze Studies*, 9: 3, pp. 424–436.

Semetsky, Inna (1999) 'The Adventures of a Postmodern Fool, or the Semiotics of Learning', *Semiotics*, pp. 477–95.

Semetsky, Inna (2006) *Deleuze, Education and Becoming*, Rotterdam: Sense Publishers.

Smith, Daniel (2007) 'Deleuze and the Question of Desire: Toward an Immanent Theory of Ethics', *Parrhesia: A Journal of Critical Philosophy*, 2, pp. 66–78.

Stengers, Isabelle (2006) 'Gilles Deleuze's Last Message', *Recalcitrance*, available at http://www.recalcitrance.com/deleuzelast.htm.

Sumsion, Jennifer (2014) 'Opening Up Possibilities Through Team Research: An Investigation of Infants' Lives in Early Childhood Education Settings', *Qualitative Research*, 14: 2, pp. 149–65.

Thompson, Greg and Ian Cook (2012) 'Spinning in the NAPLAN Ether: "Postscript on the Control Societies" and the Seduction of Education in Australia', *Deleuze Studies*, 6: 4, pp. 564–84.

Thompson, Greg and Ian Cook (2014) 'Manipulating the Data: Teaching and NAPLAN in the Control Society', *Discourse: The Cultural Politics of Education*, 35: 1, pp. 129–42.

Thompson, Greg and Ian Cook (2015) 'Producing the NAPLAN Machine: A Schizoanalytic Cartography', *Deleuze Studies*, 9: 3, pp. 410–423.

Wallin, Jason (2010) *A Deleuzian Approach to Curriculum: Essays on a Pedagogical Life*, New York: Palgrave Macmillan.

Wallin, Jason (2012) 'Bon Mots for Bad Thoughts', *Discourse: Studies in the Cultural Politics of Education*, 33: 1, pp. 147–62.

Watson, Cate (2010) 'Educational Policy in Scotland: Inclusion and the Control Society', *Discourse: Studies in the Cultural Politics of Education*, 31: 1, pp. 93–104.

Webb, P. Taylor (2011) 'The Evolution of Accountability', *Journal of Education Policy*, 26: 6, pp. 735–56.

Webb, P. Taylor and Kalervo Gulson (2012) 'Policy Prolepsis in Education: Encounters, Becomings, and Phantasms', *Discourse: Studies in the Cultural Politics of Education*, 33: 1, pp. 87–99.

Webb, P. Taylor (2015) 'Fucking Teachers', *Deleuze Studies*, 9: 3, pp. 437–451.

The Dictionaries in Which We Learn to Think

Tim Flanagan   University of Notre Dame Australia
(Fremantle Campus)

Abstract

Taking its title from the discussion of a 'new Meno' to be found in *Difference and Repetition*, through an examination of the link between learning and thinking set out across Deleuze's work this paper charts the important sense in which philosophical thought is characterised by an apprenticeship. The claim is that just as certain aesthetic and biological processes involve inscrutable and non-resembling elements that cannot be known in advance, the experience of learning is one oriented by unforseen encounters. With a view to a peculiarly heuristic use of dictionaries in the case of language learning, the paper shows how the logic (or event) of this experience is one whereby the putative meaning of things does not enjoy a priority over the immanence of their expression.

Keywords: resemblance, aesthetics, language, learning, transcendental apprenticeship

> To seek to know before we know is as absurd as the wise resolution of
> Scholasticus, not to venture into the water until he had learned to swim.

Hegel 1991: 34

First Thoughts, Initial Impressions

For Hegel the problem with Kantian thought is that its studied movement from sensibility to understanding remains always and only

Deleuze Studies 9.3 (2015): 301–317
DOI: 10.3366/dls.2015.0189
© Edinburgh University Press
www.euppublishing.com/journal/dls

ever an epistemological procedure, a practice to be forever rehearsed. The concerted undertaking to account for the appearances of things (rather than things in themselves) which animates the *Critique of Pure Reason* does not so much provide for a translation of intuitions into concepts, according to Hegel, as a gloss or marginal note which sits alongside or between the two. For while the 'synthetic' account of things that underwrite Kant's uniquely *critical* development of transcendental philosophy is characterised by the application of certain rubrics, this is not the same thing as the very synthesis by which thinking itself takes place. In this way, the proposition that these rubrics are sufficient for the decipherment of things (or at least for a reading of them which might be justified) means that in the end Kantian discourse is articulated by an accent which prevents it from being a fluent or fully articulated account of things.

In the *Science of Logic* for instance Hegel explains, with reference to what 'has always been one of the most difficult parts of the Kantian philosophy' (1969: 584), that the unity of apperception is insufficient as an account of thought since the subjectivity thereby posited is something whose transcendental contrast with what is real makes it necessarily incomplete – an 'empty identity or abstract universality' (589). In place of this provisional account of thought, Hegel posits an understanding in which the *I think* obtains in terms of a consciousness subject only to 'its own absolute character' (586). For as announced in the Introduction to this his major work, a procedure of reflection whereby the criteria or methods for thinking are set out may well be acceptable in other areas of inquiry but not in the case of that inquiry which concerns thought itself. The reason for this is that such a principle of inquiry cannot be deduced but can only be embarked upon since the knowledge it proposes is something Absolute rather than a knowledge of mere conditions – a distinction Hegel emphasises when he insists, in a subtle reversal of the 'Kantian' figure of Scholasticus, that 'this point ... must not wait to be established within *logic* itself but must be cleared up *before* that science is begun' (586). Lest thinking flounder in a knowledge of things in general, it must resolve to think what there ultimately is: things themselves.

Notwithstanding Deleuze's ultimate suspicion of Hegelian thought, this historic critique of Kant is significant for the way in which it foreshadows his own critical engagement with transcendental philosophy (especially the role of 'conditioning') taken up in a number of his studies such as *Bergsonism* (1988c: 23), *Nietzsche and Philosophy* (2002: 91), *Difference and Repetition* (1994: 173) and *The Fold: Leibniz and the Baroque* (1993: 120). Ahead of these studies, however, Deleuze's brief remarks in a 1954 review of Jean Hyppolite's *Logic and Existence* (Deleuze 2004b) merit special attention since they signal a set of points that he will draw upon in many of his later works. Furthermore, that these points are sketched in a review of a key study on Hegel helps to situate Deleuze's work within the tradition of what has come to be described as post-Kantian thought by proposing that his place within this tradition is to be understood as emphatically *non*-Hegelian.

Learning (to Think)

What makes Deleuze's review of *Logic and Existence* so significant for his own philosophical project is that it offers an alternative outlook in place of Hegel's concerns with regard to the Kantian project of critique. A glimpse of this can be seen toward the end where Deleuze remarks upon Hyppolite's attention to the sense in which 'the problem of beginning in philosophy ... is not only logical, but pedagogical'. The importance here of Hegel's work for Deleuze is that it reveals a thinking that is not what is already thought (or which might yet be thought once and for all) but rather the undertaking of 'total Thought', the 'Being that thinks itself' (2004b: 17) – one which *comes to know*.

To be sure, the grounds for such a thinking are to be found in Kantian philosophy whose achievement was to have established a form of thought which was neither simply the sheer manifold of things that gives rise to thoughts (empiricism), nor a dogmatic account of the thing that thinks them (psychology) (2004b: 15), but rather the location of one in the other which brings them both about. As Deleuze explains, 'Kant's insight is that thought is presupposed as given: thought is given because it thinks itself and reflects itself, and it is presupposed as given because the totality of objects presupposes thought as that which makes understanding possible' (16). As set out later in *Difference and Repetition*, integral to this formal development was the profoundly critical scrutiny to which Kant had subjected the Cartesian account of thought. For while the act of thinking undoubtedly implies one who thinks, the very being of the latter cannot be determined simply by the actual experience of having thoughts. It is for this reason, according to Deleuze, that there can be said to have emerged under Kant 'a fault or fracture in the *I* and a passivity in the self' (1994: 86). That this difference can even be remarked upon signals an awareness that thought itself is happening, but the strictly subjective form of this awareness in Kant assigns it to a cogito. In this way, Kant's Copernican outlook was one shot through with an epistemic parochialism since it contented itself only with the all too human form *of our subjective experience*. The contribution made by Hegel's reading is to have shown that in Kant the reality of thought is to be understood merely, as that which a thinker thinks.

Despite his critique of Descartes, no sooner had Kantian philosophy revealed that the one who thinks cannot be determined simply by having thoughts, 'the fracture is quickly filled by a new form of identity – namely active synthetic identity' (1994: 87). In other words, in view of the fact that the grounds of thought extend beyond the horizon of what can be known, the critical project had sought to establish bearings that would provide things with an orientation. But just at the moment that Kant encountered the 'unthought' in thinking – an encounter that 'constitutes the discovery of the transcendental' (86) – he undertook to furnish this rupture with a ready-made structure in the form of an I who understands. In other words, by positing (by adducing, or rather *deducing*) certain categories by which thinking is at all possible, Kantian philosophy sought to guarantee thought by proposing a legitimate place for the subject.

What makes Hyppolite's reading of Hegel so important for Deleuze then is that it proposes a real understanding in place of a justification of what can be subjectively understood; it shows that the place secured within the horizons of possible knowledge is only ever anthropological, its logical relation to any real ground is only ever synthetic. As Deleuze asks rhetorically in *Nietzsche and Philosophy*, 'what is concealed in the famous Kantian unity of legislator and subject? Nothing but a renovated theology, theology with a protestant flavour: we are burdened with the double task of priest and believer, legislator and subject' (2002: 93). In place of this *ressentiment*, however, the speculative character of Hegelian philosophy understands the very claim that thought itself makes on things to be nothing less than something real; whereas thinking in Kant was only ever conditioned, given by appearances, for Hegel thinking is oriented by nothing less than what there is. Deleuze underlines this distinction when he writes:

> Thus, in Kant, thought and the thing are identical, but the thing identical to thought is only a relative thing, not the thing-as-being, not the thing-in-itself. Hegel ... aspires to the veritable identity of what is given and what is presupposed, in other words, to the Absolute. (2004b: 16)

To borrow the legal phrasing employed by the Kantian tribunal, Hegel's claim then is one which establishes its right in the very act of making its claim – its case does not proceed by means of a 'discourse *on* humanity', a 'discourse *of* humanity, in which the speaker and the object of his speech are separate' (2004b: 15). Accordingly, the sanctions that limit Kantian thought are shown to be merely a preliminary Phenomenological moment: a *movement* that 'starts from human reflection to show that this human reflection and its consequences lead to the absolute knowledge which they presuppose' (16). The anthropology which grounds Kantian thought is thus replaced by ontology – '[philosophy] *cannot be anything else*' (16) – as thinking comes to be understood *discursively*, on its own terms, as Logic.

What this means is that the empiricism that attends the inquiry 'of' humanity and the psychologism that attends the inquiry 'on' humanity (2004b: 15) give way to a discourse of nothing less than the Absolute since it is realised 'that there is no beyond of language' (17); 'the difference between thought and being has been surpassed in the absolute by the positing of Being which is identical to difference, and which as such thinks and reflects itself *in* humanity' (18 emphasis added). Indeed this transformed understanding of thought, from something extrinsic to something intrinsic, is why for Deleuze 'Jean Hyppolite's book is a reflection on the conditions of an absolute discourse ... my discourse is logically or properly philosophical when I speak the sense of what I say, and when Being thus speaks itself' (17). But while Deleuze ultimately appreciates that the philosophical 'rationale for transforming metaphysics into logic, the logic of sense' is to escape the exteriority of essences (16),[1] the aspect of Hegel that concerns him is the way in which it despatches difference, treating it as a by-product of a more profound dialectical contradiction. No matter how radically absolute, its thinking is oriented in the end by a familiarity not dissimilar to that which was shown to occupy the anthropological subject in Kant or perhaps even the methodological cogito in Descartes.

A view of this broader concern is provided across Deleuze's later works. In particular, it is worth considering the essay on Kant (first published in English translation) that develops further the account of the 'fractured I' set out in *Difference and Repetition* (1994: 86–7). In this short essay, Deleuze augments the imagery of the important distinction between the 'I' and the self – the distinction opened up by the 'paradox of inner sense' and which follows from the Kantian account of time – by describing the way in which it 'constantly hollows us out, splits us in two, doubles us, even though our unity subsists' (1997: 31). The important thing about this relation between the self and the I for Deleuze is that it comes about 'only on the condition of a fundamental difference' (29). Crucially, this distinction between the two does not presuppose the discrete activity of an I and passivity of a self but rather attests to the paradoxical sense in which somehow the activity of the I is *spontaneously* represented in the passive self:

> I am separated from myself by the form of time and yet I am one, because the I necessarily affects this form by bringing about its synthesis ... and the Self is necessarily affected by the I as the content of this form. The form of the determinable makes the determined Self represent the determination to itself as *an* Other. (1997: 30, emphasis added)

The paradox of this unity is that, for all its passivity, the self 'actively' encounters the I of thought; the I and the self are clearly held apart, and yet *at the same time* what holds them together (and, following Kant, what provides for experience at all) is a 'fundamental difference': *an* 'Other' that exceeds variety or alterity; the Absolute of difference-in-itself. It is for this reason that, the other is no 'one' but rather something characterised purely by its structural or perhaps *structuring* character. This is why Deleuze explains, in a critical note on Sartre, that while the 'other' oscillates within the polarity of self and I (poles which may well have respective functions)[2] it is the other that establishes the poles, and not the poles that establish the other. The reason for this is that the other is the sheer expression of 'a completely different structure' which 'refers only to the self for the other I and the other I for the self' (1997: 260) – a structure he describes the following year in *Logic of Sense* as 'transcendent with respect to the terms that actualize it' (1990: 318). It would be a mistake then to view the difference between the self and the I as being a distinction *in general*. 'For it is not the other which is another I, but the I which is *an* other, fractured I' (1997: 270, emphasis added) – not 'the' other but *an* other since this 'radical difference' between the self and the I of thought is less something found 'out there' as something that is much more immediate and indeed individual.

This much is evidenced for Deleuze in the notion of a foreign language, when it becomes clear to me that I do not understand a discourse which I nonetheless find myself remarking upon. For what makes a language foreign is not so much that its unintelligibility renders it unnoticeable but that it is something we remark upon because it is unintelligible. It is not simply then that the other language given in this encounter might fail to express anything, but neither is it that this language merely expresses yet another world (one which would, after all, merely resemble our own). Rather, it expresses *an* other (whatever *this*, this other thing which is not our mother tongue, is) since however faint or fleeting there is a 'moment at which the expressed has (for us) no existence apart from that which expresses it: the Other as *the expression of a possible world*' (1994: 261).

Importantly, it is not only exotic or never-before-heard languages that attest to this intriguing and fundamental difference between our passive reception and our active incomprehension. This is why Deleuze often draws upon Proust's formulation that 'Great literature is written in a sort of foreign language' (Deleuze and Parnet 2006: 4). To be sure, many great works have been written by authors in a language other than their mother tongue, but this observation owes nothing to a predilection for a 'bilingualism or multilingualism' which would simply preserve the respective 'equilibrium' of each language (1997: 109). Instead, what makes such literature great is that its writers stretch any given language to its limit so that it begins to lose its familiarity.[3]

Accordingly, and much like the Hegelian development of Logic in Kantian thought, such literary discourse is not some extrinsic (anthropological) discourse 'on' or 'of' things but is rather the discourse *intrinsic to things themselves*. For great literature does not so much come about when writers narrate this world (or imagine other worlds) as rather when they give expression to the limits of what can be said of this world. Crucially, the important difference, however, is that whereas Hegelian discourse reveals the Identity of what we think and what there is, for Deleuze discourse reveals their Difference.

It is for this reason that the contribution of great writers is not to have managed to write in a language whose range may not be as extensive as those with a more complex grammar or a larger lexicon[4] but rather to have articulated certain intensities of tone or timbre within a given language which ultimately make that language Different from itself. These authors 'do not mix two languages together', Deleuze explains, but rather 'invent a *minor use* of the major language within which they express themselves entirely' (1997: 109). In this way these writers could be regarded as producing a stunted or pared down literature,[5] but only in the same sense that bonsai trees are at once understood as trees and at the same time confront our understanding of what a tree is.

> They are great writers because of this minorization: they make the language take flight, they send it racing a long a witch's line, *ceaselessly placing it in a state of disequilibrium*, making it bifurcate and vary in each of its terms, following an incessant modulation. (1997; 109, emphasis added)

Since they come to resemble less and less the very language they draw upon these minor literatures present a challenge to the homogeneity or 'equilibrium' of any one language, and indeed of discourse at all. But unlike the thought of Hegel that proposes to resolve itself through dialectical contradiction, these literatures exhibit the sense in which whatever has been thought or whatever can in principle be thought is not the same thing as Thought itself. In this way they render Difference.

Lest this discourse remain a murmur, it should be said that thinking is of course guided by the identity of principles and indeed these principles themselves thereby testify to a certain logical rectitude in thought. The point here for Deleuze, however, is that while the spontaneity of this active moment seems to arise from within, neither do these principles yield to the intuitions of a subjective understanding nor can the subject that knows them do so Absolutely since they are only ever to be found when they are unexpected – that is, as something other. Significantly, Hegelian thought is unaffected by things in this way for Deleuze 'since the other is *its* other' (2004b: 18); in this way, the I that thinks may well be informed or mediated by a dialectical development, yet the contradiction by which its discourse posits itself remains a familiar, inner dialogue.

In place of this dialectic of contradiction, the discourse proposed by Deleuzian logic is one whereby thought participates in what could be described as an ecology of sense: the thoughts I think are mine not simply because I happen to think but rather because *other* forces me to think them.[6] It is for this reason that I do not think each and every thought I have since, like the experience of the swimming champion set out in Kafka, many of them remain foreign to me (1997: 5).[7] It is in view of this 'minorization' or disequilibrium, and against the synthetic discourse of Kant and the dialectic of self-contradiction in Hegel, that there is revealed in language for Deleuze an *Other* thinking (one of thoughts themselves, rather than the self identity of whoever happens to think them), for:

> if an organism may be regarded as a microscopic being, how much more is this true of the Other in psychic systems. It gives rise there to local increases in entropy, whereas the explication of the other by the self represents a degradation in accordance with law ... It is true that the other disposes of a means to endow the possibles that it expresses with reality, independently of the development we cause them to undergo. This means is language. Words offered by the other confer reality on the possible as such; whence the foundation of the lie inscribed within language itself. (Deleuze 1994: 261)

There is a duplicity in discourse then since if it is natural to think, this is only because the nature of things forces us to think. *We must learn to think* since thinking is not the same thing as those orientations that can be given in advance of thought ('synthetic unity'; 'self-contradiction'), thinking is something that must *be learnt*. This much can be seen in the figure of the apprentice discussed across his later works, a figure which first emerges in the book on Proust where it receives extensive development.[8] It is taken up again in the middle chapter from *Difference and Repetition* that shares a title with a part of the earlier work on signs. And though its treatment over a decade later in *Francis Bacon: The Logic of Sensation* is much briefer, the discussion there is nonetheless worth considering since it offers a vivid account of how thought for Deleuze arises by means of an apprenticeship.

There, in his consideration of the distinction between analogical and digital methods of representation, Deleuze explains how whereas digital representation 'passes through a codification, through a homogenization and binarization of the data, which is produced on a separate plane, infinite in principle' (2004a: 116), analogical representation does not so much proceed by means of instructions as rather by 'moments' which are actual and sensible. The reason why this analogical method cannot simply be taught or acquired is that it does not obtain in relation to the abstraction imposed by digital methods of representation; 'in the absence of any code, the relations to be reproduced are produced by completely different relations, creating a resemblance through non resembling means ... instead of being produced symbolically, through the detour of the code, it is produced "sensually", through sensation' (115–6). In other words, but without recourse to other materials, the analogical method is one that must take place and indeed begin with only the immediacy of what there is (which at once provides for but also exceeds any form of subjective experience).

Pedagogically speaking this is not to say that the analogical method of representation remains a naïve imitation of things. Rather it is simply to say that it cannot be taught. This can be seen in certain works by Bacon where, following Cézanne, the conditions for the work itself (and the emergence of the painting's figure) are to be found nowhere beyond the intense chromatic complexity of the very colours by which the work was produced. In this way, painting reveals itself to be the 'analogical language par excellence' (2004a: 113); that there are those such as Bacon who have developed a proficiency in this form of expression evidences, according to Deleuze, 'the necessity of a lengthy apprenticeship for the analogical to become language' (114); what makes this apprenticeship so involved is that it must include its means in its ends. It is not something that can be imparted, but neither is it simply innate. It must be brought about in the work itself, but pass beyond it.

In the case of painting, then, the apprenticeship in colours comes to articulate a discourse in the manner of a minor literature since it 'integrates its own catastrophe, and consequently is constituted as a flight in advance' (2004a: 102–3). What this means is that the conditions of Bacon's works hold neither by means of a deduction of things in general (space, time or categories) nor in the dialectical realisation of things (by means of a self-contradiction), since in either case the proposed discourse is one whose logic does not suffice to be the articulation of what there is (the Difference of things themselves) and must posit ends beyond its means. The conditions of things in Bacon's paintings, however, emerge in the works themselves when, instead of being depicted, figures emerge through a certain colouring relation or organisation which replaces that of form and ground (118, 134). For Deleuze then, the 'analogical language' of Bacon's work is significant because the modulation of colour expresses a logic whereby the things are not so much given by terms as to be found in the encounters *between* terms.

In this way this analogical language is neither an intuitive mother tongue nor is it an object of knowledge to be understood (and in which proficiency might be acquired by means of instruction) but rather one that comes about by an apprenticeship–an encounter with an interstitial, ramifying and pullulating discourse[9] which is all too clearly not the language of common sense yet neither is it a language which might be codified through generic parts of speech.

Two Dictionaries

Despite this proscription, and working out from Deleuze's account of the diagramme (2004a: 113), there is a sense however in which verbs (rather than nouns or adjectives) might be understood as the articulation of this discourse–a discourse expressed in minor literature, colourist paintings and as announced for Deleuze in the problem of univocity, a discourse which takes place *in spite of itself*. This peculiar role of verbs is sketched across a number of Deleuze's works but a key outline is provided in *Logic of Sense* when Deleuze describes how 'the Epicureans created a model based on the *declension* of the atom; the Stoics, on the contrary, created a model based on the *conjugation* of events' (1990:

183). Anticipating the position set out in the later book on Bacon, it could be said that for Epicurean thought colour was secondary to the depiction of things but for the Stoics there was only colour. In this way, separating what are ultimately transcendent principles of generation from those that arise immanently, it can be said:

> that the Epicurean model privileges nouns and adjectives; nouns are like atoms or linguistic bodies which are coordinated through their declension, and adjectives like the qualities of these composites. But the Stoic model comprehends language on the basis of 'prouder' terms: verbs and their conjugation, in relation to the links between incorporeal events. (1990: 183)

This is not at all to say that verbs provide a didactic model for thinking. And yet their characteristic role in discourse serves as a philosophical heuristic for how things might be understood. Key to this understanding for Deleuze is the sense in which the relationships established by verbs are predicative and not attributive. The difference here is that while attributive relations take place via propositions which only ever express things from the point of view of a subject, the propositions expressed by predicative relations are themselves their own statement on things. 'The predicate *is the proposition itself*' (1993: 53). In other words, whereas the attributive scheme affirms things of a subject, the predicative scheme is affirmation itself.[10] And while it would jar with this very scheme of things to state the definition of verbs independently of their expression – to give the instruction independently of the lesson – the examples provided by two dictionaries serve as a 'motif' (2004a: 113) for what thinking in this way is like.

Indeed following Deleuze's own suggestion, Spinoza's *Compendium Gammatices Lingua-Hebraeae* merits attention for the way that it 'brings out certain characteristics that constitute a real logic of expression' (1992: 364).[11] For instance in his discussion of the six different forms of infinitive nouns (including active and passive moods) Spinoza explains that 'the Hebrews are accustomed to relate an action to the first cause which brought it into being' and yet this is not always sufficient for what is required of discourse. For this reason 'it was necessary for the Hebrews to form a new and seventh kind of infinitive which should express an action recorded simultaneously in the active and passive'. This new form combined both active and passive, according to Spinoza, since its 'imminent cause' was expressive of a certain relation that held the two together (2002: 629). Significantly, this anticipatory relation between activity and passivity could well be likened to the passive spontaneity or active passivity that attended the discovery of the transcendental Deleuze claims Kant had overlooked – a modular function whose discourse would articulate the colourist or minor literature of thought.

Albeit a fable, a second example of a dictionary somehow eliciting thought is to be found in a short story by Borges. What makes this story significant for Deleuze's thought is that it takes up the riddle posed amid his discussion of the apprentice not only in *Difference and Repetition* but also *Proust and Signs* regarding how one learns Latin.[12] In Borges' story, the narrator relates how by the time of his second visit to Fray Bentos he had:

> embarked upon a systematic study of Latin. In my suitcase I had brought with me Lhomond's *De viris illustribus*, Quicherat's *Thesaurus*, Julius Caeser's commentaries, and an odd-numbered volume of Pliny's *Naturalis historia* – a work which exceeded (and still exceeds) my modest abilities as a Latinist. (1998: 133)

After only a short while in the town he received a letter from the story's eponymous Ireneo – the once nimble youth briefly seen running through the streets during the earlier visit, nowadays consigned to bed, having since been crippled in a horse-riding accident – in which, as the narrator relates, quoting the missive in part, the boy had asked 'that I lend him one of the books I had brought, along with a dictionary "for a full understanding of the text, since I must plead ignorance of Latin"' (Borges 1998: 133). While the anecdote is well known for the extraordinary account of memory (and perception) that it goes on to detail, this epistolary request is significant in its own right.

The reason for this is that whereas at the time of writing the letter the boy admitted no knowledge of Latin, somehow, in little more than a month, he had come to be able to speak the language – having learned it, along with several others, 'effortlessly' (137). As with so many of the events from Borges' tales, little explanation is given for this feat other than the implication that Ireneo had made use of 'Quicherat's *Gradus ad Parnassum*' – an incredulity shared by the narrator who, upon receiving the letter, 'didn't know whether to attribute to brazen conceit, ignorance or stupidity the idea that hard-won Latin needed no more teaching than a dictionary could give' (133). And even though the means by which this end were reached are not detailed in the story, the clue to the boy's extraordinary ability at learning languages is given in the testimony of his memory and perception. For these are shown to signal a heightened power to be affected and indeed his experience of things is one exhausted by constantly encountering the world unexpectedly as if via an apprenticeship:

> With one quick look, you and I perceive three wineglasses on a table; Funes perceived every grape that had been pressed into the wine and all the stalks and tendrils of the vineyard. He knew the forms of the clouds in the southern sky on the morning of April 30 1882, and he could compare them in his memory with the veins in the marbled binding of a book he had seen only once, or with the feathers of spray lifted by an oar on the Río Negro on the eve of the Battle of Quebracho. (Borges 1998: 135)

These remarkable powers of mind, the narrator relates, are to be explained by the unlimited exercise of two mental faculties, each goading the other, much like the violent encounter with limits which took place in the apprenticeship of learning (Deleuze 2000: 101). Funes' 'present was so rich, so clear, that it was almost unbearable, as were his oldest and even his most trivial memories ... his perception and his memory were perfect' (Borges 1998: 135). The significance of this perfection is that it comes about through a method of exhaustion in which nothing could be forgotten since everything could be perceived, and everything could be perceived because nothing could be forgotten.

Accordingly, this simultaneity of two powers without limits (indeed their relation *in a single power*) is why in the example above Funes could contemplate the 'spray lifted by an oar' even if it had taken place forty years earlier, or the wine that had filled the glasses: he could trace the effects of events through time, since no event (let alone its effects)[13] was too subtle for him. 'His own face in the mirror, his own hands, surprised him every time he saw them ... Funes could continually perceive the quiet advances of corruption, of tooth decay, of weariness. He saw – he *noticed* – the progress of death, of humidity' (1998: 136). In short, his experience was at once so momentary and so eternal that, for Funes time did not so take place (one moment after another) as happen all at once.

Moreover, within the vortex of such an encounter with the world, this unique perspective on things is all the more acute in Funes' experience of language – and it is this that best serves to demonstrate the radical transformation of transcendental philosophy that is to be found in Deleuze. This role of language is given by the narrator's closing reflection on the boy at the end of the fable, where he notes that Funes:

> had effortlessly learned English, French, Portugese, Latin. I suspect, nevertheless, that he was not very good at thinking. To think is to ignore (or forget) differences, to generalize, to abstract. In the teeming world of Ireneo

Funes there was nothing but particulars – and they were virtually *immediate* particulars. (1998: 137)

It could be concluded following this summation that, no matter his linguistic abilities, ultimately Funes' experience was one informed by his faculties of memory and perception. But despite its impotence (relative at least to his other faculties which were without limit) Funes' faculty of natural language is key since it signals that none of the languages he knew sufficed to articulate his thoughts. In effect, then, his thoughts remained formless since they could not be designated in any way that might make things discursively understandable – and yet they were Absolutely real. That this experience exhibited a sense in which the logic of things (themselves) provides for and yet exceeds the subjective form of our discursive understanding is shown by Borges when he relates:

> Not only was it difficult for him to see that the generic symbol 'dog' took in all the dissimilar individuals of all shapes and sizes, it irritated him that the 'dog' of three-fourteen in the afternoon, seen in profile, should be indicated by the same noun as the dog of three-fifteen, seen frontally. (1998: 136)

What makes this significant for an account of transcendental philosophy is that there is here adduced in *Funes* a pronounced disequilibrium which dislocates the dialectical logic of self-contradiction in Hegel and the synthetic discourse of things guaranteed by Kant by means of a pensive (at once active and passive) anticipation of a language to come:

> In the seventeenth century, Locke postulated (and condemned) an impossible language in which each individual thing – every stone, every bird, every branch – would have its own name; Funes once contemplated a similar language, but discarded the idea as too general, too ambitious. The truth was, Funes remembered not only every leaf on every tree in every patch of forest, but every time he had perceived or imagined that leaf (1998: 136)

It may well be concluded then that that despite his linguistic abilities Funes could only think very little, but only on condition that thought here be understood as a subjective form of knowledge. Instead, Funes' unlimited perception and memory (which could only be given logical expression by a narrator) testify to an experience of thinking which takes place in light of the unexpected encounter with the Difference of things themselves.

Whether the discursive form of this encounter would include or could be found in a reading of Quicherat's *Thesaurus* or Spinoza's *Compendium* remains to be seen, since either dictionary could well serve as an 'other' for the apprenticeship of thought. What can be said, however, is that if thinking did arise from them it would do so only by virtue of this pedagogic encounter and not following any didactic intention.

Notes

1. Deleuze's enthusiasm for this project is worth noting. 'It is indeed thanks to Hyppolite that we now recognize philosophy, if it means anything, can only be ontology and an ontology of sense' (2004a: 18).
2. Deleuze explains how 'they experience qualities in general as already developed in the extensity of their system, but they tend to explicate or develop the world expressed by the other, either in order to participate in it or to deny it' (1997: 260).
3. 'This limit is not outside a particular language, nor language in general, but it is the outside of language … it is none other than the language we speak – it is a foreign language *in* the language we speak' (Deleuze 2006: 370).
4. Consider Deleuze's interest in the way in which 'American English is worked upon by a Black English, and also Yellow English, a Red English, a broken English … Oh no, it is not a question of imitating patois or restoring dialects like the peasant novelists … It is a case of making language shift, with words which are increasingly restrained and a syntax which is increasingly subtle. It is not a question of speaking a language as if one was a foreigner, it is a question of being a foreigner on one's own language, in the sense that American is indeed the Blacks' language' (Deleuze and Parnet 2006).
5. Consider Deleuze's examples from 'modern literature' such as 'Mallarmé's book, Péguy's repetitions, Artaud's breaths, the agrammaticality of Cummings, Burroughs and his cut-ups and fold-ins, as well as Rousel's proliferations, Brisset's derivations, Dada collage, and so on' (1988a: 131). In this regard consider too Jarry's project which 'is not a question of etymology, but of bringing about agglutinations in the other-language (*l'autre-langue*) so as to emerge in the-language (*la-langue*). Undertakings like those of Heidegger or Jarry should not be compared with linguistics, but rather with the analogous undertakings of Roussel, Brisset or Wolfson' (1997: 97). What these examples show, for Deleuze, is that 'language does not have signs at its disposal, *but acquires them by creating them*, when a language$_1$ acts within a language$_2$ so as to produce in it a language$_3$ an unheard of and almost foreign language. The first injects, the second stammers, the third suddenly starts with a fit' (1998: 98, emphasis added).
6. Note the 'violence' of these encounters (Deleuze 1994, 2000, *passim*).
7. Compare the remark in the lecture on Spinoza 'we use all the languages in order to try to better understand the languages that we don't know' (Deleuze 1981).
8. Consider especially the discussion of the hieroglyphics and the apprenticeship of the Egyptologist set out in the study on Proust (Deleuze 2000: 4, 92). Consider too the figure of the 'new Meno' sketched in that study (Deleuze 1994: 166, 180); given his interest later in that work of those '"things" that only an embryo can do, movements that it alone can undertake or even withstand' (215), the process by which Ideas are encountered in chapters four and five of *Difference and Repetition* and the closing lines of his essay on *The Method of Dramatization* (Deleuze 2004b: 103) could well be described as meiotic rather than maieutic.
9. Consider the respective discussions of stammering and stuttering in *Essays Critical and Clinical* (Deleuze 1997).
10. Compare how in the *Logic of Sense* Deleuze describes how 'instead of a certain number of predicates being excluded from a thing in virtue of its concept, each "thing" opens itself up to the infinity of predicates through which it passes, as

it loses its centre, that is, its identity as concept or as self' (1990: 174); 'Rather than signifying that a certain number of predicates are excluded from a thing in virtue of the identity of the corresponding concept, the disjunction now signifies that each thing is opened to the infinity of predicates through which it passes, on the condition that it loses its identity as concept and as self' (296).

11. It should be noted that in addition to this study, Deleuze later wrote a dictionary on Spinoza's philosophy (1988b).

12. 'Who knows how a schoolboy suddenly becomes "good at Latin" ...? We never learn from the dictionaries our teachers or our parents lend us' (Deleuze 2000: 22). 'We never know in advance how someone will learn: by means of what loves someone becomes good at Latin ... or in what dictionaries they learn to think' (Deleuze 1994: 165). Michael Clarke, Professor of Classics at the National University of Ireland (Galway), begins his contribution in A Companion to the Ancient Greek Language with the arresting claim that 'I do not really know Ancient Greek, nor do any of the authors to this Companion' (2010: 120). Among other things, his essay undertakes to provide a critical reflection on the dictionaries used in learning Greek, explaining that 'the standard LSJ is muddled and treacherous, especially for the commonest words, but becomes much more effective if supplemented by Chantraine's [1999] sane and sensitive Dictionnaire étymologique de la langue grecque' (132–3). The tradition that considers how learning takes place (alongside what it is that is learnt) is one surveyed in studies like those of Ong (1983) and Rossi (2006). Beyond this staple of Renaissance letters – consider Copenhaver's (1988: 107) discussion of certain middle and late fifteenth century works which 'advance[d] Europe's general command of Latin', such as De orthographia, Cornucopiae and Thesaurus linguae Graecae – even before the Greeks, the tradition of Babylonian scribal schools is to be noted in this regard. See for instance Vanstiphout's criticism of a seminal article by Kramer in which the former underlines the difficulty of learning dead and (especially given that Sumerian is understood as an isolate) foreign languages. According to Vanstiphout, Kramer 'does not explain how Sumerian was taught after its demise as a spoken language. Must we assume that this was done by means of the lists of paradigms and the "dictionaries" mentioned by Kramer ... or was this instruction in his view based on the "considerable oral and explanatory material" with which "the teacher and the assistants ... supplemented the bare lists, tables and literary texts" ...?' (1979: 118).

13. Consider Deleuze's development of the example, itself found originally from Leibniz and earlier addressed by Nietzsche, that no two leaves are the same. 'Replace two leaves with forensic scientists: no two grains of dust are exactly identical, no two hands have the same distinctive points, no two typewriters have the same strike, no two revolvers score their bullets in the same manner' (1994: 26).

References

Borges, Jorge Luis (1998) Collected Fictions, trans. Andrew Hurley, London: Penguin.

Clarke, Michael (2010) 'Semantics and Vocabulary', in Egbert Bakker (ed.), A Companion to the Ancient Greek Language, Chichester: Wiley-Blackwell.

Copenhaver, Brian (1988) 'Translation, Terminology and Style in Philosophical Discourse', in Charles Schmitt and Quentin Skinner (eds), The Cambridge History of Renaissance Philosophy, Cambridge: Cambridge University Press.

Deleuze, Gilles (1981) 'The Actual Infinite-Eternal, The Logic of Relations', Spinoza Seminar, Université de Paris VIII, 10 March, available at http://www.webdeleuze.com/php/texte.php?cle=42&groupe=Spinoza&langue=2 (accessed 7 May 2015).

Deleuze, Gilles (1988a) *Foucault*, trans. Séan Hand, Minneapolis, MN: University of Minnesota Press.

Deleuze, Gilles (1988b) *Spinoza: Practical Philosophy*, trans. Robert Hurley, San Francisco, CA: City Light Books.

Deleuze, Gilles (1988c) *Bergsonism*, trans. Hugh Tomlinson & Barbara Habberjam, New York: Zone Books.

Deleuze, Gilles (1990) *Logic of Sense*, trans. Mark Lester, New York: Columbia University Press.

Deleuze, Gilles (1992) *Expressionism in Philosophy: Spinoza*, trans. Martin Joughin, New York: Zone Books.

Deleuze, Gilles (1993) *The Fold: Leibniz and the Baroque*, trans. Tom Conley, London: Athlone Press.

Deleuze, Gilles (1994) *Difference and Repetition*, trans. Paul Patton, London: Athlone Press.

Deleuze, Gilles (1997) *Essays Critical and Clinical*, trans. Daniel W. Smith and Michael A. Greco Minneapolis, MN: University of Minnesota Press.

Deleuze, Gilles (2000) *Proust and Signs*, trans. Richard Howard, Minneapolis, MN: University of Minnesota Press.

Deleuze, Gilles (2002) *Nietzsche and Philosophy*, trans. Hugh Tomlinson, London: Continuum.

Deleuze, Gilles (2004a) *Francis Bacon: The Logic of Sensation*, trans. Daniel W. Smith, London: Continuum.

Deleuze, Gilles (2004b) *Desert Islands and Other Texts 1953–1974*, ed. David Lapoujade, trans. Michael Taormina, Los Angeles: Semiotext(e).

Deleuze, Gilles (2006) *Two Regimes of Madness: Texts and Interviews 1975–1995*, ed. David Lapoujade, trans. Ames Hodges and Mika Taomina Cambridge, MA: MIT Press.

Deleuze, Giles and Claire Parnet (2006) *Dialogues II*, trans. Hugh Tomlinson and Barbara Habberjam, London: Continuum.

Hegel, Georg W. F. (1969) *Science of Logic*, trans. A. V. Miller, London: Allen & Unwin.

Hegel, Georg W. F. (1991) *The Encyclopaedia Logic: Part I of the Encyclopaedia of the Philosophical Sciences with the Zustze*, trans T. F. Geraets, W. A. Suchting and H. S. Harris, Indianapolis, IN: Hackett.

Kant, Immanuel (1929) *Critique of Pure Reason*, trans. Norman Kemp Smith, London: Macmillan.

Ong, Walter (1983) *Ramus: Method, and the Decay of Dialogue: From the Art of Discourse to the Art of Reason*, Cambridge, MA: Harvard University Press.

Rossi, Paolo (2006) *Logic and the Art of Memory: The Quest for a Universal Language*, trans. Stephen Clucas, London: Continuum.

Spinoza (2002) *Complete Works*, ed. Michael Morgan, trans. Samuel Shirley, Indianapolis, IN: Hackett.

Vanstiphout, H. L. J. (.) 'How Did They Learn Sumerian?', *Journal of Cuneiform Studies*, 31: 2.

Classroom Video Data and the Time-Image: An-Archiving the Student Body

Elizabeth de Freitas   Manchester Metropolitan University

Abstract

Video data has now become the most common form of data for educational researchers studying classroom interaction and school culture. Software protocols for analysing vast archives of video data are deployed regularly, allowing researchers to annotate, code and sort images. These protocols are often applied by researchers without reflection or reference to the extensive philosophical work in film and media studies. Without exception, this research treats the video image as movement-image or picture, a recording of 'raw data', indexical of a given time-space relationship. In this article I situate this kind of research within the history of scientific cinema, drawing on Deleuze's books on cinema, as well as his ideas on colour and figure from *The Logic of Sensation*, to propose an alternative way of analysing video data. One of the central claims of Deleuze in *Cinema 2* is that the time-image reconfigures bodies as expressions of force – the body becomes a 'shock of forces'. I argue that such an approach allows us to study the student body as less a phenomenological organism with built-in 'I can' cognitive and motor capacities, and more an indeterminate crystalline contraction and expansion of intensity. I present an example of how to study classroom video data as time-image, and explore the implications of such work for education research.

Keywords: video data, cinema, time-image, movement-image, classroom research, student body, sensory-motor body, archive

Deleuze Studies 9.3 (2015): 318–336
DOI: 10.3366/dls.2015.0190
© Edinburgh University Press
www.euppublishing.com/journal/dls

I. Video Practices in Education Research

Video data has now become the most common form of data for educational researchers studying classroom interaction and school culture (Brophy 2004; Erikson 2006). Software protocols for analysing vast archives of video data are deployed regularly, allowing researchers to annotate, code and sort images (O'Halloran et al. 2013). Recent reviews of video research in the field identify principles for how to select an 'event' from an extensive video corpus of classroom videos, and recommend protocols for how to code these events in terms of student actions, so that 'one can interpret events as chunks of time' (Derry et al. 2010: 7). These protocols are often applied by researchers without reflection or reference to the extensive philosophical work in film and media studies (Goldman et al. 2007). The use of video analytical software without adequate attention to how such software is structuring the data becomes increasingly problematic as we begin to rely more and more on findings based on this data. Without exception, this research treats the video image as movement-image or picture, a recording of 'raw data', indexical of a given time-space relationship. An example is shown in Figure 1 that shows a sequence of video stills published as part of a study of student gesture and creativity (Sinclair et al. 2012).

Video research in education is used to document teaching experiments, design experiments, case studies and longitudinal ethnographic studies. In this article I situate this kind of research within the history of scientific cinema, and I draw on Deleuze's books on cinema (1986; 1989), as well as his ideas on colour and figure from *The Logic of Sensation* (2003), to propose an alternative way of using video data. My aim is to open up a discussion about how we might engage with video as structured light rather than as movement-image. One of the central claims of Deleuze in *Cinema 2* is that the time-image reconfigures bodies as expressions of force, as 'shocks of force' (1989: 139). I argue that such an approach allows us to study video data for how the student body is less a phenomenological organism with built-in 'I can' cognitive and motor capacities, and more an indeterminate crystalline contraction of intensity. In order to underscore the political significance of the movement-image within education research, I first discuss how this research inherits particular image conventions from early scientific cinema in which motion efficiency studies served to standardise industrial labour. I then discuss Deleuze's accounts of the history of cinema, emphasising his turn to the time-image and its potential to disrupt the fixated gaze of sensory-motor bodies. I then

Figure 1. Students discussing time graphs in a mathematics classroom (copyright of the author). A colour version can be viewed online.

present an example of how to study classroom video data as time-image, and explore the implications of such work for educational research.

II. Scientific Cinema

Cartwright (1995) uses the term 'scientific cinema' to refer to the early film recordings of moving bodies. Scientific interest in embodiment, according to Cartwright, is indebted to techniques of motion recording and observation developed by experimental physiologists, like Lumière, in France and Germany in the nineteenth century. Indeed, many of Lumière's contemporaries regarded his invention of the cinematographe as a key contribution to physiology. The Lumière laboratories manufactured film stock and equipment for science – hundreds of films in the Lumière's catalogues cover a vast array of activities or actualities of various kinds of bodily movement. This genre dominated the first decade of film, and can be seen as part of an ongoing interest in capturing and documenting the ephemeral movements of the body. The history of early cinema is thus linked with traditions of scientific experimentation. Cartwright (1995) tracks scientific cinema into the twentieth century, and argues that studies of the human body in various disciplines, education for instance, need to reckon with this history. She maps 'the history of the cinematic techniques that science has used to control, discipline, and construct the human body as a technological network of dynamic systems and forces.' (4). This tradition is one that has produced 'human life' as a dynamic entity to be tracked and studied through a cinematic lens.

The links between scientific cinema and capitalist modernity are well documented by Doane (2002) who shows how the new technology was used to restructure time and contingency in industrial labour. In the early decades of the twentieth century, cinema promised to track the

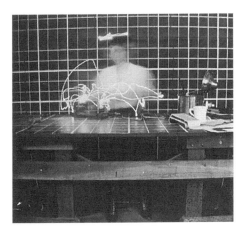

Figure 2. Motion efficiency study, 1914 (public domain). National Museum of American History, Behring Center, Division of Work and Industry Collection.

unfolding of time, and to expose the fleeting moment, the 'duration of an ephemeral smile or glance' (3). Attempts to capitalise on such knowledge were found within industries of all kinds. For instance, in 1914 Frank B. Gilbreth, a disciple of Taylor (of Taylorism) created 'cyclographs' or a 'chronocyclegraph' in which expert movements of various labourers were recorded with the aim of creating an archive of efficient motion. In each case, the body's movement was recorded by attaching a small electric light to the limb and using time exposure to generate a representation of the movement as a continuous line in space. In Figure 2, a woman is folding a handkerchief. Gilbreth's aim was to study 'perfect movement' so as to maximise efficiency of task. These were examples of how scientific cinema was used to create sensory-motor images that exceeded the perceptual capacity of the scientific observer.

According to Doane (2002), the motion efficiency studies served both the standardisation of industrial labour and also contributed to an image of time as enacted in bodily movement. Film and photography were considered exceptional technologies for the study of the human body and its unconscious capacities. The indexicality of film – its material coupling to the event – linked the cinematic record to the contingent moment, the any-moment-whatsoever. This link between the technology of the moving image and the capture of contingency was part of the rationalisation and abstraction of time that fuelled Taylorism and other capitalist flows. Thus the capturing of the sensory-motor body in its spontaneous activity was also meant to offer a trace or signature of a certain kind of temporality. Scientific cinema was deployed to capture that temporality and to code the body's movements (Sekula 1986; Foster 2004). Although video research in education continues to track the sensory-motor body and its unconscious ephemeral actions, especially in studies driven by constructivist theories of learning, there are radical differences between it and scientific cinema. Video, for instance, partakes of indexicality in an entirely different way, and allows for digital decomposition and re-assemblage of images. Of course montage – as developed by Eisenstein and others – is also a re-assembling of images, more or less experimental in its relation to human perception, but montage is never an obliteration of the image through digital decomposition. I will take up this difference in later sections, when I explore alternative ways of working with such data.

III. The Time-Image and the Body

According to Deleuze (1989), one can characterise early scientific cinema in terms of the *movement-image*, an image that answers our desire to interpret motor-activity in terms of mechanical cause and effect. I argue in this paper that this same desire fuels contemporary video research and increased educational standardisation (an extension of Taylorism), in some cases actually prescribing particular gestures and bodily movements that facilitate learning (Cook et al. 2013). Such an endeavour seems quite similar to Gilbreth's motion efficiency studies, and offers substance to Virilio's thesis, as described by Deleuze, that the movement-image was from the beginning linked to the organisation of 'ordinary fascism' (Deleuze 1989: 165).

Deleuze points to a new kind of post-war cinema that breaks with the conventions of the movement-image. This new cinema operates through the *time-image* and connects with bodies in radically different ways. In the time-image, says Deleuze, the body is no longer the obstacle that 'separates thought from itself', but precisely the passage or gateway to the unthought – or life itself. The body is no longer the sensory-motor body, the body that lends itself to control, but a body that forces us to think what is concealed from thought. The time-image is that desire to reach the body 'before discourses, before words' (1989: 172–3), to let the body speak or express itself without code. Deleuze will announce that 'to think is to learn what a non-thinking body is capable of, its capacity, its postures' (189). The time-image *forms an alliance with thought directly* rather than through the cinematic image as mediator.

If in the movement-image, characters acted and events and cameras followed, the time-image deploys instead pure optical or sound signs, akin, Deleuze suggests, to how impressionism entailed a conquering of a purely optical space. Deleuze focuses primarily on how this shift occurred within narrative cinema, pointing to Hitchcock as the harbinger, because of the way he included the viewer in the scene – and indeed in the plot. But I want to focus more on how this shift is lived outside of narrative, and perhaps contrary to narrative. An important part of this shift in cinema relates to how the sensory-motor situation is displaced and becomes 'any-space-whatever':

> Any-space-whatever … is a perfectly singular space, which has merely lost its homogeneity, that is, the principle of its metric relations or the connection of its own parts, so that linkages can be made in an infinite number of ways. (Deleuze 1986: 109)

Concerns for whether there is a subjective or objective camera at work, or to what extent the motor action propels the camera, are thus displaced, as an impersonal optical situation comes to dominate. Deleuze shows how this shift occurs in narrative cinema, but how is this shift inflected in scientific cinema? What might this mean for video research in education? I want to push the logic of the time-image into a zone where aberrant involuntary movement, precisely what early cinema aspired to capture, is affirmed as that which 'designates time as its direct cause' (Deleuze 1989: 41). In other words, the time-image breaks with the phenomenological image of the body, and its desire for presence, and directly links to the force and shock of time itself. In education video practices, this would entail studying video as a structuring of light or pure optic image, a means of dis-assembling the human body, and opening up our analysis to the fundamental difference that re-assembles and sustains bodies.

To that end, the notion of the irrational cut is crucial, as it breaks with linear causality. The 'irrational cut' creates so much rupture that it cannot belong to what has come before nor what future it seems to prolong. This concept of the irrational cut is taken from the history of mathematics – the notion of Dedekind cuts – which were an invention by Richard Dedekind in 1858 to define the real number system using open sets. Each real number – each point in the continuum – was to be uniquely identified with a cut separating the real numbers into two sets. In the case of a rational number, the number belonged to one of the two sets on either side, but in the case of an irrational number, the number belonged to neither set. Thus the irrational number was always on the outside, as Deleuze says, of both sets, which made it strangely unreachable and yet, according to the possibility of getting infinitely close to it, adequately defined. In this sense the 'irrational cut' in the new cinema is truly the place of constitution where a body is virtually produced in the singular space outside of narrative.

It is essential to note, however, that the time-image is not constituting the *presence* of the body. According to Deleuze (1989), the new cinema works the 'dancing seeds' and 'luminous dust' of *becoming*, by perturbing perception and producing 'the genesis of an unknown body' (201). The early scientific cinema might have glimpsed this radical unknown body, but it is through contemporary cinema that we begin to grasp the prospect of a new kind of *unrecognisable* body. Here Deleuze refers to Jean-Louis Schefer in *L'Homme ordinaire du cinéma* and his thesis that the object of cinema is:

> not to reconstitute a presence of bodies, in perception and action, but to carry out a primordial genesis of bodies in terms of their white, or a black or a grey (or even in terms of colours), in terms of a 'becoming of visible which is not yet a figure, which is not yet an action'. (Deleuze 1989: 201)

This is no longer a body that is the source of its will and action, but instead a Bergsonian body – a zone of indiscernability. This fact points to the undecidability of the body, 'the non-choice of the body', the body without organs. Deleuze demands that we follow the flow of intensity that contracts – provisionally – into a body. This is a body that is constantly assembling, dissembling and re-assembling.

In the next section, I explore how educational researchers might use an 'experimenting' camera to get at this Bergsonian body in classroom research. I use video data from a previously published study of student movement and gesture in the classroom.[1] In particular, I am interested in how one might relink these images in order to get at a post-phenomenological body and study the forces of affect that flow across classroom events. My aim is to pursue the time-image of 'original footage', to study the virtual image of video data, where the virtual image is a kind of pure recollection (à la Bergson). How might we encounter this crystal image where the genesis of these material relations is produced? What can we do – as researchers – that might allow one to study video data for the crystalline structure that sustains the provisional balance of individuation of a body or an action? How can we provoke or shock our 'audience' into thinking the time-image or the recollection image? If we aim to escape from the psychological automata of a movement-image that always seems to serve state-sanctioned control, then we need to be more radical in the way we work with these digital images. In the next section I offer a new method for using video data to study the potentiality of the body.

IV. Video Experiments and the Post-human Body

The method of video analysis discussed here is inspired by the Argentinian video artist Leonardo Solaas. Solaas creates social web applications and generative experiments using various computer algorithms. I have used one of his applications, available at http://www.solaas.ar.com, called Doodl, which is a tool that interacts with video images. He offers about nine such applications, and in some cases also offers the source code. Doodl is an online drawing robot that feeds on digital images. The robot acts like a swarm of 'autonomous computational agents that drift endlessly over the surface of the screen, leaving a trace' (Solaas 2011). The algorithm by which they operate decodes colours in the source image in terms of force. It quantifies the colour intensity in adjacent cells and translates that data into 'a force field' that influences the speed and direction of the flowing lines that are drawn. In other words, the robots roam randomly (and endlessly) across the image, continuously calculating a relational difference in intensity that is then translated into the speed and direction of the drawn graphic. This is not a representational tool in the strict sense of resemblance, in that the robot is generative of slightly altered and unscripted new images due to the randomness of the roaming, as well as reflecting various kinds of parameters that one can change (number of robots, speed, thickness of line, and angle of deflection). The result is always a new video that records this randomly roaming incorporation of the video data (Figure 3).

The robots incorporate the still image – in this case an image from a classroom video – and turn it into a pure event beyond the organic movement-image that is its source. The new video that is generated – as one records the Doodl event – goes on indefinitely, as the roaming is endless, and the doodling becomes harder and harder to discern in the increasingly coloured screen. Thus we can say that the drawing tool generates a dynamic diagram for this moment in the classroom interaction. When looking at these genetic images we can begin to study processes of actualisation and individuation, slowly building a very layered temporal crystal for each source image that we use. This method seems to offer us a way to tap into a new dimension for each 'frame' in

Figure 3. Four images generated from Doodl analysis of video data (copyright of the author). A colour version can be viewed online.

the video, a dimension of intensity that both cuts away and dis-invests in the usual temporal unfolding of the movement-images.

When the application begins, streams of flowing coloured lines emerge, folding and twisting across the initially white screen. Very early on in the application, one notices both the proliferation of undulating lines in a particular colour – where a solid substance slowly emerges – and the formation of border or contour lines that seem to individuate objects, but may simply mark a shadow or a fold in the surfaces as captured in the source image. These fuzzy borders remain indeterminate, no matter how long the application runs, and the smudged effect is radically different from that found in the source image where we assume the borders around tables, cups and children are fully articulated.

The processes of individuation that occur as this event unfolds, made visible through Doodl, operate through the differential of light (Figure 4). This focus on the intensity and calibration of colour shows the viewer how the gradation of light traverses the various bodies in the classroom. Assuming the duality of matter, this kind of video analysis lends itself to the study of the materiality of learning assemblages. If light is energy, then we can use this application to study the relational ontology of interaction. Not only does this application show the blurring of boundaries between objects, but it shows the *process of actualisation*

Figure 4. Flow of light/individuation (copyright of the author). A colour version can be viewed online.

in ways that representational tools do not. The application generates the image using a random walk and a sensitivity to gradations of colour. Unlike a representation of movement, this is a direct presentation of the virtuality of time in the image. This application unpacks the stillness of the video still, and generates new folds for this now singular moment. This method of video analysis is an infinite process of crystallisation (the roaming process can continue indefinitely), operating through the tiny roaming robots, each acting as a kind of Deleuzian seed which 'incorporates the environment and forces it to crystallize' (Deleuze 1989: 88).

This is an event of infolding, whereby the robots actualise the virtuality of the selected image, a virtuality that is linked to the force field of colour/light variation in the video. In *Francis Bacon: The Logic of Sensation*, Deleuze (2003) discusses how Bacon is interested in the forces that sustain a figure, while wanting to escape figuration as that which is always already immersed in narrative. Bacon, like Cezanne, wanted to paint sensation. Deleuze selects Bacon because he dwells on the figure in ways that help us think about sensation in post-humanist ways. As Smith states in the introduction to the book, Deleuze will return again and again to Bacon's interest in 'the figure, the surrounding fields of color, and the contour that separates the two' (Deleuze 2013: xii).

As a method for analysing video, Doodl has the same predilections. As Deleuze says of Francis Bacon's smudge paintings: 'create resemblances, but through accidental and non-resembling means' (Deleuze 2003: 80). And indeed these videos and the resulting images evoke the painting of Francis Bacon, operating through a kind of colourism and a disfiguration of the human body, while not completely abandoning the figure.

Doodl attends to relations of tonality. In other words, it maps the modulation of colour intensity in the image. This allows us to study the way different forces are modulated rather than mediated in the particular instant under study. Deleuze (2003) suggests that Bacon's skill at 'coloring sensation' is what allows us to get at the post-human body without organs. He says 'The formula for the colorists is: if you push color to its pure internal relations (hot-cold, expansion-contraction), then you have everything' (112). Colourism aims to show how colour itself is the variable relation or differential relation on which individuation depends. The technique of the colourist is 'the production of light and even time through the unlimited activity of color' (112). In pushing colour to function in this onto-generative way, Bacon and other colourists, and perhaps thus Doodl too, force us to encounter the image differently. In watching a Doodl video of colouring sensation, the eye is no longer the usual optic device, looking for resemblance, looking for the line, but becomes haptic. In other words, the eye touches the image, and the sense of sight behaves like the sense of touch.

This eerie 'scrambling and smudging' of an action-image gets to the heart of the time-image (Deleuze 2003: 127). During each Doodl event, time splits itself into two heterogeneous paths, one that preserves all of the past, and another that carries the present into the future. As Deleuze (1989) suggests, 'we see in the crystal the perpetual foundation of time, non-chronological time, Cronos and not Chronos' (81). But we do not always know which is which in this perpetual process of differentiation, and this ambiguity is part of the indiscernibility of the Doodl images. Doodl software underscores the many presents that are passing in any given moment, but also directly couples with the past in its entirety and preserves this virtuality in the process of aberrant drawing. In the infolding of colour, we can grasp more than the sequence of events, more than simply the anticipation of action and the coding of gesture as intention, more than the fragment of movement captured in the present moment, and we can begin to grasp as well the ways in which these many presents coexist and the way that all the presents of the past are contracted tightly in the *actual* present.

This method of video analysis demonstrates how it is 'we who are internal to time, not the other way round' (Deleuze 1989: 82). Of course there never is a completed crystal, just as the process of automated random curves can go on forever in Doodl–there is no formula for stopping, save for the reset button. In this sense, we honour the unfinished nature of both thinking and creation. But the crystal image produced by Doodl–relying on the roaming of robots that traverse the intensity of the source image–makes visible the differentiation of time in at least two flows. It underscores the present as an infinitely contracted past. Indeed, according to Deleuze (1989), it is this radical contraction that allows for the present to pass on, like the vertex of a Bergsonian cone. Such a form of video analysis explores the empty time of the event, the interstitial time, a different time revealed inside the event, made from the simultaneity of three implicated presents (will happen, is happening, and has happened), a threesome that forms the paradox of action. This video method performs the dissolution of the action-image, parallel to what Deleuze finds in, the film maker, Alain Resnais' repetitions, wanderings and immobilisations. In the context of educational research, this video method attends to the temporal depth of all activity, the contraction of time in the singular moment, the folding of dispersed energy across the field of the classroom.

Rather than a phenomenology that would invoke the 'lived body', this method attends to the 'profound and almost unlivable power' or 'vital power' of sensation (Deleuze 2003: 39). Doubtless, video will prove to be less vitally linked than future poly-sensual recording technologies, but a video analysis of this sort begins to show how sensation modulates across a classroom, and how activity is dispersed across bodies. Doodl shows us a block of sensation that is coextensive with perception and representation, generating a new intensive dimension to the screen. This has significant implications for how we consider the non-human dimensions of learning. These are images that generate the lines of force or intensity that lie within sensation, undulating lines that show how we are *always becoming non-human* just as they show us how we are also actualised as a human figure. Such a method of video analysis supports efforts to study the asymmetrical entanglements in classrooms, where assemblages are formed between human and non-human agents (de Freitas 2012; 2013). The random aspect of the robots' movement speaks to this unlivable power. As Deleuze suggests, a body is constituted through relationships of force–whether they be chemical, biological, social or political. Any two forces constitute a body as soon as they enter into a relationship. Thus a living body is the 'arbitrary product of forces of which it is composed' (Deleuze 2006: 40). This is why the body is always the fruit of *chance*, says Deleuze, and appears as the most 'astonishing' thing, much more astonishing, in fact, than consciousness and spirit.

V. Two Kinds of Automata

Deleuze argues that the new cinema offers a *direct presentation* of time rather than a *representation* of time. It does so on the basis of 'the disproportion of scales, the dissipation of centres and the false continuity of the images themselves' (Deleuze 1989: 37). While the movement-image constituted time in terms of 'a successive present in an extrinsic relation of before and after, so that the past is a former present, and the future a present to come' (Deleuze 1989: 271), the time-image operates according to a different logic of composition. This new logic is topological, probabilistic and irrational. Thus in early scientific cinema, and its continuation in current video research practice, time is always indirectly presented through movement, but in the new cinema, movement is subordinate to time. I am arguing that current video research has yet to discover the time-image, and instead it stays true to the movement-image. To be fair, there are subtle differences that distinguish the early scientific cinema and current video research on embodiment, but many of those differences have to do with the digital technology, and are yet to be adequately explored. More work needs to be done, as Deleuze suggested, on the as yet unknown aspects of the time-image.[2] In the early scientific cinema, the focus was on capturing movement, which was part of a physiological assumption that one could uncover the fundamental units of movement. In education video research, there is an increasing awareness that the scale is sliding, that the micro-gesture hides another micro-gesture, that if one selects another calibration, an infinite fold of time continues to be exposed (Nemirovsky 2013). Access to finer granularities of time is doubtless linked to particular attributes of the digital image, although not yet clearly operationalised. When we take a video and break it, that is, make it into twenty-four stills/second or whatever metric we select – and of course, it is that 'whatever' which is so important for the automaticity of film – we can no longer invest in the false continuity of the movement-image and we must draw on different energies to make sense of these images, especially as we consider using industrial cameras that can record up to 1000 frames per second.

Rather than track these frames for how the sensory-motor body acts rationally, a new video research method will explore how these frames are irrationally linked and potentially *out of order*. Instead of causally linking images, we relink them. Instead of following a linear emplotment, we 'turn around' so that time's arrow is twisted into multiple directions. The techniques of a new video method will show us how our relationship to the moving-image has changed, and thus we can begin to grasp how we might tap into the time-image in our current research. This awareness is 'a perception which does not grasp perception without also grasping its reverse, imagination, memory or knowledge' (Deleuze 1989: 245). Deleuze (1989) claims that it is 'cinema's automatic character' that gives it the capacity to explore the parallel and co-extensive choices that might normally be mutually exclusive. Thus the moving-image plants the seed of the time-image, luring us into further experiments with the cut. In post-war cinema, the irrational cut or interstice between two series of images 'determines the non-commensurable relations between images' (213). This is what makes these cuts different from the montage of Eisenstein, in which there are *rational* cuts that always determine commensurable relations between series of images. Thus in Eisenstein, time is an *indirect* representation of these commensurable images.

I am advocating for a new video research method which moves beyond the rational linkage of montage to a direct presentation of time, and this entails thought in contact with an unthought – 'the unsummable, the inexplicable, the undecidable, the incommensurable' (Deleuze 1989: 214). In the time-image, the fissure or interstice has become primary. As Deleuze (1989) suggests, 'It is the method of BETWEEN', whether it be between two images, two perceptions, two affections, two actions (180). It is the cut and the calibration 'which does away with all the cinema of the One' (180). The objective of this new research method is to make the indiscernible visible, not as presence or will, but in its pure indeterminacy. Although positivist paradigms within education research will judge the suggestion absurd – and for that reason if no other we should consider it – I believe that video researchers need to study video art. Deleuze points to the director Godard as one who explored the interstices, presenting images that belonged neither to one scene nor another. The insertion of such shots undermines any continuity of internal monologue or plot, making all claims to voice float about un-owned in any definitive way. *Educational researchers need to study Godard.*

How might we pursue these experiments in our video research practices? How might we tap into the potential of video's automatic character and its potential to directly present time? Deleuze (1989) reminds us that there are at minimum two kinds of automata – the first is the 'great spiritual automaton' which pursues the highest exercise of thought, while the second is the 'psychological automaton' who is 'dispossessed of his own thought' (263). In the first case, cinema confronts automata fundamentally. In the second case, it serves the control society and its reliance on the movement-image. These two kinds of automata are aligned with the two regimes of the image that Deleuze names, the chronic crystal regime (the time-image) and the kinetic organic regime (the movement-image). In the first case, we follow a will to art that allows us to engage with the time-image. In classroom research, this engagement can be mobilised through experiments with the digital nature of the video image. This more fundamental encounter breaks with a psychology of conceptual embodiment as well as a phenomenology of the human body as the administrator of all its participation. For the researcher, this encounter serves *the will to art*, 'aspiring to deploy itself through involuntary movements', but always risking new methods that may destroy that same will (Deleuze 1989: 266). In other words, researchers need to tap into an electronic will to art, to experiment with video, to stretch and break the digital image.

In this section, I have relied on Deleuze's account of new cinema to draw attention to how different cinematic techniques are materially implicated in the production and performance of particular images of the body. I have also drawn attention to how digital technologies are re-assembling social science methods more generally. Rather than or in addition to the slicing of the movement-image into still frames, as early scientific cinema did and as contemporary education video research continues to do, we need to explore other methods that deploy the digital. Ruppert et al. (2013) suggest that we attend to 'the lively, productive and performative qualities of the digital by attending to the specificities of digital devices and how they interact, and sometimes compete, with older devices . . . ' (22). He asks that social scientists look to work in the digital humanities and media studies so that we might begin to see how digital technologies can mobilise and materialise new social relations and new research paradigms. Savage (2013) indicates that we must examine the way that digital technologies are radically altering our methods of inquiry, and that we need to attend to the social life of research methods in the context of new media.

VI. Concluding Remarks and Provocations

The Doodl algorithm facilitates the study of the indeterminate body, a body that is produced through flowing lines and differentials. This body is no longer the centre of wilful action, but the emergent provisional body, a body that exists in potentiality. The human body is studied as a process of individuation, provisionally emergent in relation to the flow of forces across the classroom, itself another body. The student is, nonetheless, still a human body, but one that is always open to new configurations of sensory capacity – indeed one whose sensory organs are provisionally assembled. The application allows us to pursue the radical implications of cinema's 'any-instant-whatever' for, as Deleuze suggests, 'when one relates movement to any-moment-whatevers, one must be capable of thinking the production of the new, that is, of the remarkable and the singular, at any one of these moments ... ' (Deleuze 1986: 7). The specifics of the Doodl software attend to differences in colour intensity in the video image, incorporating and responding to the subtle gradations encountered in the random walk through the data. These colour gradations partake in the material individuation of bodies in the classroom, slowly vibrating around borders, surfaces and volumes. This new method of analysis gets under our perceptions of colour and begins to map the movement of sensations as they traverse a classroom encounter. The undulating lines do not follow a line of human perception, but rather a line of binding intensity. My hope is that this experimental method of studying video data will act as a catalyst for other experiments in the field of educational research.

More generally, this article calls attention to the digital aspects of video data. My aim has been to contribute to the discussion about how our current video practice serves particular kinds of learning theories and particular images of the human body, like other recent Deleuzian work on research methods in the social sciences (Maclure et al. 2010; Coleman and Ringrose 2013). Video research in education has inherited a set of data conventions from the history of early scientific cinema, a set of conventions that were used in the capitalist over-coding of the human body during twentieth century industrialisation of labour. Drawing on ideas from Deleuze, I have argued that we need to reckon with the digital potentiality of video data, in order to move beyond these cinematic conventions, so that we can begin to map new ontologies of the social and engage with the radical unthought of the time-image.

It also seems urgent that we confront the algorithmic nature of digital devices as we accept as common practice the reliance on digital data in educational research, and as we become increasingly immersed in video data and software protocols. We need to experiment with digital algorithms rather than submit to them, to enter into contact with them rather than simply submit to the software that is handed down to us. As the software theorist Lev Manovich (2013) asks:

> How does the software we use influence what we express and imagine? Shall we continue to accept the decisions made for us by algorithms if we don't know how they operate? What does it mean to be a citizen of a software society? These and many other important questions are waiting to be analyzed.

In this article, I have offered one example of how one might engage with video data in different ways, proposing Doodl as a tool. My use of Doodl is an example of what Luciani Parisi (2013) has called 'speculative computation' whereby we pursue 'the aesthetic function of algorithms in their quantitative concreteness' (xv). The term *speculative computation* supplies a way to think about such broaching experiments, a way of rethinking our relation to the digital. This article offers one breaching experiment that treats video as structured light, processing video data as a cinema of intensity rather than a movement-image.

This article poses the question to those using video data in their education research as to how they might begin to explore the crystal time-image in their work. How might we use video data without re-inscribing the phenomenological sensory-motor body all too readily controlled and archived? What sort of movement are we studying when we study video as structured light, as colourism? Doodl taps into the exaggerated, incessant and Brownian movement of life, the 'trampling, a to-and-fro, a multiplicity of movements at different scales' (Deleuze 1989: 128). My aim is to study these anomalous movements as productive rather than demote them as tangential to purposeful movement. To what extent this kind of video analysis will 'shed light' on education remains to be seen, but it does begin to embrace pure optical images, demanding that we grasp the multifarious temporal dimensions of the image, dimensions that never stop folding. These other dimensions are not spatial in the typical sense, for they twist time into alternative planes of immanence, so that a viewer falls in with the internal relations of the infolding image. Such video practices will allow us to study the heterogeneous temporalities at play in classrooms.

Notes

1. For original images, see de Freitas and Palmer (2015) and Sinclair et al. (2012: 239–52).
2. Deleuze, writing in the 1980s, states of the new digital technologies: 'An original will to art has already been defined by us in the change affecting the intelligible content of cinema itself: the substitution of the time-image for the movement-image. So that electronic images will have to be based on still another will to art, or on as yet unknown aspects of the time-image' (Deleuze 1989: 266).

References

Brophy, Jere (ed.) (2004) *Using Video in Teacher Education*, San Diego, CA: Elsevier, Inc.
Cartwright, Lisa (1995) *Screening the Body: Tracing Medicines Visual Culture*, Minneapolis, MN: University of Minnesota Press.
Coleman, Rebecca and Jessica Ringrose (2013) *Deleuze and Research Methodologies*, Edinburgh: Edinburgh University Press.
Cook, Susan W., Ryan G. Duffy and Kimberley M. Fenn (2013) 'Consolidation and Transfer of Learning after Observing Hand Gesture', *Child Development*, 84: 6, pp. 1863–71.
de Freitas, Elizabeth (2012) 'The Classroom as Rhizome: New Strategies for Diagramming Knotted Interaction', *Qualitative Inquiry*, 18: 7, pp. 557–70.
de Freitas, Elizabeth (2013) 'What Were You Thinking? A Deleuzian/Guattarian Analysis of Communication in the Mathematics Classroom', *Educational Philosophy and Theory*, 45: 3, pp. 287–300.
de Freitas, Elizabeth and Anna, Palmer (2015) 'How scientific concepts come to matter: Rethinking the concept of force', *Cultural Studies of Science Education*: 10(2), DOI 10.1007/s11422-014-9652-6.
Deleuze, Gilles (1986) *Cinema 1, The Movement Image*, trans. Hugh Tomlinson and Barbara Habberjam, Minneapolis, MN: The Athlone Press.
Deleuze, Gilles (1989) *Cinema 2, The Time Image*, trans. Hugh Tomlinson and Robert Galeta, Minneapolis, MN: The Athlone Press.
Deleuze, Gilles (2003) *Francis Bacon: The Logic of Sensation*, Minneapolis, MN: University of Minnesota Press.
Deleuze, Gilles [1962] (2006) *Nietzsche & Philosophy*, New York: Columbia University Press.
Derry, Sharon J., Roy D. Pea, Brigid Barron, Randi A. Engle, Ferderick Erikson, Ricki Goldman, Rogers Hall, Timothy Koschmann, Jay L. Lemke, Miriam Sherin and Bruce L. Sherin (2010) 'Conducting Video Research in the Learning Sciences: Guidance on Selection, Analysis, Technology and Ethics', *The Journal of the Learning Sciences*, 19, pp. 3–53.
Doane, Mary Ann (2002) *The Emergence of Cinematic Time: Modernity, Contingency, the Archive*, Cambridge, MA: Harvard University Press.
Erikson, Frederick (2006) 'Definition and Analysis of Data from Videotape: Some Research Procedures and their Rationales', in J. L. Green, G. Camilli and P. Elmore (eds), *Handbook of Complementary Methods in Education Research*, Mahwah, NJ: Erlbaum, pp. 177–92.
Foster, Hal (2004) 'An archival impulse', *October*, 110 (Fall), 3–22.
Goldman, Ricki, Roy Pea, Brigid Barron and Sharon J. Derry (eds) 2007 *Video Research in the Learning Sciences*, Mahwah, NJ: Erlbaum.

Maclure, Maggie, Rachel Holmes, Christina Macrae and Liz Jones (2010) 'Animating Classroom Ethnography, Overcoming Video-fear', *International Journal of Qualitative Studies in Education*, 23: 5, pp. 543–56.

Manovich, Lev (2013) 'The Algorithms of our Lives', *The Chronicle Review*, 16.

Nemirovsky, Ricardo (2013) 'Embodied Cognition: What it Means to Know and Do Mathematics', *National Council of Teachers of Mathematics Annual Research Conference*, New Orleans, LA.

O'Halloran, Kay, Alexey Podlasov, Sabine Tan, Marissa E, Rohanizah Ali, Mukundan Ar and Sumit Gajwani (2013) *Multimodal Analysis Video*, Singapore: Multimodal Analysis Company.

Parisi, Luciana (2013) *Contagious Architecture: Computation, Aesthetics and Space*, Cambridge, MA: MIT Press.

Ruppert, Evelyn, John Law and Mike Savage (2013) 'Re-assembling Social Science Methods: The Challenge of Digital Devices', *Theory, Culture and Society*, 30: 4, pp. 22–46.

Savage, Mike (2013) 'The "Social Life of Methods": A Critical Introduction', *Theory, Culture, Society*, 30: 4, pp. 3–21.

Sekula, Allan (1986) 'The Body and the Archive', *October*, Winter, 3–64.

Sinclair, Nathalie, Elizabeth de Freitas and Francesca Ferrara (2012) 'Virtual Encounters: The Murky and Furtive World of Mathematical Inventiveness', *ZDM – The International Journal on Mathematics Education*, 45: 2, pp. 239–52.

Solaas Leonardo (2011), *Solaas.com.ar*, available at http://www.solaas.ar.com (accessed 1 May 2015).

Slave to the Rhythm: The Problem of Creative Pedagogy and the Teaching of Creativity

Francis Russell   Curtin University

Abstract

Since the mid-twentieth century the concepts 'creativity' and 'innovation' have become increasingly significant within a host of fields, such as education, medicine, engineering, technology and science. Moreover, such terms appear to have become ubiquitous, if not hegemonic, within the contemporary discourses that inform debates that surround the allocation and cultivation of the social capital that is native to education, both tertiary and otherwise. Given that the thinking of creativity appears increasingly to be possible only within the contemporary logics of utility and productivity that inform the discussion of the 'knowledge economy', the philosophical works of Gilles Deleuze are perhaps now more vital than ever, at least insofar as he is able to provide the possibility of approaching an 'otherwise' to the contemporary thinking of 'creativity'. This paper discusses the possibility for Deleuze's discussion of *rhythm* – as can be located in his text *A Thousand Plateaus* and his work on the twentieth-century painter Francis Bacon – as providing the means for better posing the question of the conditions for the emergence of a fundamentally creative approach to teaching creativity to be conceptualized within our present situation.

Keywords: Deleuze and Guattari, creativity, innovation, knowledge economy, rhythm

Deleuze Studies 9.3 (2015): 337–355
DOI: 10.3366/dls.2015.0191
© Edinburgh University Press
www.euppublishing.com/journal/dls

According to Beckett's or Kafka's law, there is immobility beyond movement: beyond standing up, there is sitting down, and beyond sitting down, lying down, beyond which one finally dissipates. The true acrobat is one who is consigned to immobility inside the circle.

Deleuze 2005

The term 'creativity' and its contemporary couplet 'innovation' appear to have reached a state of ascendance over the course of the twentieth century, finding predominance in fields as varied as the natural and social sciences, economics, medicine, engineering, education, politics, professional sport, and the arts. Indeed, it would appear to be difficult to find a field or discipline, a subject or sequence, which has not been inculcated within the contemporary thinking of creativity. While those who consider themselves to be part of the tradition designated by the terms 'humanities' or 'liberal-arts' are now perhaps accustomed to receiving the odes to creativity that have become conventional in the disciplines of economics or business with a knowing shake of the head and a resigned sigh, the pervasiveness of the term 'creativity' appears to stretch beyond such apparent clichés.[1] Consider, for example, the writer and journalist Hans Christoph Buch's introductory essay from the text *Exodus: 50 Million People on the Move*, a collection of photographs documenting the lives of refugees. In this preliminary text, Buch argues that the collected images do not represent the third world and its inhabitants in terms of a 'conglomeration of hopeless misery' but, instead, as a 'creative chaos in which people with imagination and a talent for improvisation find a way to survive' (Kumin et al. 1997: 30). While there is much to be said for the attempt to articulate the injustices that refugees encounter daily without removing their agency and dignity, there is, nonetheless, something noteworthy about the deployment of terms such as 'creative chaos', 'imagination' and 'talent for improvisation' in order to describe the lives of those seeking refuge from war and political violence. It would appear then to be the case that this apparent convention that has taken hold within our present situation, of referring to painters, engineers, corporate bankers, *Australian Idol* contestants, and refugees alike, as being creative practitioners – that, with regards to creativity, their respective practices are different in application and not in essence – perhaps originates out of a broader shift in the conventional application of the concept of creativity. Though its ubiquity can promote a tendency to regard creativity as a necessary and a-historical concept that would be vital for adequately approaching the 'richness of human experience', the term itself, and its contemporary meaning, has, instead, gained prominence from out of the cultural and historical movements that have culminated in modernity. Indeed, despite the centrality of the term creativity to our own time, the Ancient Greeks, whose thinking is conventionally understood to be foundational for the Western tradition, 'lacked the creative apprehension of art', and, moreover, felt that 'every innovation' within the field that we would designate as 'aesthetics', 'was an outrage' (Tatarkiewicz 1980: 92). Indeed, for almost a thousand years 'the term creativity did not exist in philosophy, in theology, or in European art' and, moreover, the term's emergence with the civilisation of the Romans was limited to 'colloquial speech, *"creator"* being a synonym for father, and *"creator Urbis"* for the founder of a city' (Tatarkiewicz 1980: 250). Furthermore, the Christian notion of creation, which is perhaps the first prominent usage of the term, would set about a firm prohibition of understanding man's production in terms of the categories of the new or created. Creation was the act of God, not of man; hence, up until the Enlightenment creation would be restricted to theology (Tatarkiewicz 1980: 250). Creation, in its traditional theological conception – a conception that was dominant up until the nineteenth century – signified the production of something from nothing, and was vital for the Christian understanding of the origins of human existence and knowledge. In this model, God is posited as a transcendental and unconditioned entity that *creates* being from out of non-being; hence, *creatio ex nihilo*. For Tatarkiewicz, the thinking of modern creativity is centred on the substitution of *creatio ex nihilo* for the thinking of the production of novelty: 'creativity in the altered construction became the making of *new* things rather than the making of things from nothing' (Tatarkiewicz 1980: 252).

However, within our own time creativity, while often employed uncritically as either a psychological faculty, personality trait or as a kind of unconscious drive, is understood as vital for the production of new goods, markets, processes, and so on. As a 'senior staff member' of the Australian department of Education, Science and Technology has been quoted as saying: 'we need to keep pushing people and trying to get people to be creative, because you won't advance [in industry] if you're not creative' (quoted in Kenway et al. 2006: 80). In fact, it appears increasingly problematic to adhere to hard and fast distinctions between a concept like creativity and innovation, since there is a sense in which the two terms have come to articulate one another over the course of the twentieth century. Hence, it appears that within contemporary discourse the concept of innovation is understood to be driven by the eruptions of creative forces, whilst simultaneously the concept of creativity is understood as a resource that is to be exploited as a means of procuring innovation. Stein and Harper have argued that from a 'pragmatic perspective creativity is not enough' and that instead what is needed alongside creativity is innovation. Innovation, they write, means:

> taking the creative idea and making it *work* in your context. The more dynamic the context, the less likely that old ways will deal with the new problems, and the more important is innovative adaptation to change. (Stein and Harper 2012: 6)

This is to say that, the coupling of creativity and innovation – the idea that innovation requires creativity, and that creativity is wasted unless used to fuel innovation – appears to be made possible by a logic of utility that seemingly functions to dissimulate the possibility of divergent readings of these terms. Indeed, and as Kenway et al. have argued, the coupling of the concepts of creativity and innovation can arguably be situated within a broader incorporation of art and other creative endeavour within the broader economic system. They state that:

> In framing art as a discourse of commodity and technology, the creative industries are themselves engaged in a process of dissimulation, concealing the social, political, philosophical and critical aspects of creativity because they are inconsistent with the capitalist disposition. (Kenway et al. 2006: 82)

Indeed, it would appear to be the case that the logics of utility and productivity that seemingly shape the contemporary thinking of innovation and creativity hold as their *telos* the application of creativity as a means of enabling greater innovations and furthering efficiency and productivity. Hence it appears that for contemporary thought, creativity, which 'man' once struggled to wrestle from the clutches of a transcendental creator, has now become effaced outside of the logics of innovation, utility and productivity. Or, as Benoit Godin puts it, within the twentieth century 'creativity and productivity became one' (Godin 2008: 40). So ubiquitous have these concepts become that it is difficult to conceive of the organisation of knowledge, artistic production, and the emergence of the new as coming about in a way that is alien to the dominant and conventional thinking of creativity and innovation. For those writers concerned with this contemporary situation, recourse is often made to the works of Gilles Deleuze, a thinker who is famous for his preoccupation with the thinking of creativity and the emergence of the new. However, Deleuze appears to have become an ambivalent figure insofar as his work is discussed as being both causally and critically immanent to those logics that circumscribe the thinking of creativity – whether we refer to those logics under the banner of 'late capitalism' or in terms of 'neo-liberalism'. Indeed, while figures such as Emma L. Jeanes (Jeanes 2006) and Thomas Osborne (Osborne 2010) amongst others, affirm a host of Deleuzian concepts – the 'rhizome', the 'body without organs', 'lines-of-flight', 'becoming', 'the virtual', and 'delirium' just to name a few – in an attempt to find non-totalising approaches to creativity, for a host of contemporary philosophers – such as Simon Critchley, Slavoj Žižek and Benjamin Noys – Deleuze's privileging of pure difference and creativity is interpreted as signalling, at best, a complicity with the very repressive forces of capitalism his work attempts to subvert, and, at worse, his status as the master ideologue of 'creative' or 'late' capitalism. For example, in his text *The Persistence of the Negative: A Critique of Contemporary Continental Theory*, Noys argues that the 'irony' of the contemporary appeals made to Deleuzian difference, as a form of resistance against the seemingly hegemonic and totalising 'late-capitalist' logics of utility and productivity, is that such a strategy:

> brought this thinking into alignment with the ideology of contemporary 'creative capitalism' – one predicated on invoking the inexhaustible creating powers of novelty, production and creativity. (Noys 2010: xi)

Therefore, rather than being a means of resisting the endless production of the new – new markets for potential growth and investment, new political parties and representatives to maintain the voter's faith in the possibility of capitalism's self-development, new technologies and methodologies for the production of cheaper and novel goods and services, new iPhones, and so on – Deleuze's advocating of 'nomadic' thinking can be read as merely aligning itself with, rather than opposing itself to, the flows and cycles of 'creative capitalism'. Indeed, Simon Critchley raises this very question of 'nomadism's' relation to 'late-capitalism' when he asks:

> Might not hybridity, exile and nomadism better describe the deterriorializing force and the speculative flows of later capitalism and the theories of its management gurus and marketing consultants rather than constituting any resistance to it? (Critchley 2009: 138)

Therefore, given that Deleuze's privileging of creativity and difference is grasped both at the level of a radical opposition to *and* compliant articulation of what could be referred to as neo-liberalism, it would appear difficult indeed to attempt to decide emphatically how Deleuzian thought interacts with our present situation. However, at this juncture I wish to relocate this discussion of Deleuzian thought and the contemporary problem of creativity within a proximal contemporary problematic – namely, the problem of approaching a creative pedagogy, specifically with regards to the teaching of creativity. Given the aforementioned difficulty of approaching creativity outside the logics of utility and productivity, and given the problematic nature of Deleuzian thought, the question that I wish to pose is: how can a fundamentally creative approach to teaching creativity be conceptualised within our present situation? And, furthermore, to what extent can the thought of Deleuze be used to aid such a conceptualisation? Indeed, in posing such questions I wish to suspend entirely any critical imperative that might present the injunction to either run to Deleuze's aid by way of defending the critical import of this thinking, or, alternately, to attempt to undermine Deleuze's key concepts.

The first challenge that would face anyone who attempted to consider the potential for a creative pedagogy – and, in particular, a creative pedagogy of creativity – would be to alter, if not to overcome entirely, the seemingly intractable separation and stratification of the teacher and student. As Deleuze and Guattari point out in A Thousand Plateaus, the function of the teacher can all too often become that of providing and transmitting orders, of ordering bodies:

> When the schoolmistress instructs her students on a rule of grammar or arithmetic, she is not informing them, any more than she is informing herself when she questions a student. She does not so much as instruct as 'insign,' give orders or commands. A teacher's commands are not external or additional to what he or she teaches us. (Deleuze and Guattari 2012: 88)

On Deleuze and Guattari's account, the teacher's role is to order and shape the students, to prepare them in advance for the various roles and expectations that may await them outside the school. We are told that the teacher does not 'so much as instruct as insign', and, here, we cannot help but be drawn to 'insignia' from the Latin *insigne* meaning to mark or badge. The student is 'stamped' into the correct social, intellectual and physical form, and, when this stamping occurs with the least resistance from the student – that is to say, when the student proves to be most receptive and malleable as a material for stamping – the success warrants a stamp of approval on the behalf of the teacher. Indeed, this stamping is, for Deleuze and Guattari, the very function of the 'compulsory education machine'. Regardless of the dedication of the individual teacher, or of the spirited investment the odd student shows in their lessons,

Deleuze and Guattari's argument would appear to reveal the seemingly inevitable over-determination of ordering – that the teacher and students, despite their 'individuality', always already remain part of this broader 'ordering', of transmitting and receiving orders. While some might protest that there have always been teachers who 'put the students first' or who have maintained that 'students have as much to teach us as we them', such claims ultimately function to further, rather than equalise, the discord between the positions of teacher and student[2] insofar as the teacher's dissimulation of their power presents the possibility of disabling critique before it can ever be articulated.[3] Therefore, the question remains as to how we can conceive of something that is *against* the conventional couplet of teacher–student; something inextricably *other* than these aforementioned positions – or the relationships that occur between these positions – and yet, nonetheless, intimate to such positions and their subsistence. Here I would argue that the Deleuzian concept of rhythm, a concept that Deleuze deploys to notable affect in *A Thousand Plateaus* and *Francis Bacon: The Logic of Sensation*, can perhaps be utilised in order to provide an ontological account that disrupts the modes of separation and stratification that appear inextricably bound to the conventional thinking of the teacher–student couplet (Deleuze 2005; Deleuze and Guattari 2012). As with many of his concepts, the application of 'rhythm' is not restricted to a specific philosophical problem, or a disciplinary horizon, within the Deleuzian oeuvre. For this reason we can find within the aforementioned texts discussions of 'rhythm', applied respectively both to ontological questions regarding living organisms, and to discussions of post-impressionist and modernist painting. In *A Thousand Plateaus* rhythm is discussed in terms of the emergence and interconnected nature of various heterogeneous and pre-individual 'milieus' or environments, terms that function to produce the 'living thing' (Deleuze and Guattari 2012: 364–5). Accordingly, as the living thing is understood to emerge out of a series of interconnected environments, its 'self-identity' is radically brought into question, since, by way of its composite and heterogonous (be)coming into existence, the living thing never manifests nor subsists from out of any singular origin. We can better appreciate the consequences of such an anti-representational approach if we turn to his work *Francis Bacon: The Logic of Sensation*, where Deleuze argues that there exists a commonality or community amongst the arts insofar as they share the task of 'capturing forces' as opposed to 'reproducing or inventing forms' (Deleuze 2005: 48). Modern art, like Deleuze's philosophy, attempts to capture the productive forces of intensity that surge through milieus, as opposed to excluding such forces by way of focusing on representing supposedly 'self-identical' forms. It is in this sense that Deleuze affirms the Swiss–German painter Paul Klee's famous formulation that painting is 'not to render the visible, but to render visible' (Deleuze 2005: 48). Returning to *A Thousand Plateaus*, Deleuze and Guattari state that the living thing has four milieus: 'exterior', 'interior', 'intermediary' and 'annexed' (Deleuze and Guattari 2012: 364). Each of these milieus contains various processes – that is the living thing's interior milieu involves a series of complex and interconnected biological processes, whereas the annexed milieu contains perceptual or experiential processes – all of which are, in their interconnected affects, altering each other and, accordingly, the milieu in which they function. While, Deleuze and Guattari state that each milieu is 'coded' insofar as it becomes 'periodically defined' by the 'repetitions' of the processes that occur temporally within it, they go on to argue that, 'each code is in a perpetual state of transcoding or transduction' (Deleuze and Guattari 2012: 364). Transcoding and transduction are discussed in *A Thousand Plateaus* as being the 'manner in which one milieu serves as the basis for another, or conversely is established atop another milieu, dissipates in it or is constituted in it' (Deleuze and Guattari 2012: 364). Milieus, then, just like the processes within them, are constantly encoding, decoding and recoding themselves through their dynamic interactions with similarly heterogeneous milieus. Displaying the full extent to their affirmation of difference 'all the way down' when considering the milieus and processes that come to enform and deform the living thing, Deleuze and Guattari state that:

> The notion of the milieu is not unitary: not only does the living thing continually pass from one milieu to another, but the milieus pass into one another; they are essentially communicating. (Deleuze and Guattari 2012: 364)

Simultaneously erupting through milieu and process, and functioning as the fundamental disruption of all milieu and process, is what Deleuze and Guattari refer to as 'chaos'. Chaos is, for Deleuze and Guattari, the 'milieu of all milieus', that which all milieus are fundamentally open to and which perennially 'threatens them with exhaustion or intrusion' (Deleuze and Guattari 2012: 364). The failure for milieus to pass from or into one another, in other words, the failure for milieus to communicate with one another – and here we can note that communicate can be traced etymologically back to a notion of sharing or transmitting, such as the sharing or transmitting of a disease – presents the risk of their plunging into the dense plenum of chaos. However, out of the risk of this failure, Deleuze and Guattari argue that there is also born the possibility of the 'transcoded passage from one milieu to another, a communication of milieus'—*rhythm* (Deleuze and Guattari 2012: 364–5). Here I would argue that the Deleuzian concept of rhythm can perhaps be utilised in order to provide an ontological account that disrupts this aforementioned separation and stratification of the teacher and student. The Deleuzian notion of rhythm is discussed within *A Thousand Plateaus* as the heterogeneous movement of differentiation that allows for the possibility of communication between, and within, milieus and processes. Rather than being a specific space or process, rhythm is the dynamic movements that are always already *between* any space and process, and that allow for their co-constitution and the possibility of their dissolution. Given rhythm's fundamentally dynamic and heterogeneous nature, Deleuze and Guattari stress that the term should never be mistaken for the homogeneity of 'meter' or 'cadence' (Deleuze and Guattari 2012: 385). They argue that:

> Meter is dogmatic, but rhythm is critical; it ties together critical moments, or ties itself together in passing from one milieu to another. It does not operate in a homogenous space-time, but by heterogeneous blocks. It changes direction. (Deleuze and Guattari 2012: 365)

In a given piece of music, rhythm is the differential movement between heard elements or actual pieces of sound, and not—and this is the point Deleuze and Guattari stress—merely the ordered space of recurring points in which a piece of music can be measured in order to reveal certain structural elements, such as time signatures. Meter and cadence are presented by Deleuze and Guattari as an almost Newtonian space-as-container, in which the dynamic movements of rhythm can be thought to occur (Deleuze and Guattari 2012: 365). Rhythm, while perceptible, cannot be reduced to any concrete piece of sound that occurs within its overall movement, since such sonic elements are merely arbitrary with regards to their rhythmic status. Furthermore, it is not merely the difference of position between sounds that comprises rhythm. As the twentieth-century composer Henry Cowell argues:

> It is true that, to be realized in music, rhythm must be marked by some sort of sound, but this sound is not itself rhythm. Rhythmical considerations are the duration of sounds, the amount of stress applied to sounds, the rate of speed as indicated by the movement of sounds, periodicity of sound patterns, and so on. (Cowell 2004: 23)

Accordingly, rather than being a fixed node from which a rhythmic movement could be inferred, any discrete element of rhythm could diverge into any number of possible rhythmic movements. A way of illustrating this point would be to take a single snare hit that begins the rhythmic component of a piece of rock music and attempt to infer the entire rhythmic movement from that single piece of sound. The impossibility of such an action refers us to the dynamic nature of rhythm – that is that rhythm is something produced over time and between occurrences, and not a homogenous space in which things can be understood to occur.

The question that undoubtedly remains, however, is what this has to do with teaching creativity and the possibility of a creative pedagogy. I would argue that the concept of rhythm, as deployed in Deleuze's writing and his collaborations with Guattari, is a rich source for reimagining the conventional understandings that surround the thinking of the teaching of creativity. That this aforementioned notion of rhythm posits any supposedly necessary nodal point as being ultimately contingent, and, furthermore, that such a notion pushes the thinker to move beyond such points and to engage with the transformative and dynamic movements that occur through and between them, is significant for anyone attempting to conceive of a creative pedagogy of creativity. Moreover, given that neo-liberal educational reforms have only gained popularity over the last few decades in the USA, the UK and Australia, and given that such reforms place a great emphasis on the calculable performance of students, teachers and institutions as a whole, Deleuze's discussion of rhythm and his privileging of dynamic forces over self-identical individuals is perhaps more prescient than ever before. As Lawrence Angus has argued in his article 'School Choice: Neo-Liberal Education Policy and Imagined Futures', the logic of individualism and the push for greater competitiveness that underpins such reforms places greater emphasis on individual students, teachers and parents at the cost of reducing these terms to isolated idealisations, which are divorced from cultural, political, and economic forces (Angus 2013: 6). Angus states that through the rubric of individualism 'poor performance' becomes localised, and is assumed to be an issue for the individual school, teacher, student or parent in question, and not emergent from out of a broader context (Angus 2013: 6). Furthermore, as Polesel et al. have argued in their text 'The Impact of High-Stakes Testing on Curriculum and Pedagogy: A Teacher Perspective From Australia', one of the impacts of high-stakes testing has been the degradation of student's experiences of learning, since an ever greater portion of time is dedicated to 'cramming' for standardised tests (Polesel et al. 2013: 643). What this suggests is that isolating teachers and students from broader milieus and from the forces they contain ultimately functions to provide a misleading image of education. While this discussion of the effects of neo-liberal economic policy sits outside of the scope of this paper, the dominance of such approaches to education presents Deleuze's account of rhythm, when applied to teaching (and particularly the teaching of creativity) appears increasingly significant and untimely.

And this is effectively to argue that, when conceived in terms of this notion of rhythm, we can posit the teacher and student as being other than isolated and self-identical individuals, and we can instead approach them as being bound to the dynamic movements that occur within any attempt to teach and learn. As these points, or positions, are wholly contingent, they cannot be understood to contain any necessary or essential content or pertain to any fixed function. Just as Cowell argues that rhythm is locatable in the modifications and transformations that occur to sound over the course of a dynamic movement, similarly, teaching and learning in general, and the teaching of creativity in particular, involves a parallel set of modifications and transformations – such as discussion, confrontation, consultation, instruction, illustration, objection and reiteration just to mention a few – which occur dynamically over time. As creativity, if it is to be truly creative, is that which precisely cannot be predetermined in advance, the discussion of the creative teaching of creativity as being underpinned by a kind of dynamic and heterogeneous rhythmic movement is significant, insofar as it avoids ascribing any fixity to the contingent roles that are inherited by any set of concrete individuals. Furthermore, such a conception of rhythm avoids affixing creativity to individuals as if it were a faculty or attribute – one that some individuals merely hold by their 'nature' – and instead looks to creativity as a kind of movement that is generated 'between' rather than 'in'. Just as no single piece of sound can be used to determine in advance the movement of rhythm, neither can the teacher or student – or the knowledge that is possessed or lacked by either – be used to infer the dynamic movement that any attempt to teach creativity will take.[4] Accordingly, as neither the teacher nor the student can ground, in advance, the possibility of the emergence of the truly creative, it would appear necessary to refer to the teaching and studying of creativity as being of one and the same heterogeneous and dynamic movement. In *Difference and Repetition*, Deleuze affirms such a thinking of the 'with', of the middle ground in which teacher and student already engage in collaborative action. He states 'we learn nothing from those who say "do as I do"' and that, instead of 'proposing gestures for us to reproduce' the teacher must tell their students to 'do with me', to 'emit signs to be developed in heterogeneity' (Deleuze 1994: 23).

As with the attempt to comprehend an aesthetic object such as a work of art, there can be no appeal made to a fixed rule, which, once set in advance, can guarantee that one will be able to teach someone how to be creative. As Daniel W. Smith, the translator of Deleuze's *The Logic of Sensation*, has argued, aesthetic comprehension involves the grasping, even if unconsciously, of a rhythm, insofar as the thing to be measured and the unit of measure come to dynamically co-articulate one another (Smith 2003: xviii). Similarly, with the teaching of creativity the thing to be taught, and the method of teaching, cannot be determined from the position of the teacher or student, but, instead, manifests out of a kind of confluence and co-articulation. However, this does not mean that I, nor Deleuze, should be understood as advocating an 'anything goes' relativist approach to teaching. Indeed, it is important to have a method, and, over the course of the movement of attempting to teach creativity, one will find that certain methods simply are ineffective. However, the necessity of method does not posit the necessity of any particular method, or set of methods, but, instead, suggests simply that while particular procedures will become more effective, useful, or rich, in certain instances, there is nevertheless nothing essential or permanent about those methods. As Niall Lucy has argued in his *Introduction to Postmodern Literary Theory*, it is clear that Deleuze and Guattari stress the importance of method in their collaborative work (Lucy 1997: 187). However, and as Lucy states, 'the question remains open as to what should define this method' (Lucy 1997: 187). Perhaps this quote needs to be reread, or reemphasised, so as to stress that such a question *must* remain open, and, furthermore, that the imposition of 'necessary' methods and procedures presents the risk of simply foreclosing the emergence of something radically new. Deleuze himself raises such a problem in Claire Parnet's film *Deleuze A to Z* where he argues that the work of the genius or the great artist, in being truly new and creative, is precisely that which cannot be conceived of in advance. Speaking of the possibility of great authors emerging in the then contemporary literary scene, Deleuze states, and I quote at length:

> Yes, well ... But the Becketts of today ... Let us assume that they don't get published – after all, Beckett almost did not get published – it's obvious nothing would be missed. By definition, a great author or a genius is someone

who brings forth something new. If this innovation does not appear, then that bothers no one, no one misses it since no one has the slightest idea about it. If Proust ... If Kafka had never been published no one could say that Kafka would be missed ... if someone had burned all of Kafka's writings, no one could say 'Ah, we really miss that!' since no one would have any idea of what had disappeared. If the new Becketts of today are kept from publishing by the current system of publishing, one cannot say 'Oh, we really miss that!' I heard a declaration, the most impudent declaration I have ever heard – I don't dare say to whom it was attributed in some newspaper since these kinds of things are never certain – someone in the publishing field who dared to say: 'You know, today, we no longer risk making mistakes like Gallimard did when he initially refused to publish Proust since we have the means today ... to locate and recognize new Prousts and Becketts.' That's like saying they have some sort of Geiger counter and that the new Beckett – that is, someone who is completely unimaginable since we don't know what kind of innovation he would bring – he would emit some kind of sound if you passed it in his path (Quoted in Boutang 2012: n.p.)

What is so vital about Deleuze's remarks here is that he raises the problem of what could be referred to as the 'images of creativity' that pose the risk of creativity's heterogeneity being overlooked in favour of affirming a representation of creativity. We can better understand the limits and dangers of such representations by turning to what Deleuze calls the 'image of thought' in *Difference and Repetition*. Deleuze states that the image of thought is that set of presuppositions that we uncritically inherit and that function to determine 'our goals when we try to think' (Deleuze 1994: xvi). For Deleuze, what it means to think and what thinking can do is always in excess of our pre-philosophical understanding of what thought is. Deleuze argues that we uncritically assume that there is a clear relationship between thought and truth, as if thinking were somehow pre-ordained to strain towards and grasp that which is true (Deleuze 1994: 132). Moreover, it is assumed that the act of recognition – and the assumed identity that goes along with the recognition of a thing – has something to do with thought, or is an act of thinking. However, for Deleuze an act of mere recognition – for instance, when someone comes across a dog in the street and recognises it as cute or friendly – should not be misrecognised as being synonymous with thought. Deleuze states that 'it cannot be regarded as a *fact* that thinking is the natural exercise of a faculty ... in fact men think rarely, and more often under the impulse of a shock than in the excitement of a taste for thinking' (Deleuze 1994: 132). The image of thought as moral and natural is naturalised usually through the way we are reproached for 'not thinking'. For example, if one does the wrong thing or makes a mistake we often hear phrases like 'think before you act' or 'think you idiot!' Accordingly, the repetition of such phrases creates the impression that thinking is something that we should simply know how to do (natural) and that to not think is to do something wrong (moral). But regardless of how few mistakes we make or how much we are able to perform certain tasks that are demanded of us, such an image of thought not only tells us nothing about thinking itself, but, moreover, it hinders our ability to think thought itself. As Alberto Toscano states 'Deleuze unceasingly advocates the notion that we do not yet know what it means to think – or we do not know what thought can do' (Toscano 2010: 11).

Therefore, just as the image of thought hinders the potentialities of thought itself, so too do the images of creativity that persist within our present situation. That creativity is wedded to some notion of productivity or utility, that it is viewed as something instrumental for 'progress' – a term that is typically made synonymous with these latter terms – or as an attribute that can be predicated to individual subjects, all correspond to particular images of creativity that can ultimately tell us nothing about what creativity is or what creativity can do. Moreover, the role of the educator is thus less one of applying the necessary methods of forming a creative subject and more that of attempting to hold at bay the emergence of any dominant image of the creative. On this point I want to turn to the artist Robert Irwin, a figure who is not typically referred to as emblematic of the teaching profession, but who, nevertheless, displayed a clear concern for this question of the obligation to the openness of creativity.

Robert Irwin had a relatively short career as an educator, spread across three dispersed bursts of teaching activity: at the Chouinard Art Institute in the late 1950s; at the University of California, Los Angeles, in the mid-1960s; and at the University of California, Irvine, during the late 1960s (Weschler 2008: 123). Indeed, it does not appear to be the case that Irwin dedicated a great deal of time to the discussion of pedagogy or the teaching or creativity, and rarely has he been praised for his contribution to education in general. However, my interest in Irwin has less to do with the specific content of his teaching or his personal theories on the subject of teaching, and more to do with what I would claim is a clear example of a figure who takes this notion of an obligation to the openness of creativity as being absolutely paramount. At all of the institutions he was associated with as a teacher, Irwin favoured a process of seemingly interminable questioning that would push his students' practices through the various stylistic contours of art history (Weschler

2008: 124). However, if, over the course of his teaching, Irwin felt that students were beginning to look to Irwin for *answers*, or even to take Irwin's approach of ceaseless questioning as 'the' answer to all creative problems, then Irwin would simply leave. Irwin, in an interview with the writer Lawrence Weschler, states that over the course of his relatively short career as a teacher he encountered many students who wanted him to act as:

> their guru, and that's the last thing you can do for them, that's the worst thing. And wherever I've been, once it begins to shift from why to how, I simply leave: I'm gone. (Quoted in, Weschler 2008: 126)

Regardless of the effectiveness of Irwin's teaching style, I would argue that his commitment to an unwillingness to engage with students in terms of dogmatisms or predetermined notions of creativity – an unwillingness that resulted in Irwin only ever teaching for a total of five years in his career, and never for more than two years at any one institution (Weschler 2008: 126) – serves as a clear expression of what I would refer to as a commitment to the openness of the creative. To question whether or not Irwin was ever able to help a student produce something genuinely creative or new would be to miss the point, since such an obligation to the maintaining of the openness of the creative – that is struggling to ensure that what creativity is or means is never predetermined – is, I would argue, the true obligation of a creative pedagogy of creativity.

Therefore, rather than Irwin being able to provide us with an exemplary model for teaching creativity, I would suggest that the real lesson he has to teach is taught in the manner that a sense of obligation is communicated through their sheer unwillingness to allow something that, by its very nature, cannot be understood in advance to be predetermined. However, at this point, I feel it must be reiterated that the kind of obligation evident in a figure such as Irwin should not be misinterpreted as being a different presentation of the same tired clichés about the necessity of students and teachers interacting on a level playing field or in a non-stratified way – which, as I have stated earlier, does not seem to be possible. Instead, the kind of commitment to the openness of the creative and its irreducibility to any image of creativity that, I argue, we can find in such an example would instead function best to serve as a constant reminder to be sceptical of all facts and dogmas regarding creativity and the manner in which it 'should' be taught. Indeed, I think the fairly hackneyed quote that 'those who can do; those who can't teach' can help to illustrate this point if, instead of adhering to the conventional interpretation that serves to characterise the teacher as someone who is inept or a failure, we reinterpret this expression to mean that the teacher is the one who *resists* the urge to leap into action, who *resists* assuming the position of the 'doer' who has all the prerequisite knowledge necessary for the correct engagement and performance, and who, instead, allows for the possibility that precisely what is not known can be approached only through a commitment to an openness that would preclude every *necessary* action – that is an openness that would render every action contingent.

Interestingly enough, the very idea that we can look to Deleuze as providing a means of escaping the problem of creativity is itself centred on the need to find a 'new' theorist who can provide us with something fresh and exciting and opposed to those old and worn out theorists who cannot offer us anything that instantly looks to be new. Žižek, in the introduction to *Organs without Bodies*, answers the self-imposed question 'why Deleuze?' by stating that 'In the past decade, Deleuze emerged as the central reference of contemporary philosophy' (Žižek 2004: xxi). Against this apparent impulse to be 'timely' should we not attempt to embrace the untimeliness of every truly creative endeavour by way of resisting the contemporary neophilia that appears to surround discussions of Deleuze's work? Indeed, it is perhaps wholly arbitrary that we look to a figure like Deleuze, and that there could be any number of figures we could turn to answer these questions. Indeed, if we are to be creative with our approach to both education and to our reading of a figure like Deleuze, then we must have no preconception of what he is to teach us in advance, of what 'kind' of philosopher, or teacher, Deleuze is.[5] Returning to the question of the ambiguous status of the concept of creativity in our contemporary situation, and of the ambiguities that the likes of Badiou, Critchley, Noys and Žižek claim to have detected in Deleuze's work, it is interesting to note that we appear to have inherited the problem of creativity being both ubiquitous and enslaved to an image of the creativity as an instrument for furthering productivity. That creativity is seemingly posited as something to be found in all forms of life – from the refugee to the talent show contestant – suggests that the notion that the force of the new is to be open to only a select few talented and unique individuals is in decline. Creativity is not only waiting for us in every context but it is demanded in an ever-growing variety of fields and disciplines. Yet despite this, a particular image of creativity as being founded on the actualisation of ends dominates our understanding of what it means to be creative, and of what creativity can do. It is on this note that we can detect what is ironic about the caution with which certain figures attend to the work of Deleuze. The question should perhaps not be, what image of creativity does Deleuze provide? but instead, what forces or rhythms can we detect in our encounters with his thought, and how we can attend to them so as to release their potential for furthering a process of heterogeneity? Or, as Deleuze put it himself in his lecture series on Kant, 'the important thing is not above all to understand, but to take on the rhythm of a given man, a given writer, a given philosopher' (cited in Morin 2012: 2).

Notes

1. As Emma L. Jeanes states in her paper 'Resisting Creativity, Creating the New. A Deleuzian Perspective on Creativity': 'Pick up any text on management and you can hardly fail to notice the apparent importance of creativity and innovation to an organisation. In fact, so typical are these statements that we take them for granted, assume they are unquestionably "right". Critics of the "innovate or die" argument remain a minority voice at the edge of management discourse' (Jeanes 2006: 127).

2. Indeed, and here I am indebted to Dr Tim Gregory for the observation that, such claims could never function in the inverted form. Which is to say that, the student could not expect any impact to result from the claim that 'you have as much to learn from me as I from you', since the very claim itself is issued from a position that lacks the very authority that the teachers represents.

3. For example, the familiar phrases such as 'ultimately it is each of you who will decide for yourselves whether or not you pass or fail' whilst not a complete fabrication, nonetheless serves to dissimulate the teachers almost supreme authority in deciding who passes and fails.

4. And, I might add, anyone with even the slightest experience in teaching will know that this is true, insofar as any lesson plan, no matter how well planned or tightly coordinated will more often than not fail, given that student's simply 'don't seem to get it'. Indeed, it is at these moments that most teachers are able to do their best teaching, insofar as the failure to follow a planned instruction, illustration or lesson, will often give rise to a dynamic movement between the various positions in the class until, eventually, everyone seems to have arrived on the same page – no matter how divergent this ultimately is, and no matter how little the teacher might be able to account for or understand how everyone got there.

5. Which would mean to preclude both that Deleuze is only an 'anything goes philosopher' or a philosopher who we can only read rigorously, as 'rigorously as we would read Aristotle' as Heidegger might have said. In his introduction to *A Thousand Plateaus* Brian Massumi suggests that the text should be 'played' rather than 'read', meaning that Deleuze and Guattari's second installment of their *Capitalism and Schizophrenia* project is better approached as a Long-Player than a book conventionally understood: 'When you buy a record there are always cuts that leave you cold. You simply skip them. You don't approach a record as a closed book that you have to take or leave' (Massumi 2012: xii). However, and as Niall Lucy indicates in his *Postmodern Literary Theory: An Introduction*, the problematic nature of such a stance is that it seems to suggest that 'no less than Harold Bloom, Brian Massumi knows what "reading" is' (Lucy 1997: 185). Should it be a surprise that reading can never take the

form of Massumi's 'playing' if the former has been absolutely demarcated in advance? Is following the characters that adorn each page – starting from the left and following through to the right, page after page, until the end – of a 'closed book' reading? Does not reading always already involve the moving through associations, images, interpretations and illusions in order to construct the book?

References

Angus, Lawrence (2013) 'School Choice: Neoliberal Education Policy and Imagined Futures', *British Journal of Sociology of Education* 34: 1, pp. 1–19.

Cowell, Henry (2004) 'The Joys of Noise', in Cristoph Cox and Daniel Warner (eds), *Audio Culture: Readings In Modern Music*, New York: Bloomsbury, pp. 22–4.

Critchley, Simon (2009) *Ethics, Politics, Subjectivity: Essays on Derrida, Levinas & Contemporary French Thought*, London: Verso.

Deleuze, Gilles [1968] (1994) *Difference and Repetition*, trans. Paul Patton, New York: Columbia University Press.

Deleuze, Gilles (2005) *Francis Bacon: The Logic of Sensation*, trans. Daniel W. Smith. Minneapolis, MN: University of Minnesota Press.

Deleuze, Gilles and Félix Guttari [1987] (2012) *A Thousand Plateaus*, trans. Brian Massumi, New York: Bloomsbury.

Gilles Deleuze *From A to Z*, DVD, Pierre-André Boutang, trans. Charles J. Stivale. Los Angeles: Semiotext(e), 2012.

Godin, Benoit (2008) 'Innovation: The History of a Category', available at http://www.csiic.ca/PDF/IntellectualNo1.pdf (accessed 10 August 2013).

Jeanes, Emma (2006) 'Resisting Creativity, Creating the New. A Deleuzian Perspective on Creativity', *Creativity and Innovation Management*, 15: 2, pp. 127–34.

Kenway, Jane, Elizabeth Bullen, Johannah Fahey and Simon Robb (2006) *Haunting the Knowledge Economy*, London: Taylor and Francis.

Kumin Judith, Hans Christoph Buch and Mark Sealy (1997) *Exodus: 50 Million People on the Move*, Zurich: Edition Stemmle.

Lucy, Niall (1997) *Postmodern Literary Theory: An Introduction*, Massachusetts: Blackwell.

Massumi, Brian [1987] (2012) 'Translator's Forward: Pleasures of Philosophy', in Gilles Deleuze and Félix Guattari, *A Thousand Plateaus*, trans. Brian Massumi, New York: Bloomsbury, pp. vii–xiv.

Morin, Marie E. (2012) *Jean-Luc Nancy*, London: Polity.

Noys, Benjamin (2010) *The Persistence of the Negative: A Critique of Contemporary Continental Theory*, Edinburgh: University of Edinburgh Press.

Osborne, Thomas (2010) 'Against "Creativity": A Philistine Rant', *Economy and Society*, 32: 4, pp. 507–25.

Polesel, John, Suzanne Rice and Nicole Dulfer (2013) 'The Impact of High Stakes Testing on Curriculum Pedagogy: A Teacher Perspective From Australia', *Journal of Education Policy*, 29: 5, pp. 640–57.

Smith, Daniel W. (2003) 'Translator's Introduction', in Gilles Deleuze, *Francis Bacon: The Logic of Sensation*, trans. Daniel W. Smith. Minneapolis, MN: University of Minnesota Press, pp. vii–xxvii.

Stein, Stanley M. and Thomas L. Harper (2011) 'Creativity and Innovation: Divergence and Convergence in Pragmatic Dialogical Planning', *Journal of Planning and Research*, 32: 1, pp. 5–17.

Tatarkiewicz, Władysław (1980) *A History of Six Ideas: An Essay in Aesthetics*, The Hague: Martinus Nijhoff.

Toscano, Alberto (2010) 'Everybody Thinks: Deleuze, Descartes and Rationalism', *Radical Philosophy* 162, pp. 8–17.

Weschler, Lawrence (2008 [revised edition]) *Seeing is Forgetting the Name of the Thing One Sees: Over Thirty Years of Conversation with Robert Irwin*, California: University of California Press.

Žižek, Slavoj (2004) *Organs without Bodies: On Deleuze and Consequences*, London: Routledge.

Saints, Jesters and Nomads: The Anomalous Pedagogies of Lacan, Žižek, … Deleuze and Guattari

jan jagodzinski   University of Alberta

Abstract

In this essay I bring together Lacan, Žižek, Deleuze and Guattari as mediators and intercessors for one another. The tensions that exist between them still continue to reverberate throughout the academic community. The intent is to query their pedagogies in what they are trying to 'do' within the context of capitalism in particular. I have called their pedagogies anomalous in keeping with their thrust of becoming other in their own particular ways through what I take to be three pedagogical conceptual personae: saint, jester and nomad. I try to show how Deleuze and Guattari managed to supplant and perhaps overcome Lacan's own pedagogical project to have psychoanalysis as a way out from capitalism, which has been continued today by Žižek. I do this by showing how Lacan's mathemes, used in his four discourses, can be understood as having been deterritorialised by Deleuze and Guattari to present us with a counter-actualised pedagogy that challenges psychoanalysis as presented by both Lacan and Žižek. Nevertheless, reconciliations between the thought of Deleuze, Guattari and Lacan are possible. The reader will also find that particular door open, yet not fully explored here.

Keywords: Lacan, Žižek, Deleuze and Guattari, pedagogy, mathemes, capitalism

Deleuze Studies 9.3 (2015): 356–381
DOI: 10.3366/dls.2015.0192
© Edinburgh University Press
www.euppublishing.com/journal/dls

The idiot is the private thinker, in contrast to the public teacher (the schoolman): the teacher refers constantly to taught concepts (man – rational animal), whereas the private thinker forms a concept with innate forces that everyone possesses on their own account by right ('I think'). Here is a very strange type of persona who wants to think, and who thinks for himself, by the 'natural light.' The idiot is a conceptual persona.

Deleuze and Guattari 1994: 62

To make oneself understood is not the same as teaching – it is the opposite. One only understands what one thinks one already knows. More precisely, one never understands anything but a meaning whose satisfaction or comfort one has already felt. I'll say it to you in a way you won't understand: one never understands anything but one's fantasies. And one is never taught by anything other than what one doesn't understand, that is to say, by *nonsense.*

Lacan 1990: xxvi

The word 'nonsense' has been emphasised from Lacan's oddly stilted televised presentation where he answered, somewhat oblivious to television's prosody, pre-set questions asked by his son-in-law, Jacques-Alain Miller, on ORTF (French public TV) in 1973. It was a failed, somewhat humorous attempt at a traditional 'interview'. Basically, Lacan 'lectured' with the oratorical, theatrical panache he was known for. 'Nonsense' will be a trope that appears throughout this essay that will help bring together three distinct styles of anomalous pedagogies[1] in terms of what these *do* through the conceptual personae of jesters, saints and nomads. *Sens* (Fr. for sense) is one of those words whose meaning is never precise. In the 'hands' of Lacan and Deleuze it quivers between meaning and meaningless, between common sense and nonsense. This ambivalence is crucial when it comes to their 'teachings' given the indeterminacy of borders where 'learning' takes place.

While the intent of this issue of *Deleuze Studies* is devoted to exploring Deleuze's pedagogy, the tact I take is to bring Lacan and Deleuze into the mix for two specific reasons: Deleuze and Guattari made a gradual theoretical break with Lacan after the publication of *Anti-Oedipus*: schizoanalysis begins its own journey as it departs from psychoanalysis. This raises a different pedagogy in terms of what schizoanalysis *does*. Lacan, however, never stopped developing a 'reply' to their boldness, coming up with the concept of the *sinthome* via James Joyce as a way of overcoming 'the desire of the Other'. Such a development also means that pedagogy only succeeds at the point of 'failure' in the future when some master (Other) stops insisting. The 'subject who is supposed to know' drops away; a rupture takes place as the 'student' walks away having come to grips with an unanswerable question. The rift between Lacan and Deleuze and Guattari did not and has not stopped: Lacan's radical humanism based on the 'signifier' of language became pitted against the equally more radical machinic posthumanism of Deleuze and Guattari. Their neurological musings and variations on complexity theory have not been taken up with the same rigor by the post-Lacanian generation as they have by post-Deleuze and Guattarians. What are the implications of this tension pedagogically? This leads me to the second reason: Žižek's attempt to 'Hegelianise' Deleuze and side with Lacan has ended badly.[2] There have been too many misreadings and sharp commentators have now called his bluff. Profound differences remain.[3]

It is impossible to articulate a comparative pedagogy between Lacan, Žižek and Deleuze if the issue of 'knowledge' is placed on the table between them. *The question should be at the level of form rather than content.* What is the generic place of 'knowledge' within their respective systems? Each of these 'teachers' has chosen their path by conversing with an entirely different philosophical tradition. Lacan's 'return to Freud' is as compelling as Žižek's 'return to Hegel' (German idealism), as is Deleuze's 'return to Spinoza'. All three develop concepts that further their particular paths. One chooses their counsel as to how compelling they make their argumentation that is to be followed often on the vagaries of belief. The choice of position in terms of pedagogy has ethical and political consequences, within the Academy and beyond, for questions concerning globalised capitalism. But that is not all: each teacher has had an 'event' that fated their lives, which led them to pursue a particular direction as they worked through their own *amor fati.* With Lacan this was in 1953 when a political rift in the psychoanalytic organisation took place;[4] with Žižek (I hazard a guess here) this was when he was barred from getting a university post in Ljubljana (or at least not immediately) due to his ideologically unsuitable position on French structuralism, as developed in his *Habil* during the mid-1970s, and then his subsequent political involvement in the Slovenian League of Communists and eventual running for public office.[5] For Deleuze, aside from a famous ten-year hiatus where he was 'silent', it was the meeting with Guattari in 1969 that politicised him. I do not, of course, attempt some impossible biography here, which would be certainly a silly thing to do. Rather I note that these events are unquestionably turning points that have fated these three brilliant philosophers in the directions they took. Such an 'event' raises ethical and political questions as to how one remains 'worthy' of it, rather than simply demonstrating fidelity towards it, despite the major rupture events cause in the seemingly habitual flows of life. This too has pedagogical consequences in the way an event is to be approached.[6]

Lacan: The Saints Go Marching In

When it comes to Lacan, Douglas Aoki (2002) has it right: as a teacher he is a 'prick', but qualified as a 'charming prick'. Lacan was a flirt, a 'ladies' man' and 'always embroiled in coquetry' (Gallop 1992: 35). Arrogant and demeaning, is not the 'sort' of teacher one would want, or would one? In his seminars, Lacan belittled and insulted his audience, yet the halls were filled with an adoring audience despite his nastiness and 'in large part *because* he was a prick' (Aoki: 37, original emphasis). Aoki (2000) evokes the difficulty of style that Lacan intentionally used in his teachings so that, when it comes to the 'art of teaching', the act of translation plunges what is intelligible and legible into disarray. Lacan's nonsense forces the listener or learner (should they be willing to engage) into an impossible situation. One can never 'master' his texts.[7] Those who do embrace him, often end up writing in a style just as difficult, a good example being Ellie Ragland.[8] Aoki makes a strong case that the teaching and pedagogy that follow in Lacan's style leads to the difficulties as to what knowledge is, what precisely does it mean to communicate ideas, and whether 'to communicate' is indeed the operative word here since Lacan taught that language is what we use to construct the world, and hence we shape ourselves through it, yet it is precisely language that fails us. It is inadequate for the task of communication.

To 'express' the discourse of the unconscious, it is necessary to be incomprehensible. When the unconscious 'speaks', it does not make [common] sense. It 'speaks' nonsense. So the 'art of teaching' from this perspective comes across as somewhat of an anti-pedagogy in terms of the way we use the language of common sense. Unconscious pedagogy as opposed to conscious pedagogy requires other strategies and tactics. Lacan becomes a mixture of showman, trickster, comedian and juggler, playing a language game on the edge between clarity and what appears as obfuscation or jargon through the use of puns, logical contradictions, allusions, jokes and language games in order to claim that glimpses of 'truth' come through. This is an extremely frustrating pedagogical 'experience'. Yet, paradoxically alluring.

Lacan could never be a Lacanian, consequently those who follow as 'teachers' or 'pedagogues', 'operationalise' the particular typology he developed. One certainly can argue that Lacan exemplifies the 'Discourse of the Master',[9] which is the grounding discourse of fantasy. Master signifiers (S_1), within his teaching, are such *mathemes* such as phallus (ø), *object a*, *jouissance*, Big Other (A), master signifier (S_1), barred or split subject ($), *sinthome*, and so on. These signifiers give meaning to other signifiers since they stand for nothing but themselves. Signifier and signified refer to one another; they are the same. The point to note is that these master signifiers are nonsensical. They are 'devoid of reasoning' (Fink 1995: 75, n.2). These are functional concepts that are at 'work' within Lacan's own symbolic order. Hence we can think of Lacan as an 'idiot' here in the sense that to ground a new typology requires dismissing or overriding previous master signifiers. Freud is 'stood on his head', so to speak, although he is *carefully* read. Pedagogically then, an ethical choice is made as to which master signifiers are accepted. Why choose Lacan over Deleuze or vice versa? The choice has consequences for pedagogy when a particular typological grasp of unconscious desire is developed: the unconscious as a 'theatre' (Freud) or 'factory' (Deleuze and Guattari) remain at the level of metaphorical representation. The level of abstraction, it seems, is never enough when articulating the unconscious.

In the master discourse, S_2 is the knowledge generated from master signifiers (S_1) so that $S_1 \rightarrow S_2$ 'produces' a (the *objet a* 'cause' of desire). Knowledge (S_2) is both conscious and unconscious as there is always something going on below the level of consciousness that escapes capture; at the unconscious level, Lacan sets up the fantasy scenario that is filled up via the Imaginary and Real registers ($ \leftarrow a$). The 'truth' of S_1 is the barred subject ($). There is a 'passive' subjective sense to all knowledge that some educators have called 'hidden curriculum', which can be loosely equated with Žižek's take on the 'sublime object of ideology', for it is here where the fantasies of fulfilment and satisfaction take place. As is well known, the split subject for Lacan is a result of being 'socialised' through the signifiers of language (by the Other). Some part of the 'self' has to be 'given up'. Desire becomes 'extimate' (which comes from 'extimacy' (*extimité*), a portmanteau of 'extimate' and 'intimacy'), that is, desire rests with the Other. We are given Lacan's maxim: 'the desire of the Other', and the rhetorical '*Che Voui?*' as the give and take tension between the subject and the Symbolic Order or Big Other.

To accept Lacanianism means to buy into the master–slave relationship, a Hegelian form of desire as lack. The subject is split, meaning it is void, a subject devoid of any content, which then begins 'filling up' with language and is shaped by it. In brief, the view that the subject is alienated, not 'whole', castrated, that there was a primordial unity identified with the maternal body, is a fantasy that emerges below the level of consciousness – the desire to be whole, the 'cause' of which is *objet a*. The split of subjectivity is the desire to be whole (S). Desire then is to give body to negativity via the satisfaction of an object of desire (that object 'containing' the 'positivity' desired). What is crucial to understand in the Lacanian typology is that this object is 'forever' lost. The object that is the 'cause' of desire is perpetually missing – a positivised loss. The 'cause of desire' is thus a *metonymy for lack*. In relation to anti-pedagogy then, the fantasy of knowledge fulfilment becomes an impossibility; technically speaking, learning objectives are *never* achieved.

The master discourse, as has become historically evident, has evolved into the Discourse of the University (DU) since the 'student [slave] revolts' of 1968 where the master signifier (S_1) falls out and becomes veiled by a body of knowledge (S_2). But this has changed once again in the contemporary context of the Internet where the Discourse of Capitalism has taken over and the Discourse of the Master begins to fade, while the Discourse of the University is perpetually challenged via difference and diversity.

The master discourse, however, holds a pedagogical paradox. The 'subject who is supposed to know' (as master) must abandon this position in the Discourse of the Analyst so that the analyst is able to take on the desire of the analysand. The analyst's duty is to empty his or her own ego and listen and ascertain the analysand's *objet a*, his or her cause of desire. Surprisingly, as Miller (1990) informs us about Lacan's television appearance from which this essay started, psychoanalysis was to be the way out of capitalism, which was already underway in some sense in the years after 1968. The antinomy between psychoanalysis and capitalism enters in the guise of sainthood. 'There is no better way of placing him [the analyst] than in relation to what was in the past called: being a saint' (Lacan 1990: 15). Psychoanalysis as an ethical attitude is pitted against the 'ethical attitude' of capitalism as the order of exploitation of production whose law is profit, as desiring 'more' (*jouissance*). Psychoanalysis is taken outside the realm of pure therapy and capitalism is taken outside the realm of pure sociology and political science.

Lacanian pedagogy of the analyst has taken two directions. The most prominent has been the direction taken by Žižek, which is extensively discussed below as a move from the saint to the jester following one of Lacan's hints regarding the 'sainthood' he had in mind. 'The more saints, the more laughter; that's my principle, to wit, the way out of capitalist discourse – which will not constitute progress, if it happens only for some' (Lacan 1990: 16). The saint in this case is not a producer in relation to capitalism, which is marked by intensive production. The saint's very uselessness, finds true usefulness to others. Like Diogenes, a true cynic, 'such a saint transforms himself into a testimony and a cause of the desire of the Other' (Miller 1990: 9). Such a saint, being a non-producer within the capitalist system, he or she becomes a 'remainder' – simply trash, refuse or a reject to be tossed away. This is the path Žižek chose.

There are other forms of sainthood, however, saints who tried, through their activism, to create social security, medical care and social justice by creating and instituting convents and monasteries around the world. Pedagogically, the Discourse of the Analyst as a teacher who helps students deal with the symptoms of their own desire (the Real of their existential lives), not in therapeutic terms, but in terms of overcoming the 'desire of the Other', so that they might become *independent thinkers* was spearheaded by Mark Bracher (1999, 2006; jagodzinski 2002). Bracher's particular sainthood revolved around an unequivocal social justice position, furthering what was an over-sociologised pedagogical critical theory as developed by Henri Giroux, for instance. To that end, through his attempt to strengthen the worth of the self, he was accused of falling into the traps of psychology, seemingly emphasising the ego, which did not sit well with Žižekians, splitting the field of psychoanalytic pedagogy. The writing of Mari Ruti (2012) has attempted to continue this other train of thought, which has closer affinities with Deleuze and Guattari through the concept of singularity. It is at this point we can bring in Slavoj Žižek's particular form of pedagogy that now intervenes and supplements Lacan's edifice of teaching.

Žižek: From Saint to Jester

Žižek is not a master like Lacan but has been elevated to an 'intellectual rock star', and is seen by many as a radical hip priest and saviour of the Left. Yet, Žižek does not develop a set of new 'concepts' over his long career, what might be identified as a consistent metaphysics. Interpassivity comes from the work of Robert Pfaller. Subjective destitution can be found in Lacan's ethical development of Antigone's 'act', as can many other concepts he utilises in his applications to popular culture, political theory, Marxism, German idealism and Enlightenment rationality. His 'return to Hegel' (Žižek 2012) is a strong defence to keep *representational thought* alive, as well as preserve a strategy to occupy the position of the *analyst* who never gets 'caught', but remains in the 'dummy' position (as in the card game of bridge) occupying the position of '*a*'. From this non-place position, Žižek can move over the landscape of capitalism dropping explosions of insight to end its demise. As the book jacket on *Less than Nothing* says, 'Slavoj Žižek was born, writes books, and will die.' But this is *not* a heroic position, although many transfer heroic worship onto him.[10] The desire of the analyst as 'teacher' not only refuses to take up a position of authority, he must disidentify both love and identification with analysands. No small feat. Further, the analyst can be reduced to 'trash' (*déchet*) as Lacan says in the *Television* lecture. The business of the analyst is that of the 'saint' (1990: 15–16). As a 'reluctant hero', the analyst is both a saint as well as a 'fool' or jester, since he will be eventually rejected (by the student/analysand) and experience 'unbeing' [*desêtre*], or 'subjective destitution' as Žižek formulates it.

Žižek (2006a) clearly states:

> The analyst's discourse stands for the emergence of revolution-ary-emancipatory subjectivity that resolves the split of university and hysteria. In it, the revolutionary agent –*a*– addresses the subject from the position of knowledge that occupies the place of truth (i.e., which intervenes at the 'symptomal torsion' of the subject's constellation), and the goal is to isolate, get rid of, the master signifier that structured the subject's (ideologico-political) unconscious (unpaginated).

The master signifier here is obviously capitalism. As a pedagogue, Žižek would simply drive you 'mad' in the classroom, as he tries to drive capitalism 'mad', so to speak. There is no way of pinning him down as classically shown in the many books, chapters and essays that have tried; perhaps as is most evident in *The Truth of Žižek* (Bowman and Stamp 2007), which has Žižek answering back just as vehemently as the many authors who criticise him within its pages.

In terms of content then, it is foolish to enter the same territory as Žižek occupies for it is a non-place. As he himself admits, there is no 'dialogue' with him. He fills the airwaves and 'performs' his lectures. There is no pretence of seminars as in Lacan's case, although he may be on a 'panel' at a conference. Žižek's 'pedagogy' is not one of dialogue, it is more of an exposition aimed at some particular political or cultural situation. One could see this being another form of engaging with the 'stupidity' of common sense so as to create the nonsense that Žižek is able to generate through the many contradictions that emerge in his discourse. Rather than the analyst's 'silence' you have generative 'noise' that can be rather upsetting, but tolerable as the 'charming' side emerges through jokes: the jester or fool teasing and playing 'with' Authority (S₁). The Fool can play with power by emptying himself of it. He himself admits that he never 'answers' a question, and is suspicious of any 'simple' narrative. He simply 'throws' the question back at those who ask it. While the transference, by those on the Left who admire him, is to that of a 'hero' fighting against the capitalist symbolic order, he avoids that mantel, tries to 'joke' it off and maintains that he is a misanthrope. What then does he do as a pedagogue?

In a surprising move, Žižek (2007a) maintains Hegel's master–slave dialectic has been somewhat misinterpreted. There is:

> an unheard-of *third* version: the way to resolve the deadlock is to engage oneself neither in fighting for the 'good' side against the 'bad' one, nor in trying to bring them together in a balanced 'synthesis,' but in opting for the *bad* side of the initial either/or. Of course, this 'choice of the worst' fails, but in this failure it undermines the entire field of alternatives and thus enables us to overcome its terms. (12, author's emphasis)

The 'act' of the analyst is to take a position that escapes the defined field of coordinates that is defined by the antagonism of the either/or. By doing so, the unthought of the system introduces new possibilities, which may be well part of disavowed presuppositions. Common sense tells us that in this defined field of the master–slave it is always necessary to 'save oneself' within it. This is the 'choice without a choice' as in Lacan's (1977: 212) well-known example: When faced by a street mugger who says, 'Your money or your life!' Who would want to 'give up their life?' If you choose the money, you loose both (money and life). If you choose life, you have life without the money, a life deprived of something. Either way you are about to be parted from your money. Yet, the Lacanian 'act' opens up the choice of death as well. In contrast, by immediately taking the 'good' option, the systemic ideology continues to remain the same. We will continue our own oppression and desire what is expected of us. In brief, the fantasy of organic 'wholeness' is thus sustained. Some object, or knowledge fills us up and satisfies us. Hence, today we are told that we need continuous 'learning to learn' only to find ourselves entering the ranks of the post-doctoral 'holding tank', remaining freelancers, adjuncts and positionless without a tenure track. This choice can appear to be without a choice if we wish to sustain this fantasy. But then the ideology is sustained.

Žižek's basic stance maintains that antagonism is a structural feature of the system, but what I find most surprising is the way his Hegelianism turns into a Deleuzianism! This is most evident when he talks about 'open systems' in order to avoid the Hegelian organicism and teleology ('the acorn becomes an oak') that is often associated with nineteenth-century system's talk of genus and genius. In *The Parallax View* (2006b), after dismissing a system of pure differentiality where there is no antagonism, and a system where there is only antagonism (Us and Them), he states: 'but *there is no "primordial" unity of poles in the first place, only the inherent gap of the One ...*' (36, author's emphasis). But, this is precisely what the gap of the fold is for Deleuze (1993). 'The tension between immanence and transcendence is thus secondary with regard to the gap *within immanence itself*: "transcendence" is a kind of perspective illusion, the way we (mis)perceive the gap/discord that inheres to immanence itself' (36, second italic is my emphasis).

The molar–molecular 'antagonism' in Deleuze and Guattari is precisely of the same order – a both/and logic where the 'gap' is the 'line of flight' out of the system for change, equivalent to Žižek's analyst taking a non-position within the gap or void, or Deleuze's *unthought* as the 'outside' that is already 'inside' in an immanent system. For all the disparaging talk of the Deleuzian problematic 'One', especially as contested by Badiou, it has *nothing to do with 'unity'*. For Deleuze the One is *always* n-1. Here is Žižek utilising the same construct. Given the structural incompleteness of the system, the One differs not only from others but also foremost from itself. 'Becoming' has now snuck in. Identity *and* difference are simultaneous, a Deleuzian construct. At any given time the 'molar' structure is identified, but simultaneously it is undergoing a becoming at the molecular level. This is fundamental to chaos theory. A living organism at the 'edge of chaos' must maintain both its stable strata as well as its unstable deterritorialising flows.[11] Without stability the system dies (becomes totally nonsensical), and without the latter it is unable to regenerate, innovate and renew. It falls into orthodoxy, mindless repetition, cliché and platitudes, which means it 'dies' as well. In this reading, Hegel's 'third' position that Žižek advocates for analysis becomes a Deleuzian proposition. Who's 'buggering' whom?[12]

Now that I have turned Žižek into a Deleuzian (something I have tried before, see jagodzinski 2010a),[13] at least for the time being, what does this say about pedagogy? I think the question boils down to what kind of analyst of the capitalist order does one want to be, pedagogically that is, since the ethical and political questions are on the table. In the Hegelian sense Žižek's *an sich* does not match his *für sich*. He says he is an analyst (for-himself) in the Lacanian sense but does something quite different (in-himself). The first is conscious claim, and the second is unconscious expression. My contention is that in-himself, Žižek's unconscious is more Deleuzian than he will ever admit. Levi Bryant (2008) has tried to expose this 'other side' of Žižek, and in what is remaining of this essay I intend to contrast and show the similarities between Žižek and Deleuze and Guattari in the way each attempts to overturn the capitalist machinery for pedagogical purposes. In the end, however, I side with those post-Deleuze and Guattarians who develop an *affirmative nomadology*.

Deleuze and Guattari: From Saints and Jesters to Nomads

The Deleuze and Guattarian paradigm also offers an anomalous pedagogical 'toolkit', one that challenged both Lacan and the Hegelian master–slave dialectic as it is 'commonly' understood. The prime difference is that there is no talk of lack concerning desire; desire is always theorised in the affirmative sense. The toolkit consists of an array of concepts: *Bodies without Organs* (BwO), war machine, becoming woman, child, animal and imperceptible, striated–smooth space, rhizome, 'joy', affect rather than *jouissance*, schizoanalysis as opposed to psychoanalysis, and so on. Most importantly is that they make no differentiation between 'man' and 'nature'. Everything is machinic. Lacanian mathemes become 'desiring machines', and their entire arsenal of concepts is aimed at the capitalist system. To see their worth as to what their pedagogy can do, I would like to develop the Discourse of the Capitalist and then show Žižek's refinement of the analyst within that discourse. Then I will introduce the way Deleuze and Guattari and their followers can be understood as overturning Lacan–Žižek within the capitalist discourse as well.

Lacan (1972) developed a 'Discourse of the Capitalist', a fifth discourse, which surprisingly is seldom explored or mentioned comparatively to the other four (see Bianchi 2010). In the position of the agent, the worker ($) sets about producing knowledge (S_2). What is produced by this relationship ($\$ \rightarrow S_2$) is a. This is the product (of desire) as surplus profit for the reinvestment by the corporation (the shareholders) (S_1). So in the unconscious position we have ($S_1 \leftarrow a$). Given that this libidinal object of fantasy grips *everyone*,

Lacan (1974) maintained that capitalists were proletarians as well (in Declercq 2006: 80). In machinic terms, we have a desiring machine that generates surplus-value so that constant expansion can take place. However, the constant accumulation also requires constant destruction or deterritorialisation, decoding as well as coding, and hence the 'product' produced (a) is extremely ambiguous in a competitive market. It is both positive (profit) and negative (a loss of profit as the commodity is dated or becomes evacuated of desire and becomes 'shit'). As the productive remainder, this surplus (a) is a double-edged sword – both surplus-profit (gold) and/or surplus shit, you cannot get rid of the stock, for the stock s(t)inks (which is a portmanteau of sinks and stinks). The relationship between worker and knowledge under global capitalism ($\$ \rightarrow S_2$) has a huge pedagogical component. As Deleuze says, in a control society, nothing is ever 'finished'. The worker has to continually produce new technologies and innovations that produce (a), the object of desire for consumption, and profit as well as waste. Capitalism only works by 'breaking down' as Deleuze and Guattari state in *Anti-Oedipus*.

Given that the 'truth' of the capitalist machinery is the insatiable superego (S_1) that can never be satisfied, but commands 'enjoyment!' or *jouissance* as Žižek further developed; the sustained drive of capitalism is based on *desire as lack*. The *object a*, which is the product of knowledge of the managerial elite of the capitalist order remains a *lost object*, split between an object that *temporarily satisfies* (through commodity consumption), but only to be eventually *evacuated of desire*, which then turns the product into shit (waste), making any object of fantasy ambiguous and paradoxical. The managerial discourse that generates knowledge (S_2), as Foucault (1990) maintained, is a form of bio-power where the techniques that are produced enable even more production to take place via a multiplier effect. Such 'immaterial labour' has become the 'knowledge' of the creative class within designer capitalism where 'affect' is manipulated so as to achieve satisfaction, excitement and passion – the packaging of 'experience' (jagodzinski 2010b). Economic, political and socio-cultural life are collapsed together producing social-life under capitalism.

Given this capitalist machine, the question can certainly be raised as to whether the constitutive void of the subject as an emptiness without positive content, the 'hard' kernel of the Real as both Lacan and Žižek claim, is merely identifying the capitalist subject ($\$$) within this machinery, or whether this is an *ontological universal claim*. In a 'post-Oedipal' world of neoliberalism, the divided subject in capitalism is endlessly pursuing some signifier that assigns its place in the symbolic order.[14] Both Lacan and Žižek make much of the death drive when it comes to this endeavour, where the subject is faced with lack that generates the excesses of *jouissance* of painful pleasure, where every 'drive' is a death drive in pursuit of fulfilment. Within this framework, Žižek highlights the 'surplus' *jouissance* that revolves around the lack theorised as a fundamental antagonism: master–slave.

The pedagogical thrust of Žižek, as analyst within this system, his *an sich* position, can be articulated as a modification of the analytic discourse within the discourse of capitalism (see Bryant 2008). Žižek, as in the Discourse of the Analyst, takes the position of the *objet a* as the agent. This means that knowledge (S_2) is evacuated from the agent and becomes the 'truth' of the agent (a/S_2). As agent (a), Žižek is a subject who is 'supposed to know' and yet does not know. The agent-analyst reduces himself to the void so that the Other (addressee) is provoked into confronting the truth of his/her desire. Authority is thus ambivalent here and paradoxical, and we see this throughout Žižek's 'pedagogy' as simply being elusive, 'funny' and provocative, all rolled into one. No one can pin him down or get the 'right' answers from him. Most of his provocation is through parataxis. The addressee, however, in Žižek's case is not the split subject ($), rather it is the master signifier (S_1) of capitalism ($a \rightarrow S_1$). Žižek, in effect, analyses how we 'desire' in a capitalist system, the 'product' of such analysis being the split subject ($). The idea is then to worry the consumer culture of capitalism by being in the position of exploring its traumas and symptoms, the master signifiers (S_1) of desire (as nonsense). Through his performances and writings (as it is claimed) new possibilities are opened up once the common sense 'closed' subject ($) 'opens' up (S) as to how capitalism structures desire that is duping the populace. The transferences by the Left who read and listen to Žižek as being someone who is an 'Authority' and reaches a stage where he 'must' reject all transferences that are bestowed on him.[15] The desire of the analyst is simply to reach that point where those he addresses must take on knowledge by themselves (S_2). His is a perpetual performative act of provocation, which can be viewed as a 'pedagogical sacrifice' of sorts. The saint is trashed. The end of the analysis is the execution of an 'act' when his 'students' (S) choose *not* to buy into the capitalist order, and become 'revolutionary' subjects. He then has effectively done his psychoanalytic 'job.'

Deleuze and Guattari radically differ in their typological system to do battle with capitalism that is defined by a society of control where the 'dividual' is being manipulated through the space–time of modularity of what they call 'control society'. Schizoanalysis challenges psychoanalysis leaving Lacan behind by fundamentally treating desire in the affirmative sense. In the Lacanian–Žižekian system there are generally two modalities of the Real that are at play: a Real 'before the letter' (R_1) and a Real 'after the letter' (R_2) (see Fink 1995: 24–5). R_1 is the unmediated connection with the body. This distinction is played with, back and forth, by Žižek throughout his many writings depending on how he wishes to continue his provocative game, which also includes the 'symbolic Real' (capitalism), and 'Imaginary Real', making it that much harder to pin him down as the bearer of Truth. Deleuze and Guattari are primarily concerned with the R_1, which Lacan also maintained as having an 'extimate' relationship to the Symbolic Order. They however part company with Lacan and Žižek, who call for the sacrifice of enjoyment (*jouissance*) by way of castration as the subject enters the symbolic order when acquiring language. The intensity of 'affect' of the intrinsic body (R_1) replaces the negativity of *jouissance,* making a distinction between *Zoë* and *Bios* when it comes to theorising 'life'. Symbiotic affirmation replaces castration. The idea is to open these flows that are capable of affecting and changing the system. The relationship between R_1 and R_2 is modified into the virtual–actual relationship within spacio-temporal terms.

Given Žižek and Lacan's propensity to dwell on R_2, which results from the 'drop' or 'cut' of the linguistic signifier, R_1 becomes characterised in terms of 'pure' *jouissance* and the death drive because the subject is 'castrated' (one could also say 'civilised') by entering into the Symbolic Order. Desire becomes a lack. Deleuze and Guattari are more interested in a 'virtual' Real–the R_1; they make no distinction between the psychic and the social, the personal and the social unconscious. All desire is productive. It is an affirmative force, and R_1 is a nonrepresentational realm where affect and joy replace *jouissance.* More importantly, the stress is on the *creation of the new* that emerges from the release of desire via this 'virtual Real'. The 'virtual' is a dimension that is *real*. It informs the empirical identities that are *actualised*, and vice versa within the temporality of becoming. It is a realm of *sens* that generates the 'fourth dimension' of language, thereby leaving Lacan's linguistic structuralism behind.[16] The virtual Real, as a realm of multiple intensive processes of individuation that can be actualised, holds the potential for transformative change, emerging from the *molecular level*, which is always already embedded within the molar structures. Taking this emancipatory 'line of flight' along molecular lines is what Deleuze and Guattari take to be 'minoritarian politics'. We therefore have a *pedagogy of creation* rather than a representational critical Discourse of the Analyst as in Žižek's case. Poiesis (creative making of ideas) is stressed over praxis (execution of existing ideas).

Hysterical Inversion

If I were to plot Deleuze and Guattari in relation to Lacan's four discourses in response to the capitalist fifth discourse, what would emerge is an inversion of the 'hysterics discourse' to answer and intervene with the capitalist machinery.[17] Within the hysterics discourse, as developed by Lacan, the barred subject understands that her desire is the desire of the Other. Learning of this relationship, she is forced to confront it. The barred subject acts as an agent questioning the master signifier (S_1 or Law, Big Other) ($\$ \rightarrow S_1$). The truth of the agent ($\$$) is a, as the object cause of desire, which *is* the subjective desire the Law has barred. The agent ($\$$) speaks from a position of pain given this barring of desire, and her truth is 'that' which has been barred. The product of this discourse is a new type of knowledge represented as S_2. S_2 is the barred knowledge that has now become accessible.

So one way to rethink pedagogy from a Deleuze and Guattarian machinic stance is to claim that the hysterical discourse is *inverted* to expose capitalism. The agent position is taken on as 'a', just like the analyst's discourse. However 'a' here is R_1 (*avant la lettre*), the domain of the virtual Real, the domain of potentiality and multiplicity in a time of Aion[18] as opposed to Chronos. This is a creative realm that is to be actualised into S_2, the newly created knowledge, with new concepts and new relations ($a \rightarrow S_2$). The 'a' is modified. It is *not* the hard kernel of the Real (R_2) but a virtual multiplicity (R_1). R_1 refers to the *quasi-cause* in Deleuze's system where the virtual Real as the potential of actualisation is open and contingent.[19] The product of this inverted discourse is not the hysterical subject but a *schizo* subject ($\$$). As in Žižek's modified analytic discourse, the $\$$ is also 'open' to new potentialities rather than possibilities as a result of the actualisation of virtual Ideas to generate the new S_2 knowledge. The 'truth' of the virtual Real (R_1) is the master discourse (S_1). In other words, Deleuze and Guattari are advocating the creation of a philosophy – new concepts, new master signifiers that are the formulation of the *minoritarian political* position that is embedded within global capitalism. Their 'antagonism' is an 'emergent becoming'. Just as the hysterical discourse is described as an 'artistic' one because it offers creative freedom generating a new discourse, so it is also with Deleuze and Guattari who advocate the creation of a *new future* – utopian not utopia; that is to say, Samuel

Butler's nihilistic tendencies in *Erewhon* that refer not only to no-where but also to now-here (Deleuze and Guattari 1994: 100). Such an atopic now-here refers to 'the constitutive relationship of philosophy and *nonphilosophy*. Becoming is always double, and it is this double becoming that constitutes the people to come and the new earth' (109, added emphasis).

The irony in all of this rests on the latter Lacan who adds a fourth 'band' in response to Deleuze and Guattari's challenge by changing his typography from a Borromean knot to a *chain*, when he introduces the *sinthome* in an attempt to break with the 'desire of the Other'. The *sinthome*, in the figure of Joyce, introduces creativity and art as a way that, in a sense, can break with the Other and explore the virtual Real (R_1). It leans towards poiesis rather than praxis. Pedagogy is essentially the creation of new potential futures that can break with global capitalism, which relies on surplus expansion.

The creation of new concepts as 'nonsense' signifiers has nothing to do with 'truth', but with the 'powers of the false', with creation itself. Deleuze and Guattari therefore *also invert* Lacan's Discourse of the Master.

$$\frac{\text{(agent: minoritarian subject) } \$}{\text{(truth powers of the false) } S} \quad \substack{\rightarrow \\ \leftarrow} \quad \frac{\text{quasi-}a \ (R_1)}{S_2 \text{ (product: creative knowledge,}}$$

intensities)

In the place of the master signifier (S1) they have a minoritarian political subject ($\$$) as the addresser of the virtual Real realm [quasi-a (R_1)] of affect (not *jouissance*) in order to *creatively* 'produce' knowledge (S_2) – the forces 'underneath matters and forms' (Deleuze 1994: 38), a 'sub-representative' domain of differences (178). So these concepts (S_2) are not 'representational functions, they are forces of intensity – they 'do' something, not 'mean' something. The position of 'truth' is replaced by the 'powers of the false' (S_1). The nonsense master signifier is a *created* concept. This development simply confirms what Lacan noted: that the master discourse after 1968 began to wane, being replaced with the university discourse, which in turn has been continually challenged by a string of agencies to its Authority: the hysteric's discourse as adopted by some feminists,[20] the queer challenge to sexuality, identity politics of every sort, and so on. A managerial elite (World Bank,

The International Monetary Fund) attempt to balance the vicissitudes of power via pluralist forms of democratic rule, playing a game of difference within representational sameness. While Žižek developed an analytic discourse to challenge the discourse of global capitalism, Deleuze and Guattari not only inverted the master discourse through their own minoritarian politics, but they also inverted the Discourse of the Hysteric to produce a schizo-subject to change global capitalism, avoiding any forms of representational structuralism.

The Pedagogy of Nonsense

It would be instructive to read the sections where Deleuze and Guattari enter into Žižek's Magnus Opus on Hegel, *Less than Nothing*, in order to recognise his continual persistence, as first developed in *Organs without Bodies,* that somehow Deleuze can be 'buggered' into being a Hegelian. This insistence on the negative has consequences as to what Žižek's particular anomalous pedagogy can *do* when he addresses the crowds that come to his 'lectures as performances' and staged conferences, for he has become an itinerant intellectual. *Should the Left follow Žižek's lead?* Žižekian politics rests on the claim that class struggle is the Real of a fundamental antagonism within global capitalism, making it somewhat, as a number of critics have pointed out, impossible to generate any sort of political practice.[21] Which is not, as I have claimed, his desire. The pedagogical strategic processes are all disruptive ones: via the act (to transverse the fantasy), a politics of withdrawal (a refusal to participate in capitalist order à la Bartelby), and the practice of concrete universality (where that 'part', which forms the antagonistic element within the capitalist system belongs to the Real, has the possibility of transforming the system). Žižek's pedagogy always insists that capitalism can only be broken through an awareness of its own limits. He never offers an 'action research plan' or an ideological manifesto (unlike his comrade Badiou, for example, regarding the 'Idea of Communism' that is ideologically carried out by a 'collective subject' who have a fidelity to the Event). Žižek is the consummate analyst offering a negative ontological politics (via the signifier) where the aim is always to disrupt capitalist fantasy life and expose its symptoms. Following on from Badiou, his own 'communist hypothesis' (to follow Jacques Rancière here) refers to 'the part that has no part', the exclusionary lumpenproletariat whose bodies 'exist' extimately in the Real. They have 'no place'. While offering no course of action, a 'utopian impossibility' via their 'utopian demand' becomes the potential for change (for a review see McMillan 2011). Their demand suggests a new imaginary that will supersede global capitalism.

For me, this last position by Žižek is an 'endgame' for the analytic discourse and a *skewed* nod in the direction, once again, of Deleuze and Guattari. While it is not possible to develop this fully here, there is a significant difference between Deleuze's development of *fabulation* (see Bogue 2010) and Lacanian fantasy. Fabulation, once more, sees the play of the virtual Real (R_1) in an attempt to establish an intervention from the minoritarian political position to develop an imaginary that actualises political minoritarian changes. In contrast to Badiou's 'communist hypothesis' of the Event, and unlike Hardt and Negri's Deleuzo-Guattarian inspired strategy for communism in *Empire* (2001), which posits yet another game-changing Event,[22] Eugene Holland (2011) develops an 'affirmative nomadology' of 'free market communism'. He shows that there are all sorts of alternative nomadic groups, practices and institutions that already exist as *creative inventions*. They can be united and knotted together to develop broader relations to create a critical mass.[23] This is a 'slow-motion' minor change by those in a *minoritarian position* who are certainly engaged in a 'fundamental antagonism' within global capitalism, but this is change via affirmative desire. Spinozian 'joy' replaces Lacanian *jouissance*. The category of:

> minority for Deleuze and Guattari does not refer to any specific ethnic or other identity groups, nor necessarily to a lumpenproletariat. Rather it refers to the 'multiplicities or nondenumerable sets . . . *related difference* that cannot be homogenized and counted, and hence exploited and commanded, by the axioms of capital or the State'. (Holland 2011: 157, original emphasis)

Deleuze and Guattari offer a different typology than that of 'the part that has not part' in its negative sense. Again, it is a minoritarian struggle 'within' the axioms of capital and the state. 'The power of . . . minorities is measured not by their capacity to enter and make themselves felt within the majority system . . . but to bring to bear the force of the nondenumerable sets, however small they may be, against denumberable sets' (1987: 471). 'War machines' bring on such force of nondenumerable sets.

Deleuze and Guattari do not dismiss the 'axiomatic' struggle of representation, but avoid any top-down organisation that Badiou proposes and that Žižek avoids (knowing better) supporting. Rather, it is Deleuze and Guattari's utopian (not utopia) potential for a 'new earth' where 'pure becoming of minorities' can be brought into convergence and interconnection. Such an anomalous pedagogy asks for a different strategy, a 'slow-motion' strategy, and the marshalling of 'war machines' that do not have 'war' necessarily as their object.[24] The *nomadic* pedagogy of such a 'war machine' sets out to form alternative organisations of social relations operating in 'smooth space' before it closes, the spaces of the unthought within capitalism and the State. It is a creative and nonreactive pedagogy that attempts to map out positive instances of a 'nomadism' that creatively modify (and adapt if necessary) within existing empirical conditions, to map the virtual potentials as alternatives to capitalist and state norms. While this is a modest and less flashy proposal than the performative antics of Slavoj Žižek, it is the one I support.

Notes

1. By anomalous pedagogy in the title I am referring to the power of attraction these figures had in the academy and beyond, in the way they *affected* their audiences through their performative teachings. 'The anomalous is neither an individual nor a species; it only has affects, it has neither familiar nor subjected feelings, nor specific or significant characteristics' (Deleuze and Guattari 1987: 244). The conceptual personae (jesters, saints and nomads), which appear now and again throughout this essay, manifest as a non-teleological movement where their teachings construct new positions and concepts of identity that function as vectors for becoming. While the medium of television was a 'bust' for Lacan (although his lectures were packed), and Deleuze did a series of television interviews with Claire Parnet (*L'Abécédaire de Gilles Deleuze* produced by Pierre-André Boutang in 1988–9) that was more 'successful' (his lectures were packed as well), we had to wait for the public attention garnered by Žižek via contemporary social media to experience the full reach that has now become possible via repetitive repackaging of books, films, conferences and YouTube posts. The halls are now likewise full when he performs. For Žižek's amazing output see http://www.egs.edu/faculty/slavoj-zizek/videos/.
2. Developed in his *Organs without Bodies* (2004). Deleuze again appears many times throughout Žižek's magnum opus, his 1000 pages on Hegel (2012). I will address this when I come to Deleuze. A partial listing of those who have questioned Žižek's response to Deleuze include Berressem (2005), Crockett (2013), Buchanan (2005), Sinnerbrink (2006), Smith (2004) and Walsh (2008).
3. If we were to add Alain Badiou into this mix, the conversation regarding public pedagogy becomes that much more complex and perhaps even more muddled and irresolvable than it already is. Badiou has no 'truck' with Deleuze (although he praises him in good academic fashion for his 'failures'). Badiou is equally critical of his master, Lacan, for not going far enough concerning 'subjectivity', and Žižek, despite the friendly demeanour towards Badiou as an ally to develop a new invigorating 'communism', has equally criticised

Badiou's position concerning his communist manifesto, as any good comrade should.

4. 'So far as my *place* is concerned, things go back to the year 1953. At that time, in psychoanalysis in France, we were in what might be called a moment of crisis' (Lacan 2008: 6, added emphasis). Quotes drawn from this book, *My Teaching*, are rather significant as Lacan uses quite direct language. As he puts it, 'I allow myself this prosopopoeia simply to make what I am saying comprehensible to those of you who have not heard it before' (28).

5. Ian Parker (2004: 11–35) has attempted to develop this background that, at one point, angered Žižek regarding the interpretation of his involvement with *Neue Slowenische Kunst* (NSK) as well as a joke that he was a 'commissar' at the Institute of Sociology, University of Ljubljana. The sensitivity that surrounds this period is hinted at in Žižek's reply to Parker, which was short and swift: 'First, which "department" should be mine? In Yugoslavia, I was never employed at any university department – how could I then be active there as a "commissar"? Second, from (at least) the middle of the 1980s, the Communist party effectively lost control over the employment politics at the university' (Žižek 2009).

6. Here I evoke two competing notions of 'event' as developed by Deleuze and Badiou respectively, siding with Deleuze. Deleuze develops being 'worthy' of the event in the twenty-fourth series of *Logic of Sense* (1990), while Badiou's fidelity to the Event is developed throughout his Magnus opus *Being and Event* (2007). On his part, Žižek (2000: 260–4) develops the 'act' rather than dwelling on event.

7. Lacan (2008) says so himself when referring to *Écrits*: 'we agree to consider these *Écrits* unreadable; people at least pretend to read them, or to have read them ... As you may have noticed, this book has not had many reviews. Probably because it is very thick, difficult to read, obscure. It is not designed for everyday consumption at all' (62).

8. Ragland, a long time reader and interpreter of Lacan, presents many challenges of comprehension. A good example of such difficulty can be found in the way she attempts to address the question of the 'veil', a long-standing concern for feminists (Ragland 2008).

9. All the discourses discussed in this essay are attached as an appendix.

10. There is some irony to this assertion as Žižek reflexively plays with his elevated status. To sell his books, early cover copy would regularly announce, 'The giant of Ljubljana.' There are many blog sites and magazines that sing his praises and where you can read great admiration for his (often) outrageous claims. ('Žižek leaves no social or cultural phenomenon untheorized, and is master of the counterintuitive observation', *The New Yorker*; 'Unafraid of confrontation and with a near-limitless grasp of pop symbolism', *The Times*; 'Žižek is one of the few living writers to combine theoretical rigor with compulsive readability', *Publishers Weekly*.) Jonathan Rée (2012) of *The Guardian* writes, 'He has become the *saint* of total leftism: a quasi-divine being, than whom none more radical can ever be conceived' (added emphasis). Either that approach or a sense of total disgust that his analysis is simply bullshit. Rée ends his review with, 'In the past I have found it hard to dislike Žižek, but after a month's forced march through *Less Than Nothing* it seems to be getting easier.'

11. An explication of Deleuze and chaos theory is developed by Bell (2006).

12. In *Organs without Bodies*, Žižek (2004) has taken great pleasure in Deleuze's off-remark of 'buggery' that takes place by taking a philosopher 'from behind' when it comes to appropriating thought, which Žižek then proceeds to do with Deleuze by 'Hegelianising' him. An explanation of the syntax of Deleuze's

remark and Žižek's misreading of it can be found at http://terenceblake.
wordpress.com/2012/02/25/keziz-zizek-gets-it-backwards-1-deleuzes-buggery-
quote-retranslated/ (accessed 13 June 2013).

13. This was approached in the context of examining Žižek's ideology critique. As
far as I know, there is no other person foolish enough to call Žižek a repressed
Deleuzian.

14. Here I am equally suspicious of the Derridean open system that is formed by
difference and deferral because of a negation of an Other (that is an original
absence), which sets up the initial difference. The system is perpetually open
because of this absence preventing its closure (see Derrida 1976: 23).

15. Some examples in relation to his dread of students come to mind: 'I was shocked,
for example, once, a student approached me in the US, when I was still teaching
a class – which I will never do again ... I especially hate when they [students]
come to me with personal problems. My standard line is: "Look at me, look at
my tics, don't you see that I'm mad? How can you even think about asking a
mad man like me to help you in personal problems, no?"' (Žižek as reported in
Aitkenhead 2012).

16. In Seminar XX, Lacan introduces *lalague* as a way to counter their development.

17. Refer to the Appendix for the Discourse of the Hysteric and the 'machinery' of
its inversion.

18. Deleuze introduces Aion as the time of virtuality, meaning it is contingent and
'timeless'.

19. It should be noted here that the *quasi-cause* refers to the virtual multiplicity
and cannot be equated with the Lacanian Real (R_2), as Žižek claims in *Organs
without Bodies* (2004: 27) when he states that, 'the quasi-cause fills in the gap of
corporeal causality'. This again places the Real (*objet a*) as a lack, whereas quasi-
cause here is a positive multiplicity. The virtual is equated with *potential* whereas
Lacan and Žižek's Real is equated with *possibility*, which Deleuze critiques in
Difference and Repetition (1994: 211). The former is an open future, the latter
is 'open' future as well, but foreclosed in terms of various 'possibilities' that
will be determined within a range of outcomes that are nevertheless resolvable
solutions. Žižek's key refusal is to accept the transcendental virtual realm as
anything but (in a strict Kantian sense) the *a priori* conditions of possibility
of constituted experience (Žižek 2004: 4). Yet Deleuze is adamant in inverting
Kant's transcendental position so that it becomes a 'transcendental empiricism'
where it is not an *opposition* between the two realms (introducing negativity
and lack), but recognition that there is a creative dynamic between the virtual
and actual, that is between the non-existent and the existent. The transcendental
is not the *a priori* condition of possible experience. It is the condition of 'real'
experience without prior conceptual possibilities being traced out empirically.
The virtual is 'real', and opposed to the 'actual', whereas the 'real' is opposed
to the possible. This means the actual becomes the fulfilled *potential* of the
multiple differences within the virtual. Each can influence the other, and vice
versa.

20. Lacan's matheme for the hysteric's discourse that challenges the phallic Symbolic
Order (S_1) has often been equated with generic 'feminism' as a form of continual
resistance. This begins as early as Toril Moi (1990). For a review of this concept
see Showalter (1993). However, not all feminists are in agreement with such
an assessment because it remains symptomatological and pathological, which is
inadequate for a feminist subject (see Campbell 2004: 77–9). Lacan, however,
equates the hysteric's discourse with the *feminine* subject, but not as *female*.

This conceptual difficulty has proven troublesome for feminists engaged in sorting out whether Lacan's position retains any force of viability.

21. His sharpest critics being: Boucher (2004), Bowman (2007), Bowman and Stamp (2007), Sharpe (2004) and Sharpe and Boucher (2010). The subsequent debate between Critchley (2009) and Žižek (2007b), after his critique of Critchley's book *Infinitely Demanding*, offers perhaps a vivid example of the tensions between revolutionary violence and non-violence as the obsessive deadlock Žižek maintains between Bartelbian inertia and the divine ultra-violence of revolutionary change, in short: no power or state power, which he always wavers between. In contrast Deleuze and Guattari's minoritarian politics operates to open up a space, an interstitial distance, between the law and life.

22. Hardt and Negri write: the actions of the 'multitude becomes political' when there is 'the construction, or rather the insurgence of a powerful organization' (2001: 339, 411).

23. While this sounds like the early post-Marxist political socialist strategy of Ernesto Laclau and Chantal Mouffe, which involves the development of strategic coalitions, it is a very superficial comparison. Laclau and Mouffe's position is to formulate a place of universality based on an empty signifier as the point of lack in society so that 'society does not exist' and remains an impossible battle of hegemony. Affirmative nomadology is an emergent molecular structure within molar capitalism that is opening up an interstitial gap between molar law and molecular life.

24. See Holland (2011: 26–7) for a clarification of Deleuze and Guattari's differentiation of war machines with war as their object and those without.

References

Aitkenhead, Decca (2012) 'Slavoj Žižek: "Humanity is OK, but 99% of people are boring idiots"', *The Guardian*, 10 June, available at http://www.guardian.co.uk/culture/2012/jun/10/slavoj-zizek-humanity-ok-people-boring (accessed 13 June 2013).

Aoki, Doug (2000) 'The Thing Never Speaks for Itself: Lacan and the Pedagogical Politics of Clarity', *Harvard Educational Review*, 70: 3, pp. 347–70.

Aoki, Doug (2002) 'The Teacher is a Prick', in jan jagodzinski (ed), *Pedagogical Desire: Authority, Seduction, Transference, and the Question of Ethics*, London and Westport, CT: Bergin & Garvey, pp. 33–44.

Badiou, Alain (2007) *Being and Event*, trans. Oliver Feltham, London: Continuum.

Bell, Jeffrey (2006) *Philosophy at the Edge of Chaos: Gilles Deleuze and the Philosophy of Difference*, Toronto and Buffalo: University of Toronto Press.

Berressem, Hanjo (2005) '"Is it Possible not to Love Žižek?" on Slavoj Žižek's Missed Encounter with Deleuze', review of *Organs without Bodies: On Deleuze and Consequences*, by Slavoj Žižek, New York: Routledge, 2003, available at http://www.electronicbookreview.com/thread/endconstruction/stringency (accessed 13 June 2013).

Bianchi, Pietro (2010) 'The Discourse and the Capitalist: Lacan, Marx, and the Question of Surplus', *Filozofski Vestnik*, XXXI, pp. 123–37.

Bogue, Ron (2010) *Deleuzian Fabulation and the Scars of History*, Edinburgh: Edinburgh University Press.

Boucher, Geoff (2004) 'The Antinomies of Slavoj Žižek', *Telos*, 129, pp. 151–72.

Bowman, Paul (2007) 'The Tao of Žižek', in Paul Bowman and Richard Stamp (eds), *The Truth of Žižek*, London: Continuum, pp. 27–44.

Bowman, Paul and Richard Stamp (eds) (2007) *The Truth of Žižek*, London: Continuum.

Bracher, Mark (1999) *The Writing Cure: Psychoanalysis, Composition, and the Aims of Education*, Carbondale, IL: Southern Illinois University Press.

Bracher, Mark (2006) *Radical Pedagogy: Identity, Generativity, and Social Transformation*, New York and London: Palgrave Macmillan.

Bryant, Levi R. (2008) 'Žižek's New Universe of Discourse: Politics and the Discourse of the Capitalist', *International Journal of Žižek Studies*, 2: 4, available at http://www.zizekstudies.org/ (accessed 13 June 2013).

Buchanan, Ian (2005) 'Žižek and Deleuze', in Geoff Boucher, Jason Glynos and Mathew Sharpe (eds), *Traversing the Fantasy: Critical Responses to Slavoj Žižek*, Aldershot: Ashgate, pp. 69–88.

Campbell, Kirsten (2004) *Jacques Lacan and Feminist Epistemology*, London and New York: Routledge.

Critchley, Simon (2009) 'Violent Thoughts about Žižek', *Naked Punch*, available at http://www.nakedpunch.com/articles/39 (accessed 13 June 2013).

Crockett, Clayton (2013) *Deleuze Beyond Badiou: Ontology, Multiplicity, and Event*, New York: Columbia University Press.

Declercq, Fédéric (2006) 'Lacan on the Capitalist Discourse: Its Consequences for Libidinal Enjoyment and Social Bonds', *Psychoanalysis, Culture & Society*, 11, pp.74–83.

Deleuze, Gilles (1990) *Logic of Sense*, trans. Mark Lester, New York: Columbia University Press.

Deleuze, Gilles (1993) *The Fold: Leibniz and the Baroque*, trans. Tom Conley, Minneapolis, MN: University of Minnesota Press.

Deleuze, Gilles (1994) *Difference and Repetition*, trans. Paul Patton, New York: Columbia University Press.

Deleuze, Gilles and Félix Guattari (1987) *A Thousand Plateaus*, trans. Brian Massumi, Minneapolis, MN: University of Minnesota Press.

Deleuze, Gilles and Félix Guattari (1994) *What is Philosophy?* trans. Hugh Tomlinson and Graham Burchill, London and New York: Verso.

Derrida, Jacques (1976) *Of Grammatology*, trans. Gayatri Chakravorty Spivak, Baltimore: John Hopkins University Press.

Fink, Bruce (1995) *The Lacanian Subject: Between Language and Jouissance*, Princeton, NJ: Princeton University Press.

Foucault, Michel (1990) 'Right of Death and Power over Life', in Michel Foucault, *An Introduction, vol. 1, The History of Sexuality*, New York: Vintage Books, pp. 135–59.

Gallop, Jane (1992) *The Daughter's Seduction*, Ithaca, NY: Cornell University Press.

Hardt, Michael and Antonio Negri (2001) *Empire*, Cambridge, MA: Harvard University Press.

Holland, Eugene W. (2011) *Nomad Citizenship: Free Market Communism and the Slow-Motion General Strike*, London and Minneapolis: University of Minnesota Press.

jagodzinski, jan (ed.) (2002) *Pedagogical Desire: Authority, Seduction, Transference, and the Question of Ethics*, London and Westport, CT: Bergin & Garvey.

jagodzinski, jan (2010a) 'Struggling with Žižek's Ideology: Deleuzian Complaint, Or Why Slavoj Žižek is a Deleuzian in Denial', *International Journal of Žižek Studies* 4: 1, available at http://www.zizekstudies.org/ (accessed 13 June 2013).

jagodzinski, jan (2010b) *Art and Education in an Era of Designer Capitalism: Deconstructing the Oral Eye*, New York and London: Palgrave McMillan.

L'Abécédire de Gilles Deleuze, Film, Pierre-André Boutang. France: La Femis et Sodaperaga Productions, 1988–9.

Lacan, Jacques (1972) *On Psychoanalytic Discourse (Milan): 12th May 1972: Jacques Lacan*, transcripts by Julia Evans, trans. Jack W. Stone, Columbia, MO: University of Missouri, available at http://www.lacanianworks.net/?p=334 (accessed 13 June 2013).

Lacan, Jacques (1974) Proceedings of the Conference held at the French Cultural Centre, 30 March, Rom, Unpublished.

Lacan, Jacques (1977) *The Seminar of Jacques Lacan, Book XI: The Four Fundamental Concepts of Psychoanalysis*, Jacques-Alain Miller (ed), trans. Alan Sheridan, New York: W. W. Norton and Company.

Lacan, Jacques (1990) *Television: A Challenge to the Psychoanalytic Establishment*, ed. Joan Copjec, trans. Denis Hollier, Rosalind Krauss, Annette Michelson and Jeffrey Hehlman, New York and London: W. W. Norton & Company.

Lacan, Jacques (2008) *My Teaching*, Preface by Jacques-Alain Miller, trans. David Macey, London and New York: Verso.

McMillan, Chris (2011) 'The Communist Hypothesis; Žižekian Utopia or Utopian Fantasy?', *International Journal of Žižek Studies* 5: 2, available at http://www.žižekstudies.org/index.php/ijzs/article/viewFile/301/399 (accessed 13 June 2013).

Miller, Jacques-Alain (1990) 'A Reading of Some Details in Television in Dialogue with the Audience', *Newsletter of the Freudian Field*, 4: 1–2, pp. 3–29.

Moi, Toril (1990) *Feminist Theory and Simone de Beauvoir*, London: Basil Blackwell Publisher.

Negri, Tony and Michael Hardt (2004) *Multitudes: War and Democracy in an Age of Empire*, New York: The Penguin Press.

Parker, Ian (2004) *Slavoj Žižek: A Critical Introduction*, London: Pluto Press.

Ragland, Ellie (2008) 'The Masquerade, the Veil, and the Phallic Mask', *Psychoanalysis, Culture & Society*, 13, pp. 8–23.

Rée, Jonathan (2012) 'Less Than Nothing by Slavoj Žižek – Review', *The Guardian*, available at http://www.guardian.co.uk/books/2012/jun/27/less-than-nothing-slavoj-zizek-review (accessed 13 June 2013).

Ruti, Mari (2012) *The Singularity of Being: Lacan and the Immortal Within*, New York: Fordham University Press.

Sharpe, Matthew (2004) *Slavoj Žižek: A Little Piece of the Real*, Aldershot: Ashgate.

Sharpe, Matthew and Geoff Boucher (2010) *Žižek and Politics: A Critical Introduction*, Edinburgh: Edinburgh University Press.

Showalter, Elaine (1993) 'Hysteria, Feminism, Gender', in Sander L. Gilman (ed.), *Hysteria Beyond Freud*, Berkeley, CA: University of California Press, pp. 286–344.

Sinnerbrink, Robert (2006) 'Nomadology or Ideology? Žižek's Critique of Deleuze', *Parrhesia*, 1, pp. 62–87.

Smith, Daniel (2004) 'The Inverse Side of the Structure: Žižek on Deleuze on Lacan', *Criticism*, 46: 4, pp. 635–50.

Walsh, Maria (2008) 'Žižek, Deleuze, and the Feminine Cinematic Sublime', *Rhizomes*, 16, available at http://www.rhizomes.net/issue16/walsh/index.html (accessed 13 June 2013).

Žižek, Slavoj (2000) *The Ticklish Subject: The Absent Centre of Political Ontology*, London and New York: Verso.

Žižek, Slavoj (2004) *Organs without Bodies: Deleuze and Consequences*, New York: Routledge.

Žižek, Slavoj (2006a) 'Jacques Lacan's Four Discourses', available at http://www.lacan.com/zizfour.htm (accessed 13 June 2013).

Žižek, Slavoj (2006b) *The Parallax View*, Cambridge, MA: The MIT Press.

Žižek, Slavoj (2007a) 'Introduction', in Mao Tse-Tung, *On Practice and Contradiction (Revolutions)*, London and New York: Verso.

Žižek, Slavoj (2007b) 'Resistance is Surrender: What to Do about Capitalism', *London Review of Books*, 29: 22, available at http://www.lrb.co.uk/v29/n22/slavoj-zizek/resistance-is-surrender (accessed 13 June 2013).

Žižek, Slavoj (2009) 'A Short Clarification to Ian Parker', *Lacanian Symptom 9*, available at http://www.lacan.com/thesymptom/?page_id=513 (accessed 13 June 2013).

Žižek, Slavoj (2012) *Less than Nothing: Hegel and the Shadow of Dialectical Materialism*, London and New York: Verso.

Appendix

Lacan's General Structure of the Discourses

$$\frac{\text{Agent} \quad \rightarrow \quad \text{Other}}{\text{Truth} \quad \leftarrow \quad \text{Product/Loss}}$$

Discourse of the Master

$$\frac{(S_1 \quad \rightarrow \quad S_2)}{(\$ \quad \leftarrow \quad a)}$$

Discourse of the Hysteric

$$\frac{(\$ \quad \rightarrow \quad S_1)}{(a \quad \leftarrow \quad S_2)}$$

Discourse of the University

$$\frac{(S_2 \quad \rightarrow \quad a)}{(S_1 \quad \leftarrow \quad \$)}$$

Discourse of the Analyst

$$\frac{(a \quad \rightarrow \quad \$)}{(S_2 \quad \leftarrow \quad S_1)}$$

*Žižek's Modification of the Discourse of the Analyst
within Capitalism*

$$\frac{(a \quad \rightarrow \quad S_1)}{(S_2 \quad \leftarrow \quad \$)}$$

*Deleuze and Guattari's Modification of the Discourse of the Hysteric
within Capitalism (control society)*

$$\frac{(a \quad \rightarrow \quad S_2)}{(S_1 \quad \leftarrow \quad \$_{schizo})}$$

*Deleuze and Guattari's Modification of the Discourse of the Master
within Capitalism (control society)*

$$\frac{(\$ \quad \rightarrow \quad a_1)}{(S_1 \quad \leftarrow \quad S_2)}$$

Assemblage Theory and Its Discontents

Ian Buchanan   University of Wollongong

At least since the publication of Taylor Webb's landmark work *Teacher Assemblage* there has been a high level of interest in Deleuze and Guattari's work in Education Studies. Undoubtedly the major reason for this interest is the perceived close connection between Deleuze and Guattari's concept of the assemblage and Foucault's concepts of power and governmentality. Webb explicitly situates his work at this intersection of these three concepts, with the aim of using the combination to map the effects of surveillance on teachers (Webb 2009: 30). Webb's work offers a salient reminder too that assemblage theory, at its origin in the work of Deleuze and Guattari, was always concerned about questions of power. This aspect of assemblage theory is all too often forgotten, making the assemblage seem as though it is merely another way of saying something is complicated. This reminder is urgently needed because assemblage theory is rapidly gathering a significant following in the human and social sciences. My university library catalogue lists over 8000 journal articles across all disciplines with the word 'assemblage' in the title. There can be no question that it has generated interesting and important new ways of thinking about the complex nature of social reality but it has also drifted a long way from its origins and in doing so a number of both small and large misprisions of Deleuze and Guattari's work have slipped under the radar and embedded themselves as 'truths'.[1]

I have never been one to think that there is no such thing as a 'right' or a 'wrong' reading, so I am going to simply go ahead and say assemblage theory makes two kinds of error in their appropriation of Deleuze and Guattari: (1) it focuses on the complex and undecidable (Actor Network Theory); and/or (2) it focuses on the problem of emergence (DeLanda). It may be that these are providential errors because they

Deleuze Studies 9.3 (2015): 382–392
DOI: 10.3366/dls.2015.0193
© Edinburgh University Press
www.euppublishing.com/journal/dls

give rise to new and interesting ways of thinking in their own right, though I have my doubts on that front, but they nevertheless cloud our understanding of Deleuze and Guattari and in that regard call for our critical attention. One may well say that Deleuze and Guattari do not call for our strict adherence to their ideas (this is certainly true), but such an argument misses the more general point Deleuze and Guattari make about concepts, that they should have cutting edges. It should always be possible to determine with precision the specific characteristics and features of a concept. And that is not always the case with assemblage theory's deployment of assemblage.

Assemblage is now so widely used as a term it is generally forgotten that in spite of its francophone appearance, it is actually an English word. Assemblage is Brian Massumi's translation of the French word *agencement*, which, as John Law has noted, encompasses a range of meanings that include 'to arrange, to dispose, to fit up, to combine, to order' (Law 2004: 41). It could therefore just as appropriately be translated as arrangement, in the sense of a 'working arrangement', provided it was kept clear that it described an ongoing process rather than a static situation. It could also be thought in terms of a 'musical arrangement', which is a way of adapting an abstract plan of music to a particular performer and performance. Arrangement is in many ways my preferred translation for these reasons. This is not to say I disagree with Massumi's choice, which like all translations has its problems but is very far from being wrong or inappropriate. It is considerably better than several other choices that have also been tried. For example, *agencement* has also been translated as 'layout' and 'ensemble' both of which are too static in my view. Layout implies something much flatter and more fixed than an arrangement, which can at least imply a temporal as well as spatial aspect. The word 'ensemble' is similarly problematic because it lacks the contingency of arrangement, which can always fail. Assemblage is problematic for these reasons too, albeit much less so, which is why I ultimately favour arrangement.[2]

It is worth adding that *agencement* is Deleuze and Guattari's own translation, or perhaps re-arrangement would be a better word, of the German word *Komplex* (as in the 'Oedipal complex' or the 'castration complex'). Despite the fact it is Guattari himself who defines the assemblage this way in the various glossaries he has provided, the connection between Freud's complex and the concept of the assemblage has been almost completely ignored. This may go some way toward explaining the origin of the two kinds of errors I will discuss in what follows – it appears to me that the term assemblage has been taken at face value, as though the concept was somehow self-explanatory. Yet that is far from the case.

At the very least it fails to take into account Guattari's comments on art assemblages in his essay 'Balancing-Sheet Program for Desiring Machines' (which was appended to the second edition of *Anti-Oedipus* and can therefore be read as a kind of bridging piece linking *Anti-Oedipus* to *A Thousand Plateaus*). Referring to Man Ray's collage 'dancer/danger', Guattari observes that what is crucial about this piece of sculpture is the fact that it does not work. He means this quite literally. The working parts, its cogs and wheels and so on, do not turn or intermesh with one another in a mechanical fashion. It is precisely for that reason, he argues, that it *works* as a piece of art (Guattari 1995: 120). It works by creating an association (that is, a refrain) between the human dancer and the inhuman machine, and thereby brings them into a new kind of relation which Deleuze and Guattari would later call the assemblage, but in their first works they called the desiring-machine. The only time they make a direct comparison between the unconscious and actual machines is when they compare it to the absurd machines of the Dadaists, surrealists, as well as the infernal machines imagined by Buster Keaton and Rube Goldberg (Guattari 1995: 135).[3] And again, what is crucial is that these machines do not work. In other words, the obvious mechanical explanation of various machines is precisely *not* what Deleuze and Guattari had in mind when they conceived of the concept of the assemblage and its forerunner the desiring-machine. Yet this is precisely how assemblage tends to be treated.

Let me quickly turn to Freud to try to re-orient thinking about the assemblage. According to Laplanche and Pontalis's exhaustive account, there are three senses of the word complex in Freud's writing: (1) 'a relatively stable arrangement of chains of association'; (2) 'a collection of personal characteristics – including the best integrated ones – which is organised to a greater or lesser degree, the emphasis here being on emotional reactions'; (3) 'a basic structure of interpersonal relationships and the way in which the individual finds and appropriates his place' (Laplanche and Pontalis 1973: 72–4). Laplanche and Pontalis also note that there is an underlying tendency toward 'psychologism' inherent in the term. Not only does it imply that all individual behaviour is shaped by a latent, unchanging structure, it also allows that there is a complex for every conceivable psychological type. The key point I want to make here is that none of these ways of thinking about the complex actually requires that we give any consideration to a material object.

This is not to say material objects cannot form part of an assemblage because clearly they can, and Deleuze and Guattari give several examples of this, but it is to say – no doubt provocatively – that the assemblage is not defined by such objects and, as Bettelheim's case history of 'little Joey' demonstrates, can function perfectly well without them.[4] As Deleuze and Guattari's discussion of 'little Hans' makes clear, the assemblage is a 'living' arrangement. Hans' agoraphobia is an arrangement he has with his anxieties, his neuroses, it is as much an attempt at self-cure (as Freud might put it) as it is a symptom. Whatever it is that underpins his anxiety, whether it is Oedipally motivated or not, it is nonetheless assuaged by putting in place an arrangement that inhibits the degree to which he has to confront that anxiety. By limiting his encounter with 'the street' he limits his anxiety. This is how the assemblage works. It always benefits someone or something outside of the assemblage itself (the body without organs); along the same lines, the assemblage is purposeful, it is not simply a happenstance collocation of people, materials and actions, but the deliberate realisation of a distinctive plan (abstract machine); lastly, the assemblage is a multiplicity, which means its components are both known and integral to its existence, not unknown and undecided.

The conflict here between Deleuze and Guattari's conception of the assemblage and assemblage theory's conception of the assemblage is obvious: the latter celebrates something that is inessential in the former. One of the great insights of assemblage theory, particularly its more materialist permutations in the hands of Bruno Latour, is that it shows that material objects can and frequently do have agential power. This idea is far from being incompatible with Deleuze and Guattari's thinking, but one should be wary of making it the central point of analysis as ANT does. This is not to say that the search for non-human actors is not an important project, but it is to say that it misses what is central to the assemblage. One might say this is the nub of what ANT gets wrong with respect to the assemblage, but the problems run deeper than that because ANT uses the assemblage to name a complex form of causality which Jane Bennett (2010) usefully defines as distributive because of the way it rejects both direct and indirect causality in favour of a third option which attributes causality to the whole network of interacting elements. To take an illustrative case in point, John Law uses assemblage to deal with complex social and cultural situations or problematics which can neither be reduced to a single instance, object or truth nor allowed to remain indefinite, undecidable or purely perspectival as though to say (*pace* Derrida) that there is no discernible object, instance or truth.

Law's 'gold standard' test case, if you will, is the Ladbroke Grove train crash in 1999, which killed twenty-three people and injured 414 others (Law 2004: 93). As he notes, a single or definitive explanation of the cause of the accident is impossible, and not only because both the drivers involved died in the crash. There were simply too many factors that could have been the cause for any single factor to be singled out and blamed, ranging from driver error to machine or system failure. Yet given the need to learn from the disaster, and thereby prevent a recurrence of this type of tragedy, forensic analysis needed to produce something more solid than an open-ended 'anything is possible' finding. As Law explains, there are in effect two kinds of problem here – the first can be solved rather easily, instead of a single answer, we can offer multiple answers, or rather multiple explanations, and this is precisely what the inquest did. But this raises a second and much trickier problem because multiple explanations tend to give rise to the perception of imprecision and indefiniteness, thus making the findings seem less credible for being multiple, even though in point of fact the explanation is more likely to be multiple than single. Deleuze and Guattari's solution, which Law partially adopts, is to 'trouble' the distinction between single and multiple:

> [T]he absence of singularity does not imply that we live in a world composed of an indefinite number of disconnected bodies ... It does not imply that reality is fragmented. It instead implies something much more complex. It implies that different realities overlap and interfere with one another. Their relations, partially coordinated, are complex and messy. (Law 2004: 61)

Deleuze and Guattari's solution is in fact more radical than Law's – where he is only prepared to trouble the distinction between single and multiple, they reject it altogether. By postulating multiple, overlapping realities, Law cannot evade the charges of pluralism, perspectivalism, and relativism that he hopes to escape by exactly this means. The train drivers did not have a separate reality from each other, nor did they have a separate reality from the signal switch that may or may not have failed, and so on. Similarly Deleuze and Guattari insist that there is no such thing as 'psychic' reality, which would somehow be different from other kinds of reality (Deleuze and Guattari 1983: 27). There is only one reality, but that reality is multiple in and of itself and we need conceptual tools like Deleuze and Guattari's concept of the assemblage to disentangle it and render visible its constitutive threads. If we stay with Law's train crash example, we can say that the drivers perhaps saw things differently from each other – they were travelling in different directions with different destinations – but that very difference in perception is constitutive of the reality they shared. The signal system was part of that reality, as was the whole rail network, and behind that the whole hinterland (as Law usefully calls it) of the drivers' training, the design and manufacture of the trains, and so on.

To describe the crash fully, then, one has to follow the multi-various lines that twist and turn and finally intersect to produce the event we know as the Ladbroke Grove train disaster. To give this a more human scale, one might think of the countless mini-decisions, chances and coincidences that led to those twenty-three people being on those trains at that particular time. Had any one of them missed their train that day they might have cursed their luck, until they discovered that chance had saved their life. But these decisions are essentially random – they are only held together by the event itself. Had the trains not collided, these people would not have died in this way, and their lives would not have intersected in this way either. My point is that while it is an undoubtedly complex event, with a great many elements, there is no particular analytic advantage in describing it as an assemblage. It lacks the necessity of the 'true' assemblage – it is an accident, not an arrangement. There is nothing deliberate about it, therefore, strictly speaking, it is not an assemblage. Law's version of the assemblage is clearly not the same as Deleuze and Guattari's – this does not mean that the way he uses it is problematic in and of itself. It obviously works very well in an ANT context.

The same cannot be said for the second error – it reduces assemblage to the status of adjective. The central exhibit here is Manuel DeLanda's *A New Philosophy of Society*. As I will briefly explain, it typifies a general problem in the reception of the concept of the assemblage. Aligned with Deleuze (and quite pointedly *not* Guattari), it tactfully or perhaps tactically positions itself as 'Deleuze 2.0', and instructs us to feel free to ignore its connection to Deleuze altogether. Doubtless this is because conceptually it owes very little to Deleuze. As even a casual inspection can confirm, Braudel, Goffman and Weber, among others, are much more central to DeLanda's formulation of the assemblage than Deleuze. The problem here is not simply that something that is not Deleuzian is presented *as* Deleuzian, again it runs much deeper than that. The real problem is that 'Deleuze 2.0' is conceptually stunted in comparison with the 'original'. DeLanda 'improves' on Deleuze and

Guattari by reformulating their concept in such a way that it lacks all analytic power.

DeLanda treats the assemblage as an aggregate, albeit a complex aggregate of the variety of an ecosystem. Nonetheless, for DeLanda the assemblage is an entity that grows in both scale and complexity as components are added. In his view, assemblages are 'wholes whose properties emerge from the interactions between parts'. He suggests they can be used to 'model' 'entities' such as 'interpersonal networks', 'social justice movements', 'cities' and 'nation-states' (DeLanda 2006: 5–6). Central to DeLanda's thinking about assemblages is Deleuze's idea (drawn from Hume) that relations are exterior to their terms. This enables DeLanda to offer an account of assemblages as ontologically 'unique, singular, historically contingent, [and] individual' (DeLanda 2006: 40). More particularly, though, DeLanda frames the assemblage as a new way of thinking about part-whole relations, essentially pitching it as a new kind of causality, one that acts without conscious intention or purpose:

> For example, during the seventeenth and eighteenth centuries in Europe the authority structure of many organisations changed from a form based on traditional legitimacy to one based on rational-legal bureaucratic procedures. The change affected not only government bureaucracies, but also hospitals, schools and prisons. When studied in detail, however, no deliberate plan can be discerned, the change occurring through the slow replacement over two centuries of one set of daily routines by another. Although this replacement did involve decisions by individual persons ... the details of these decisions are in most cases causally redundant to explain the outcome ... (DeLanda 2006: 41)

There are a number of problems here, but I will focus on just three 'fatal flaws' in DeLanda's account: first, the assemblage does not constitute a part-whole relation; second, the assemblage is not the product of an accumulation of individual acts; and third, the assemblage does not change incrementally. To say that a bureaucratic structure of authority was constituted by and ultimately transformed by myriad individual acts says nothing but the obvious. One does not even need a concept to make this claim. This is history in the mode of one damn thing after another (as Arnold Toynbee famously put it). Focusing on the 'how' question as insistently as he does obscures the deeper and more interesting 'what' question. Worrying about *how* a particular authority structure actually changes forgets that the real question here, at least insofar as assemblage theory is concerned, is *what* is that structure of authority? How is it constituted?

Let me turn briefly to Deleuze and Guattari's account of the formation of the state in *Anti-Oedipus*. As will be immediately obvious, it follows a path that is diametrically opposite to the one mapped out by DeLanda. 'The State was not formed in progressive stages; it appears fully armed, a master stroke executed all at once; the primordial *Urstaat*, the eternal model of everything the State wants to be and desires' (Deleuze and Guattari 1983: 217). History is *in* the *Urstaat*, in its head, not the other way round: primitive society knew about the terrors of the state, Deleuze and Guattari argue (following Pierre Clastres), long before any actual states existed. Primitive society's rituals and customs, centred on the destruction of accumulated 'wealth' (that is, seeds, weapons, furs and so on) so as to institute a socially binding debt relation within the 'tribe' and between 'tribes', can be seen as staving off the formation of an actual state, which requires wealth to come into being. It is the idea of the state that concerns Deleuze and Guattari, not the practical matter of its coming into being.[5]

DeLanda thus departs from Deleuze and Guattari in three crucial ways: first, he always proceeds from the concrete to the abstract, whereas Deleuze and Guattari (following Marx's famous reversal of Hegel) tend to proceed from the abstract to the concrete – the state is first of all an idea, it only subsequently functions as a structure of authority; second it seems he cannot countenance a purely immanent form of organisation that is not somehow undergirded by the transcendent 'real', whereas Deleuze and Guattari say the exact opposite – the state can only function as it does to the extent that it can become immanent; and, third, he reverses the actual-virtual relation – he assumes that the concrete 'bits and pieces' are the actual, whereas for Deleuze and Guattari it is the structure of authority that is actual and the 'bits and pieces' that are virtual.[6] Marcus and Saka, indirectly following DeLanda, thus write that the assemblage 'is a topological concept that designates the actualizations of the virtual causes or causal processes that are immanent in an open system of intensities that is under the influence of a force that is external (or heterogeneous) in relation to it' (Marcus and Saka 2006: 103). But this is precisely the wrong way round: *only the actual elements can be causal*. It is very clear in Deleuze and Guattari's discussion of the 'actual factor' in desiring-production that the actual is what is self-generated and therefore active in the unconscious, while the virtual is the imported and therefore inert or 'dead' element in the unconscious (for example, they describe the Oedipal complex as virtual) (Deleuze and Guattari 1983: 129).

What then does Deleuze and Guattari's assemblage consist of? In brief, it is derived from a combination of Stoic language philosophy, speech-act theory and Hjelmslev's so-called glossematics. In practice, the assemblage is the productive intersection of a form of content (actions, bodies and things) and a form of expression (affects, words and ideas). The form of content and the form of expression are independent of each other – their relationship is one of reciprocal presupposition (one implies and demands the other but does not cause or refer to it, for example a sunset is an array of colours produced by the diffraction of light, but this does not cause us to see it as beautiful or melancholic; by the same token, our concepts of beauty and melancholy do not compel us to apprehend sunsets in this way). Let me illustrate this with a very brief example.

In 1923, George Mallory made headlines around the world when in response to the question 'Why do you want to climb Mount Everest?' he said 'because it's there'. People at the time, and still, were both dumbfounded and immediately comprehending of his seemingly blank statement, which appears to be uninterested in and not a little contemptuous of the actual physical features of the mountain, beyond its imperious height. They were dumbfounded because they expected him to say that it was the ultimate challenge or something that directly acknowledged the scale of the accomplishment were he to be able to pull it off; but they also immediately comprehended the fact that he did not have to say anything like that because everyone already knew that it was a monumental challenge. One senses too that Mallory's insouciance is gesturing to something beyond the actual physical challenge of climbing Mount Everest to what we might call its virtual or symbolic dimension. By virtue of its size, Mount Everest's 'there-ness' in Mallory's sense consists in its capacity to confer upon anyone who scales it the attribute of having climbed the world's highest peak. Mallory knew that everyone knew that by being the first to scale the world's highest peak his body would acquire a new attribute – he would instantly become the first man to have climbed Mount Everest. That incorporeal transformation, as Deleuze and Guattari usefully call it, would stay with him for eternity. It is that aspect of its 'there-ness' that everyone instantly grasps. This is the form of the expression.

The physical effort required to climb Mount Everest is the price of admission to the symbolic realm of the select group of people who have conquered that peak. This amounts to saying actual effort is required to enter the virtual realm, which is also to say that events always occur on two planes at once – the empirical plane of consistency (the physical effort of climbing the actual mountain) and the abstract plane of immanence (the symbolic achievement of having climbed a symbolically significant mountain). Effort is the form of content. There is a feedback loop between these two forms. If the symbolic accolade (form of expression) is not great enough, then the effort (form of content) will seem out of proportion; by the same token, if the effort (form of content) required is not great enough, then the symbolic accolade (form of expression) will seem undeserved. This can manifest itself in interesting ways. For example, apart from its height, Mount Everest is not regarded as the most difficult of the fourteen above 8000m climbs – that honour usually goes to K2, which has a one in four fatality rate. If actual physical effort was the foundation of symbolic attainment, then K2 should rank above Mount Everest, but it does not except perhaps in the very small community of 8000-ers. The prestige of climbing the world's highest peak remains so great that overcrowding on the climb is now more imperilling than the physical hazards from ice and rock. That prestige would evaporate, though, if one could simply take a helicopter to the peak, or ride some kind of funicular car to the top, making the journey as simple as getting to the airport or train station on time. So the effort required to get to the top is not unimportant, by any means, but it always sits in a dialectical relationship with the symbolic dimension. The two planes must be adequate to each other. Anything that interrupts or interferes with this dialectical relationship between the forms (expression and content) is known as an assemblage converter.

In conclusion, then, however useful and analytically revealing assemblage theory can be, in practice its use of the concept of the assemblage is often indistinguishable from that of an adjective, serving more to name than frame a problem. Therefore, rather than opening a problem up it tends to close it down. Instead of a new understanding of the problem, it simply gives us a currently fashionable way of speaking about it. This issue becomes more urgent the more widely assemblage theory is embraced. If everything is or must be an assemblage then the term loses precision, indeed it loses its analytic power altogether.

Notes

1. Indeed, the problem is endemic and known to be so. In their 2006 summary of assemblage theory's applications in anthropological research, Marcus and Saka make the following interesting and I suspect quite accurate observation: 'None of the derivations of assemblage from Deleuze and Guattari of which we are aware is based on ... a technical and formal analysis of how this concept functions in their writing. Few in the social sciences who have found the modernist sensibilities embedded in the concepts that Deleuze and Guattari deploy for

their purposes to be attractive have appreciated, understood or incorporated those purposes in their own. Rather, it has been the power and often beguiling attraction of Deleuze and Guattari's language that has encouraged the piecemeal appropriation of certain concepts for the remaking of middle-range theorizing that informs contemporary research projects.' (Marcus and Saka 2006: 103).

2. See also Alliez and Goffey's (2011: 10–11) discussion of the problems with 'assemblage' as a translation of *agencement*. In particular they note that it obscures the obvious implication that *agencement* concerns questions and issues relating to agency, which is obviously important.

3. In the text Guattari actually refers to Julius Goldberg, but from the discussion that follows it is clear he meant Rube Goldberg.

4. See my discussion in Buchanan 2013.

5. For a more detailed account of this process see Buchanan 2008: 88–116.

6. For a more detailed account of this argument see Buchanan 2011: 17–18.

References

Alliez, E. and A. Goffey (2011) 'Introduction' in Alliez and Goffey (eds), *The Guattari Effect*, London: Continuum, pp. 8–14.

Bennett, J. (2010) *Vibrant Matter: A Political Ecology of Things*, Durham, NC: Duke University Press.

Buchanan, Ian (2008) *Deleuze and Guattari's Anti-Oedipus*, London: Continuum.

Buchanan, Ian (2011) 'Deleuze and Ethics', *Deleuze Studies*, 5: 4, pp. 7–20.

Buchanan, Ian (2013) 'Little Hans Assemblage', *Visual Arts Research*, 40, pp. 9–17.

DeLanda, M. (2006) *A New Philosophy of Society: Assemblage Theory and Social Complexity*, London: Continuum.

Deleuze, Gilles and Félix Guattari (1983) *Anti-Oedipus: Capitalism and Schizophrenia*, transRobert Hurley, Mark Seem and Helen R. Lane, London: Athlone.

Freud, Sigmund (1985) *Penguin Freud Library*, *vol.* 12, trans. J. Strachey, London: Penguin.

Guattari, Félix (1995) 'Balancing-Sheet Program for Desiring Machines', in *Chaosophy*, trans. R. Hurley, New York: Semiotext(e), pp. 123–50.

Laplanche, J. and J-B. Pontalis (1973) *The Language of Psycho-Analysis*, trans. D. Nicholson-Smith, New York: Norton.

Latour, B. (1999) 'On recalling ANT', in J. Law and J. Hassard (eds), *Actor Network Theory and After*, Oxford: Blackwell Publishing, pp. 15–25.

Law, John (2004) *After Method: Mess in Social Science Research*, London: Routledge.

Marcus, G. and E. Saka (2006) 'Assemblage', *Theory, Culture & Society*, 23: 2–3, pp. 101–6.

Webb, T. (2009) *Teacher Assemblage*, Rotterdam: Sense Publishers.

Schizo-Feminist Educational Research Cartographies

Jessica Ringrose   University College London Institute of Education

Deleuze and Guattari have set the onto-epistemological ground for much of the enlivening new work that is happening in the 'affective', 'non-representational', 'posthuman', and 'new material' 'turns' in educational research. However, where I think discussion needs to gain ground is around the ethico-political dimensions of Deleuze and Guattari's thought for conducting research in relation to the conceptual apparatuses outlined in their treatises on schizoanalysis. It seems what is lacking in some of the take-up of Deleuze's solo philosophy, for instance his treatise on 'societies of control' as well as perhaps Deleuze and Guattari's later, *A Thousand Plateaus*, is adequate attention to the *psyche and subjectivity*, which was paramount in *Anti-Oedipus*. While their work is celebrated for 'flattening out of the social and psychical so that there is neither a relation of causation (one- or two-way) nor hierarchies, levels, grounds, or foundations' (Grosz 1994: 180), flattening does not mean eschewing attention to the psyche-subjectivity.

To address my concerns about the sometimes missing dimensions of *subjectivity* in the take-up of Deleuze and Guattari in some educational research, in this short article I would like to return to the basic premises of schizoanalysis as outlined in *Anti-Oedipus* and Guattari's later *Schizoanalytic Cartographies* – both issue radical calls to engage with the complexity of the social field, capitalism and the unconscious and explore the conditions through which schizoanalytic change is made possible. My aim is not to define or defend the correct schizoanalytic tasks or methodological rules but to show how this orientation may be experimented with through assembled relations that make up the apparatus of conceptual inquiry: 'The most desirable effect that can be anticipated in the conceptual field is not in the order of comprehension

Deleuze Studies 9.3 (2015): 393–409
DOI: 10.3366/dls.2015.0194
© Edinburgh University Press
www.euppublishing.com/journal/dls

but in the form of a certain efficiency "it works or it doesn't work"' (Guattari 2009: 22).

My interest in this paper is in putting schizoanalysis 'to work' alongside feminist desires to push back and through binaries and dualisms. A number of feminist philosophers have suggested Deleuze and Guattari's work can be appropriated for feminism because it involves challenging Oedipal logics and bourgeois repression, and capitalist territorialisations of sexuality, which reinstate and naturalise gender binary machines, for example masculinities vs femininities (Braidotti 1994; Grosz 1994; Lorraine 2008). The basic challenge to binary formations of gender identity and the proposition of 1000 tiny sexes as the schizophrenic model for posthuman sexuality (Beckman 2011); offering a fantastic war machine against the stranglehold of compulsory gender binaries that dictate gender 'roles' and 'behaviours' but also normalise these binaries as a legitimate realm of inquiry (think of all statistical, bio-political attempts to measure naturalised gender differences in educational research and policy, for instance in performative audits of exam success by gender).

To challenge the great molar aggregate of gender binaries, the philosopher Tamsin Lorraine suggests (2008: 80):

> Feminism could be seen as an untimely schizo practice designed to intervene with contemporary configurations of modern subjectivity that involve suppression and oppression of subjects that deviate from a majoritarian norm with the fault lines of sexed, gendered and sexual identity as its starting point.

Lorraine speculates on the 'life affirming potentialities' of schizoanalysis as offering us concepts that help us to perceive and map different ways of doing and breaking apart gender. Developing the concept of alternative feminist 'figurations' to resist the constellation of bodies, things and desires that are bound up in the Oedipal formations, Rosi Braidotti notes 'The rejection of the principle of equation to and identification with a phallogoncentric image of thought lies at the heart of the nomadic vision of subjectivity that Deleuze [and Guattari] propose as the new, postmetaphysical figuration of the subject ...' (Braidotti 1994: 101). Elizabeth Grosz notes similarly (1994) that Deleuze (and Guattari) are useful for corporeal feminism because they blow up binaries and classification hierarchies like those of gender. Their framework:

> de-massifies the entities that binary thought conterposes against each other: the subject, the social order, even the natural world are theorized in terms of the microprocesses, a myriad of intensities and flows, with unaligned or unalignable components ... the body and subjectivity excessive to

hierarchical control ... the body as the realm of affectivity is the site or sites of multiple struggles. (Grosz 1994: 181)

I wish to follow these ideas to think about how what I will call schizo-feminist research can operate as a 'mapping' tool – a cartographic experiment to re-think the 'appearance of "data"' that emerges from feminist research processes (St Pierre 2013). How can research map gender territorialisations as well as discover–create new formations of gendered and sexed becoming-(post)human (Braidotti 2013)? Which feminist figurations are apparent or not in what we find? What can gendered bodies become – do and not do (Coleman 2009)? To think through these questions I will briefly review some key ideas from *Anti-Oedipus* and *Schizoanalytic Cartographies*.

Schizoanalysis: Mapping Libidinal and Political Economies and Investments

From the first time I read *Anti-Oedipus* I was enthralled. It was revolutionary poetry in motion! It joined up many of the conversations I had emerged from in graduate school and which informed my PhD thesis, including: anti-racist Marxist feminist pedagogy (Bannerji 1995), object-relations feminist psychoanalysis (Benjamin 1998) and free association psychosocial research methodologies (Hollway and Jefferson 2000). Deleuze and Guattari's materialist semiotics and ontology offers a profound challenge to individualising egoic subjects by insisting we explore the *libidinal and political* economy simultaneously as *non-discrete processes* or becomings (Holland 1999). Their schizoanalysis is complex: it outlines multiple directions of thought-action through the two tasks and four theses, which I want to go through with the specific aim of drawing out what is useful for schizo-feminism.

As a feminist the first task of schizoanalysis, the 'negative' task of destroying the dominant social order or 'insanity' of capitalism, was enormously appealing. I confess to seizing upon impassioned (and manic) passages like this one with glee:

> [S]chizoanalysis must devote itself with all its strength to the necessary destructions. Destroying beliefs and representations, theatrical scenes. And when engaged in this task no activity will be too malevolent. Causing Oedipus and castration to explode, brutally intervening each time the subject strikes up the song of myth or intones tragic lines, carrying him back *to the factory* ... Oedipus and castration are no more than reactional formations, resistances, blockages and armourings whose destruction can't come fast enough ...

the psychoanalyst reterritorializes on the couch, in the representation of Oedipus and castration. Schizoanalysis on the contrary must disengage the deterritorialised flows of desire, in the molecular elements of desiring-production. (Deleuze and Guattari 2004: 345–6)

How much this type of call fired up my radical feminist inclinations! I was pumping to crush all the vertical power relations that express themselves through phallogocentrism (Oedipal and phallic-oriented power relations) festering in the striated (stratified) intra-personal spaces of 'the factory' (the mind, school, workplace, family, peer group, social network . . .).

But there was more! Joining the negative and destructive task were the double positive tasks of schizoanalysis: (1) discovering the desiring machines bound up by Oedipus (and the phallic signifier); and (2) the call to break down the duality and structural distinction between the two poles of molar and molecular to understand how the investments of libidinal and political economy work together. Paranoid, sedimentary and bi-univocalising, reactionary and fascist tendencies *as well as* schizophrenic, nomadic and polyvocal deterritorialisations can live out at the molar and molecular level, and the implications of Deleuze and Guattari's schizoanalysis are that we must map the operations at multiple levels (Holland 1999). To try to clarify the complexities of the second positive task, Deleuze and Guattari introduce four theses:

1. The first thesis is that every psychic investment is simultaneously social (Deleuze and Guattari 2004: 373) (despite the apparent segregation of familial desire from society at large). Capitalist power relations work through *political and libidinal* economies that must be taken apart together. Capitalism effects a massive deterritorialisation of flows by taking away the major codification systems from previous formations of savagery and despotism. Money, for instance, reduces all codes and meanings opening up flows due to an 'axiomatization of abstract quantitates' (Holland 1999: 116): 'Patriarchy certainly does not disappear under capitalisms; it merely goes underground: it becomes psychological rather than socio-cultural or institutional.' Schizoanalysis needs to grasp and track the potentialities of the schizophrenic desiring machines to break out of paranoiac formations through new bodily (partial object) relations, sensations and intensities (the body without organs).

2. The second thesis is that we must distinguish the preconscious investment of class or interest, from the unconscious libidinal investment of desire, 'desire and interest always co-exist but do not necessarily coincide' (Holland 1999: 103). Preconscious investments may be revolutionary

in content (let's rid the world of hunger) yet molar and repressive in form (let's do it through relations of dominance). There are two corresponding kinds of revolutionary breaks or rupture – unconscious revolutionary breaks which operate in the promotion of molecular desire, subordinating molar forms to the subversive free-play of desiring production and preconscious breaks which enact new forms of codification or axiomatisation (Holland 1999). For revolution to occur the two kinds of break must coincide – new freedoms *and* new rules – to create the conditions under which new formations of subjectivity may be possible.

3. The third thesis is that libidinal investments are primarily social and only secondarily familial. However, as we saw, libidinal relations are continuously over-coded by familial terms because of the primacy of the nuclear family as the conduit of desire under capitalist, privatised relationality. The Oedipal triangle is a socio-historical-material construct that operates the actual relations of dependency (desire, money, and so on) that are materialised in the nuclear family. These tripartite affective relations are between Mommy, Daddy and me (what they also term Mr Capital, Mrs Earth and Worker Child) as sites where we find the over-investing of familial bound desire. Patriarchal and Oedipalised subjectivity produce not just a hierarchical gendered identity but oppressive value orientation and 'identifications' with either the domineering father or conversely the subjugated figure of the victim (Holland 1999: 118). Eugene Holland warns that this exclusive identification with victimisation of the subjugated (for example women/girls) is a potential pitfall of some versions of feminism.

4. The fourth thesis explains that there are two poles of libidinal social investment paranoia and schizophrenia, and each pole can be analysed in terms of its characteristic mode of psychic functioning as well as its social function (Holland 1999: 93). Two types of revolutionary groups are discussed: subject groups are characterised by unconscious investment of schizophrenic form, while subjugated groups operate according to preconscious investments of paranoid form (Holland 1999: 103). Important for this chapter, Deleuze and Guattari warn that the 'researcher' and the (social) scientist need to be aware of the libidinal conflict between a paranoiac-Oedipalising element of science and a schizo-revolutionary element. Rather than the 'great social axiomatic that retains from science what must be retained in terms of market needs and zones of technical innovation' (Deleuze and Guattari 2004: 406), as with art, we must develop methods of scientific *experimentation* but not '*without aim or end*' (406–7).

So to summarise, schizoanalysis is a call for a (social) science of experimentation with revolutionary scope that creates and maps different formations (arrangements or assemblages). Schizoanalysis as a practice is to interfere in some way in the Oedipal, Capitalist capture of desire (the familial – sociodesiring libidinal investments) through the 'disintegration of the normal ego' which can show that 'neither men nor women are clearly defined personalities, but rather vibrations, flows, schizzes, and "knots" … everyone is a little group (un groupuscule) and must live as such' (Deleuze and Guattari 2004: 396). Deleuze and Guattari offer the useful concept of 'orphan desire' and 'orphan libido' which moves outside Oedipal binds/bounds:

> what the orphan libido invests is a field of social desire, a field of production and anti-production with its breaks and flows, where the parents are apprehended in nonparental functions and roles confronting other roles and functions. (Deleuze and Guattari 2004: 389)

Demonstrating or finding evidence of the schizzes and orphan desire contributes to a schizoanalytic project. When, for instance, do we find evidence of something different within research accounts (for instance a qualitative research interview)? When can we see lines of flight outside of the great molar aggregate of gender differences, constructed through paranoiac, neurotic formations of desire? When are different partial object bodily relations made possible? What are the de-re-territorialising rhythms involved? And as we will see next, Guattari was even more concerned with *the conditions* that allow for such schizzes and breaks to unfold.

Schizoanalytic Cartographies

Guattari went on to specifically call his guide to undertaking such maps *Schizoanalytic Cartographies*. Schizoanalysis needed a second term to reference the conditions that could enable possibility for subjective-social change. What was primary for Guattari, as (anti)psychiatrist was in creating the conditions that would allow for both *safety and disruption* of the norms and power striations (Walkerdine 2012). For example, through his re-routing of the tasks performed by patients, staff and doctors, at the clinic La Borde, with a new circulating '*la grille*' or 'grid' of tasks and activities he sought to directly challenge vertical power relations through his notion of transversality (Genesko 2009: 51). According to Gary Genesko (2009: 51) one of Guattari's most significant contributions is 'the political idea of (non-hierarchical) transversal relationships'. Transversal is that which defies vertical relations of managerial pyramid structures as well as pure horizontality among groups of senile patients for instance, 'transversality is a dimension that strives to overcome two impasses: that of pure verticality or simple horizontality. Transversality tends to be realised when maximum communication is brought about between different levels and above all in terms of different directions' (2009: 51). So transversality operates between hierarchy and accommodation where openness is introduced through variations in relationships that disrupt, rework but also productively inhabit hierarchies. Guattari showed how specific and tangible manifestations can foster institutional changes that enable 'mutually enriching encounters ... so that individual did not fall back into old roles and the repressive fantasies attached to them or succumb to retrogressive habits of how to respond to authority and fixed ways of communicating' (56). Through the famous examples of the patient becoming 'cook for the day' Guattari discussed how changes in role could allow for new connections and subjective potentialities to emerge. This was not an isolated case but took place within a reconfigured set of social relations where the patient was *psychically contained* enough to engage in the experiment (Walkerdine 2013). Indeed, to get at the transience of these affective relations Renold and Ivinson (2014) call them 'transversal flashes', which may resonate with pure desire.

Seeking to elaborate the abstract grid of relations that might make deterritorialisations of subjectivity and transversal relations possible, Guattari envisioned a four-field map of figuring out the coordinates of subjectivity as a way of deciphering the singular factors in play in creating *psychical and social* flux:

Concrete and abstract machinic phylums	Virtual universes of value
• The 'general intellect' and its creative applications	• Worlds of senses and feeling, aesthetic images conjured forth
Material, energetic and semiotic fluxes	Finite existential territories
• The movement, circulation and change of all things	• Feelings of familiarity, belonging, the sense of 'homeland'

Reading this table[1] clockwise these quadrants translate into developing research methods as: (1) mapping the phylum or knowledges or systems of thought that are constructing the situation (discourses/representations, for instance a policy is a technology or phylum organising thought/action); (2) mapping how value is accrued and attributable through aesthetical/image bound processes (systems of exchange and reward, for instance fashion media could over-code wearable aesthetics); (3) mapping the familiar territories and repetitions (the phenomenological, embodied, everyday ground of existence and context in play); (4) mapping out the material, affective and semiotic flows of practices (the assembled relations in process). Guattari called these the four 'functors of deterritorialisation' – aspects that would help us to map 'the configurations of subjectivity, desire, drive energy and the diverse modalities of discourses and consciousness relating to them' (1989: 26).

To develop schizoanalytic cartography as a feminist research method means trying to engage with these various levels of social-subjectivities. For instance, Watson (2015: 108) suggests that 'All assemblages require components from all four quadrants in order to function effectively, although components from any one quadrant may dominate or recede with any given assemblage'. It may not be possible to keep all the elements of this complexity theory in play within the one dimensionality of scientific writing, hence the propensity to extract aspects of assemblages. A schizo-feminist research method brings certain quadrants into focus, whilst attempting to keep the complexity of the whole assemblage in the foreground.

Indeed, for the remainder of this paper I want to outline several areas of qualitative research in gender, sexuality and education where I have begun to think about how the negative and positive tasks of schizoanalysis and attending to the various schizoanalytic research quadrants can help in making perceptible new figurations of subjectivity, as well as the conditions (technological, pedagogical, relational, and so on) that may make such change possible.

Beyond Bullying Binaries: Schizoid Subjectivities and Orphan Desire

One area where my work both solo (2011) and with Emma Renold (for example: 2008, 2011, 2012) has consistently sought to map out territorialisation and deterritorialisation is through critiques of psychological, binary driven school psychology research and policies on bullying and cyberbullying. We have consistently critiqued the machinic phylum of psychological school bullying categorisations that artificially separate conflict into victim, bully and bystander. These discourses work through the binaries critiqued in the second thesis of schizoanalysis, discussed above where victim status is binarised (and can be attached to as morally superior) seeking to make simple sense of the complex power relations governing group cultures. School bully discourses/policies also unfold via Oedipalised gender binaries to construct a normal, phallic oriented violent boy and a normal passive, subservient yet therefore relationally (repressively and internalised) aggressive girl.

Using schizoanalysis has allowed us to map how affects do not simply flow, 'travel' or stick in only in predictable ways, however. Sexual subjectification exceeds the discursive regulation through complex flows and molecular lines of flight where the affective assemblages end up rupturing and sometimes 'queering' (that is mix-up, complicate and subvert) conventional meanings of gendered norms as they unfold in live time (Renold and Ringrose 2008, 2011; Ringrose and Renold 2012). We developed the concept of 'schizoid subjectivities' to *empirically demonstrate*, what Grosz philosophises, that feminine subjectivity is not reducible to a pathological symptom of patriarchy, rather girls are managing schizoid conditions in the performance and doing of intelligible femininities in relation to age and sexuality in a context of mass panic over girls' 'sexualisation' in the anglophone West.

To take one of my favourite empirical examples where we mapped disruptions of the Oedipal and gender binary relations of desire, we explored (through interviews and online observations) a friendship pair of teen girls, Daniella and Sadie, who purposefully call themselves whore and slut on each other's social networking profiles to occupy these subject positions. This is an assemblage since their online profiles are co-created they have a shared subjectivity – they literally write the identities on each other's pages, and they take back the terms of injurious sexual subjectification saying they are EACH OTHER'S WHORE AND SLUT, rather than in relation to male gaze/possession. This can be theorised as a form of orphan desire articulated by Deleuze and Guattari where Daniella and Sadie try out forms of sexual subjectivity that break away from the mommy-daddy-me formation of Oedipalised phallic oriented desire. However, they do not simply inhabit these spaces as the security to do so partly depends on their relational attachments to popular boys (the phallus) in the peer hierarchy, recalling Gayle Rubin's (1984) charmed (Oedipal) circle. The girls also revert back to appropriate child subjectivities and binary modalities of relating to child and parent functions/roles through other subjective states expressed online, when for instance they assemble photos of themselves in their school uniforms, angel wings for Halloween and post a poem entreating one of their friends to stop dating her older boyfriend, beseeching her to 'come back to them', to 'have good times' and 'do childish things like the children that we are'. By seeing disruption as a perceptible variable *flow of deterritorialisation and reterritorialisation* – the answer is not mass organised revolution but micro ruptures which portend new formations of subjectivities. We can show and therefore enable the possible re-valuing of new empirical figurations like digital slut.

Organs without Bodies and Post-Oedipal Parodies

In my recent youth 'sexting' research the two areas anxiety about aggressively sexual femininity (potential deterritorialisations?) and the repeated sexual re-regulation of femininity (reterritorialisation) back into the fictive box of childhood feminine sexual innocence, come together quite profoundly in the constructions of the illegal teen girl selfie sexter. Entering into a highly contested set of legal and educational rules and media debates (machinic phylum and existential territories of meaning) over youth digitally mediated sexuality we see the public pedagogy of anti-sexting repeatedly trying to re-position teen girls into the victim binary as melancholic target of having a future spoiled sexual reputation via boys/men passing around images of their bodies (Albury and Crawford 2012; Dobson and Ringrose forthcoming). Critics have challenged the construction of the young girl sexter as a self-exploiting criminal (Karianan 2013), but the sexual volition or agency of 'underage' girls' self-produced 'sexy' selfie images dramatically challenges the socio-legal discourses/policies of child protection at school (Ringrose et al. 2012).

If we follow the negative and positive tasks of schizoanalysis through the phenomena of teen sexting: the negative task is to deconstruct the regulative discourses about sexting (official phylum and aesthetic constructions of morality) with their life and energy destroying psychosocial material-affective effects upon young people. Interrupting the binary machines of gender that materialise through the discourses of sexting is not just a representational task, but research mapping means rendering perceptible the striations and affective territorialisations of technologically mediated sexual communication.

Despite the rather idealised notion that capitalism does not need gender, since it will take any unit of labourer (Holland 1999) we see renewed gender binaries in the territories of value in social media ecology. For instance the compulsory 'sharing' in social media platforms like Facebook, through digital affordances like photo posting and tagging and 'likes', can operate as new forms of phallic touch (Renold and Ringrose, forthcoming) hardening new gender dualism machines. Take the production of 'sexy selfies' Laura Harvey and I (2015) have shown how images of 'sexy selfies' (Tiidenberg 2014) of breasts, butts, six packs and bits (dick-pics) take on differential value in social networks through processes of over-investment and reterritorialisation of Oedipal, phallic oriented desire. So rather than a body without organs we find organs without bodies (Braidotti 1994) and what I have termed commodified 'intensive body parts' of breasts and penises re-territorialising the symbolic and material terrain. Girls are called upon to produce, share and post images of their breasts and butts, yet this is typically subject to sexual re-regulation, since it is girls who self-display or post such images who are regularly slut-shamed across various international studies (Ringrose et al. 2012; Daniels and Zurbriggen 2014). However, reinstating patriarchal hierarchies of existential value, the same dynamics of territorialising sexual shame do not surround the display of boys' six-pack selfies online, although their 'manly bits' may be judged too small (see Ringrose and Harvey 2015). Thus, despite the potentially smooth space offered by the digital affordances of technological platforms as places to perform multiplicitous identities (Van Doorn 2011), we see new striations of space and matter where Oedipal logics continually draw us into a phallogocentric object relations where the breast is semiotically–materially linked back to the phallus, the female body is understood primarily as a site for male gaze/penetration, where a teen girl's self-produced image can be read as evidence of shamefulness, looseness re-drawing coercive hierarchies of value in line with heteronormative power relations.

Of course lived desire relations *exceed* the logic of commodification, fetishisation and exchange and the affective economy of sexual shame and blame. Young people refuse the construction of sexual images of their body as shameful and exploitative in many ways. Some girls responded to Oedipal requests to produce images of their bodies by sending an image of their cat (here's my pussy) or an alien (what inventive parodies of posthuman sex!) Some suggested that sexting images were evidence of creativity in negotiating intimacy and sex and if you were in a trusting relationship an image was like a gift. However, like Daniella discussed above it is the charmed circle of Oedipal protection of the heterosexual relationship that provided the ground for the confidence for sharing images for girls. It was not apparent in any of the sexting data so far that girls could confidently proclaim themselves able to send a picture of their breasts to anyone they wish, since that image would continue to represent a reputational risk of codifying the body-image as slutty.

Schizo-Feminist Assemblages in School

To conclude my discussion of the possibilities offered by schizo-feminist research cartographies, I must stress we take seriously how to feed data 'findings' through and back into a wider set of power relations in policy, media, institutional structures, and so on. Research is not generated in a vacuum and needs to exceed the boundaries of the academy: science must experiment in new feminist worldings (Haraway 1996). Thus schizo-feminism following Guattari's call for transversalising of social relations, needs to *do something* to effectuate interruptions of the same. Schizo-feminist research is always part of a wider feminist assemblage, working in relation to the four quadrants, where various intra-acting (Barad 2007 in Lenz-Taguchi and Palmer 2013) agents co-constitute the lived social relations of gender and education. To try to put the impact aspect of schizo-feminist research into action myself with a group of academics and teachers recently assembled a schizo-feminist project to develop experimental 'Feminism in school' para-educational lunch or after school clubs in six schools across England and Wales.[2] These groups operated as a form of consciousness-raising, where young people (including a group at an all-boys' school), teachers and academics developed experimental discussion groups to explore feminism (or issues of 'gender equality' where feminism was too incendiary) for a minimum of six weeks of group meetings. Echoing Guattarian inspired experiments in schooling such as the Freinet movement, which drew on the radical pedagogy of Celestin Freinet to resist 'the alienation of the institutional subject from the social fabric of the institution and collapse the student–teacher dyad' (Wallin 2012: 12), our programme operated as an example of schizo-cartography and transversalising of relations through meetings with students, teachers and academics. Breaking down hierarchies was attempted through switching teacher–student roles around who would lead conversations, select topics for engagement, and creative productions. For instance girls initiated creating new objects like a curvy Barbie doll; recreating the Tumblr meme 'I need feminism because' and transmitting it through one of the schools television systems, and using and social media like Twitter and Facebook to communicate their 'feminist' views.[3] The teachers, students and academics also worked on impromptu in-group writing experiments including poems and blogs.

It is the latter aspect of the assemblage – the writing experiments that I want to focus on briefly to explain how it provided a channel for dialogue and dissemination via a 'transversal' exchange of knowledge between academics, high school teachers and students to disrupt the 'general dissociation between schools and students' but also between academics, schools and teachers (Wallin 2012). In one example that demonstrates how the group discussion and writing pieces practices could disrupt both hierarchical adult–child and student–teacher relations in the classroom as well as phallogocentric and Oedipal power relations in the outside world, in the entry 'Your personality isn't your sex!' Nihinsa writes about the time her dad yelled in the car that woman drivers were crazy and how it made her 'fuming inside'. She describes the need for people to stop referring to 'weak, soft or crazy (as in emotionally unstable) for women' and 'strong, or rough or crazy (as in wild or reckless) for men'. Space is opened here to dispute men and women as 'clearly defined personalities' and to explore the 'vibrations, flows, schizzes, and "knots"' (Deleuze and Guattari 2004: 396) of Oedipal power relations alive in the family car. The car and driving as spatial domain allowed teachers, academics and students to explore Oedipal investments and how to re-think femininity and masculinity in the family and beyond.

In another example there was hot debate around whether feminine body hair was 'disgusting', something that the teachers, academics and students argued over at length. Pavlova then wrote about body 'Hair', noting:

> We all have hair all over our body. It grows everywhere except for our palms, lips and the soles of our feet. But for some reasons as time has gone by it has become the norm for women to take it all off. Well it started with woman however now some men feel the need to as well!

She continues by listing many of the amazing functionalities of hair to protect our bodies against the elements, but laments:

> I have sadly given in to society's low expectations and I have recently taken the hairs off my legs because I felt judged and the idea of having 'hair on your legs makes you look like a boy' has already been drilled into my brain since I was very young. Even though I have given into it I wouldn't want the same for future generations ... why should the body always be seen as a sexual object, in the same way why is hair on your body apart for your head seen as 'horrible' or 'unfeminine'? We have also got to accept the fact that we are never going to stop the world from spinning but we can at least make it better for future generations! Go Natural!

This discussion and writing then led to students making several posters for their art room which parodied the depilation practices. In one, for instance, an ambiguously gendered celebrity figure accepts an academy award in an evening gown with unshaven leg hair.

These are but two brief and incomplete accounts of where the group discussion and writing exercises provided space for girls and women teachers and academics to disrupt the gender binary machines of gender as well as question power dynamics regulated through Oedipal relations (adult–child, student–teacher, academic–teacher and so on). Nihinsa's challenge to why her dad 'assumed the driver was a woman' was felt as a transversal flash where the academics, teachers and students shared their resistance to reducing the personality to feminine or masculine 'sex'.

Pavlova's schizo-address encouraged discussion of the affective dynamics of wanting to 'Go Natural' – at the same time as she and others in the room were caught in a psychosocial web of capture through the mediated gaze ordering feminine depilation. She finds space to move about amongst the 'spinning' of the world.

Conclusion

As all the examples drawn from my research and collaborations aimed to demonstrate the ethico-political imperative of schizoanalysis – to grasp how the psychical and libidinal economies and investments work together in the contemporary context of advanced capitalist privatisation of social relations organising gender and sexuality. It looks for and enacts ruptures and breaks (the negative tasks). But also seeks to perceive and create conditions for something anew (the positive tasks). Thus, schizoanalysis or the transmogrified mix of schizo-feminist research cartographies are working to reconfigure what research is and can look like and what it can do.

Indeed in this article I have charted a journey from my own previous scholarship that modelled how to plug Deleuze and Guattari into research data in order to find 'evidence of something different within research accounts (for instance a qualitative research interview)' to how schizo-cartographies can be set into motion within the institutional cultures and spaces of schools. Thus we see how the work of Deleuze and Guattari and schizoanalysis not only lends insights into the analysis of data but also the ways that combining research, activism, art and writing, through new feminist assemblages in schools, might enable new transversal flashes and disruptions. As one of the helpful reviewers noted, this article seems to be on the precipice of documenting the unfolding of the schizo-feminist cartographic process where data moves from an object to an event. The after-school feminist clubs were a form of schizoanalytic cartography in action – our writings can be seen as constituting data-events where something different happens although the wider effects are not yet known. Yet I agree with the reviewer's estimation of this capturing of the research being on the 'precipice' because data-events are unfoldings in action and we do not know the possible effects and we freeze their movement to tell our stories. Moreover the capacity to sustain experimental methodologies surges and wanes. What is clear, then, as with Deleuze and Guattari's own mappings – is these are contextually specific and unfinished thought-activity experiments. It is up to each of us to find how our research thinking, writing, speaking, and research activities are part of wider projects of immanent becoming and may hold capacity for transversal transformation in the socio-political terrain of educational studies and beyond.

Notes

1. Table derived from 'How does Schizoanalysis Work? Or, "How do you Make a Class Operate Like a Work of Art"', available at http://deterritoriali nvestigations.wordpress.com/2013/05/15/how-does-schizoanalysis-work-or-how-do-you-make-a-class-operate-like-a-work-of-art/ (accessed 10 May 2015).
2. Originally the assemblage included a corporate women's fashion magazine that in part mobilised the undertaking. However, we 'split off from each other', as the features editor put it, when the Corporation wanted to brand (territorialise) educational materials with their logo but refused to provide any financial backing or even media exposure for the project. The data collection was enabled through the project 'Feminism in Schools: Mapping Impact in Practice' Funded by Cardiff University and led by Professor Emma Renold.
3. Please see Ringrose and Renold (forthcoming) for a more extensive discussion of how social media practices such as Facebook comments and Tweeting worked to transmit the feminist views of students to the wider community in a posthuman digital transformation of Freinet's printing press (Wallin 2012). The chapter explores how the contemporary digital affordances of social media are a platform for sharing affect and thought experiments around the inside and to the outside of the school space.

References

Albury, Kath and Kate Crawford (2012) 'Sexting, Consent and Young People's Ethics: Beyond Megan's Story', *Continuum*, 26: 3, 463–73.

Bannerji, Himani (1995) *Thinking Through: Essays on Feminism, Marxism, and Anti-racism*, Toronto: Women's Press.

Beckman, F. (2011) 'Introduction', in F. Beckman (ed.), *Deleuze and Sex*, Edinburgh: Edinburgh University Press.

Benjamin, Jessica (1998) *Shadow of the Other: Intersubjectivity and Gender in Psychoanalysis*, New York: Routledge.

Braidotti, Rosi (1994) *Nomadic Subjects: Embodiment and Sexual Difference in Contemporary Feminist Theory*, Cambridge: Columbia University Press.

Braidotti, Rosi (2013) *The Posthuman*, London: Polity Press.

Coleman, Rebecca (2009) *The Becoming of Bodies: Girls, Images, Experience*, Manchester: Manchester University Press.

Daniels Elizabeth A. and Eileen L. Zurbriggen (2014) 'The Price of Sexy: Viewers' Perceptions of a Sexualized Versus Nonsexualized Facebook Profile Photograph', *Psychology of Popular Media Culture*. doi: 10.1037/ppm0000048 (accessed 10 May 2015).

Deleuze, Gilles and Félix Guattari [1984] (2004) *Anti-Oedipus: Capitalism and Schizophrenia*, London: Continuum.

Dobson, Amy and Jessica Ringrose (in press) 'Sext Education: Sex, Gender and Shame in the Schoolyards of Tagged and Exposed', *Sex Education*.

Genesko, Gary (2009) *Félix Guattari: A Critical Introduction*, Northhampton: Pluto Press.

Grosz, Elizabeth (1994) *Volatile Bodies: Toward a Corporeal Feminism*, Bloomington, IN: Indiana University Press.

Guattari, Félix (2009) *Soft Subversions*, London: Semiotext(e).

Guattari, Félix [1989] (2013) *Schizoanalytic Cartographies*, London: Bloomsbury.

Haraway, Donna J. (1996) *Modest_Witness@Second_Millennium.FemaleMan©_Meets_Oncomouse*, New York: Routledge.

Holland, Eugene (1999) *Deleuze and Guattari's Anti-Oedipus: Introduction to Schizoanalysis*, London: Routledge.

Hollway, Wendy and Tony Jefferson (2000) *Doing Qualitative Research Differently: Free Association, Narrative and the Interview Method*, Thousand Oaks, CA: Sage Publications.

Karaian, Lara (2013) 'Policing "Sexting": Responsibilization, Respectability and Sexual Subjectivity in Child Protection/Crime Prevention Responses to Teenagers' Digital Sexual Expression', *Theoretical Criminology*. doi: 10.1177/1362480613504331 (accessed 10 May 2015).

Lenz-Taguchi, Hillevi and Anna Palmer (2013) 'A More "Livable" School? A Diffractive Analysis of the Performative Enactments of Girls' Ill-/Well-being With(in) School Environments', *Gender and Education*, 25: 6, 671–87.

Lorraine, Tamsin (2008) 'Feminist Lines of Flight from the Majoritarian Subject', in Claire Colebrook and Jami Weinstein (eds), *Deleuze and Gender*, Edinburgh: Edinburgh University Press.

Renold, Emma and Gabrielle Ivinson (2014) 'Horse-girl Assemblages: Towards a Post-human Cartography of Girls' Desire in an Ex-mining Valleys Community', *Discourse Studies in the Cultural Politics of Education*, 35: 3. doi: 10.1080/01596306.2014.888841 (accessed October 2014).

Renold, Emma and Jessica Ringrose (2008) 'Regulation and Rupture: Mapping Tween and Teenage Girls' "Resistance" to the Heterosexual Matrix', *Feminist Theory*, 9: 3, pp. 335–60.

Renold, Emma and Jessica Ringrose (2011) 'Schizoid Subjectivities?: Re-theorising Teen-girls' Sexual Cultures in an era of 'Sexualisation', *Journal of Sociology*, 47: 4, pp. 389–409.

Ringrose, Jessica (2011) 'Beyond Discourse? Using Deleuze and Guattari's Schizoanalysis to Explore Affective Assemblages, Heterosexually Striated Space, and Lines of Flight Online and at School', *Educational Philosophy & Theory*, 43: 6, pp. 598–618.

Ringrose, Jessica and Laura Harvey (2015) 'Boobs, Back-off, Six packs and Bits: Mediated Body Parts, Gendered Reward, and Sexual Shame in Teens' Sexting Images', *Continuum Journal of Media and Cultural Studies*, 29: 2, 205–17.

Ringrose, Jessica and Emma Renold (2012) Teen Girls, Working Class Femininity and Resistance: Re-theorizing Fantasy and Desire in Educational Contexts of Heterosexualized Violence, *International Journal of Inclusive Education*, 16: 4, 461–77.

Ringrose, Jessica and Emma Renold (forthcoming) 'Cows, Cabins and Tweets: Posthuman Affect in Feminist Research Assemblages', in Carol Taylor and Christina Hughes, *Posthuman Research Practices in Education*, London: Palgrave.

Ringrose, Jessica, Rosalind Gill, Sonia Livingstone and Laura Harvey (2012) A Qualitative Study of Children, Young People and 'Sexting', London: NSPCC, available at http://www.nspcc.org.uk/inform/resourcesforprofessionals/sexualabuse/sexting-research-report_wdf89269.pdf (accessed 10 May 2015).

St Pierre, Elizabeth A. (2013) The Appearance of Data, *Cultural Studies ↔ Critical Methodologies*, 13, 223–7.

Tiidenberg, Katrin (2014) 'Bringing Sexy Back: Reclaiming the Body Aesthetic via Self-shooting', *Cyberpsychology: Journal of Psychosocial Research on Cyberspace*, 8: 1, article 3. doi: 10.5817/CP2014–1–3 (accessed February 2015).

Van Doorn, Neils (2011) 'Digital Spaces, Material Traces: How Matter Comes to Matter in Online Performances of Gender, Sexuality and Embodiment', *New Media, Culture and Society*, 33: 4, pp. 531–47.

Walkerdine, Valerie (2013) Using the Work of Felix Guattari to Understand Space, Place, Social Justice, and Education, *Qualitative Inquiry*, 19: 10, 756–64.

Wallin, Jason (2012) 'Getting Out from Behind the Lectern: Counter-cartographies of the Transversal Institution', in David Masney (ed.), *Cartographies of Becoming in Education*, London: Springer.

Watson Janell (2015) MULTIPLE MUTATING MASCULINITIES of maps and men, *Angelaki: Journal of the Theoretical Humanities*, 20: 1, 107–21. doi: 10.1080/0969725X.2015.1017387 (accessed 5 May 2015).

Producing the NAPLAN Machine: A Schizoanalytic Cartography

Greg Thompson and Ian Cook   Murdoch University

We live today in the age of partial objects, bricks that have been shattered to bits, and leftovers. We no longer believe in the myth of the existence of fragments that, like pieces of an antique statue, are merely waiting for the last one to be turned up, so that they may all be glued back together to create a unity that is precisely the same as the original unity.

Deleuze and Guattari 1983, p. 42

This paper addresses the proliferation and intensification of testing, both global and national, that functions as a 'regulatory mechanism for nations in terms of the scaling and rescaling of educational accountabilities' (Lingard et al. 2013, p. 4). Our argument is that testing has become a central process in the production of subjectivities in schooling that exemplify Deleuze and Guattari's schizophrenic society, which manifests 'increasing disharmony and discord at every level' (Deleuze and Guattari 1983, p. 34). We apply Guattari's speculative schizoanalytic cartography to ask what 'opens' education, and teachers in particular, to these regimes of standardised testing. This 'opening' is affected through bodies, so we use schizoanalytic cartographies to "forge new coordinates" for reading those testing↔schooling↔teaching↔learning↔desiring education machines (Guattari 2013, p. 17).

Education, in particular schooling, is undergoing a change in the production of desire, or the 'set of passive syntheses that engineer partial objects, flows, and bodies, and that function as units of production' that results in the 'autoproduction of the unconscious' (Deleuze and Guattari 1983, p. 26). There has always been a coupling of schooling and desire-production to produce disciplinary effects as

Deleuze Studies 9.3 (2015): 410–423
DOI: 10.3366/dls.2015.0195
© Edinburgh University Press
www.euppublishing.com/journal/dls

various machines connect, form, re-form, fold and re-fold, producing certain kinds of employable and governable knowledges, bodies and dispositions. New couplings and de-couplings, however, are part of 'a general breakdown' that Deleuze argued disciplinary logics of schooling were 'in the midst of' as 'control societies are taking over from disciplinary societies' (Deleuze 1995, p. 178). A control society is characterised by 'ultrarapid forms of apparently free-floating control' whose machines are digital, and deploys the language of reform, competition and continuation (Deleuze 1995, pp. 178–9). Our argument is that within this complex, ultrarapid, continuousness of education reform and competition high stakes testing regimes like NAPLAN[1] have acquired a special significance as they change teacher subjectivities. In this context, we require new cartographies that help us to 'get our bearings' within the 'created, smooth frictionless spaces that hurry the postmodern subject onward' (Buchanan 2005, p. 19). This requires a schizoanalysis to make intelligible the machinic processes and desire productions of 'our universal schizophrenia' that are always immanent and powerfully evocative (Buchanan and Lambert 2005, p. 6).

This schizoanalysis reflects Guattari's contention that production machines that operate at a national and/or global scale but have local impacts, like testing, represent the 'molecularization of the human elements in the various machines of industry, the economy, education, the media and so on' (Guattari 1984b, p. 224). In education, this may be seen in the shifts from teaching to teacher quality, from school-based assessment to testing regimes like NAPLAN and the Programme for International Student Assessment (PISA), from inspection to professional accreditation:

> No longer does a person communicate with other persons: organs and functions take part in a machinic 'assembly' which puts together semiotic links and a great interweaving of material and social fluxes. Having broken up the traditional human territorialities, the forces of production are now in a position to liberate the 'molecular' energy of desire. (Guattari 1984b, p. 223)

Standardised testing machines like NAPLAN are machines of desire-production that code and encode, albeit within the continuation of pre-existing signs and assemblages. NAPLAN induces a particular subjectivity, the challenge for a schizoanalysis of NAPLAN is to chart the ways that machines of capture operate within certain modes of desiring-production. Our cartography, which expresses the negative task of schizoanalysis, maps a space of the formation and deformation of a subject manifesting through three voice-pathways. We chart the way that the voice-pathways, or spheres, of 'power', 'knowledge' and 'self-reference' organise, via neurotic and psychotic affects, a teacher opening to regimes of standardised testing.

Schizoanalysis

Schizoanalysis is fundamentally and self-consciously a 'mapping', or cartography, of the various interactions of desire, subjectivity, semiotics and bodies that operate as a fundamental questioning of liberal/capitalist subjectivity. Schizoanalysis aims to recognise the affect of capitalist pragmatics and axiomatics that produces individualisation and specific desires.

Molar and molecular forces are machinic and constantly interact, communicate and striate the spaces and territories in which bodies move. 'Molar structures and molecular machinisms ... are "piloted" either beginning with visible stratified assemblages or beginning with "stratified powers"' (Guattari 2011, p. 150). Guattari posited metamodelling or mapping as a device to understand these machinic interactions and connections. Schizoanalysis determines 'the principal micropolitical lines of the assemblages of enunciation and power formations even at the most abstract level' (Guattari 2011, p. 170). In each instance and in each circumstance in which we examine subjectivity, a new map must be drawn, a 'map of the unconscious' (Guattari 2011, p. 170). This cartography 'will not "decipher" an already constituted, self-enclosed unconscious, it will construct it and will compete in the connection of fields' (Guattari 2011, p. 171).

This mapping, of a machinic unconscious, its rules and codes, moments, shifts, possibilities offers a new machine to understand NAPLAN, not as a set of individual practices, but as a complex interweaving of molar and molecular power; micro- and macro-fascisms if you will. A schizoanalysis does not concern the individualisation of education, nor has it to do with the collective and/or systemic institutionalisation of education. It is both and more. Ultimately, though we cannot follow this line here, it is a map that shows how to move beyond the specific past-future machines that have come to dominate our present, charting lines of flight for thinking, and moving beyond to a new plane of teaching, or education or schooling. As its final stage, schizoanalysis promotes depersonalisation and the release of flows that do not return those normal subjectivities and objectivities supported and regulated by the machines of capitalism. The ultimate goal of schizoanalysis, then, is to register the effects and affects of the various machines at work in terms of their flows, blockages and the lines of flight they prefigure to move beyond the 'capitalist order', where 'desire, once freed from the control of authority, can be seen as more real and more realistic, a better organiser and more skilful engineer, than the raving rationalism of the planners and administrators of the present system' (Guattari 1984a, p. 86).

Partial Objects and Voices/Pathways

To map the flows, blockages and escape routes in which subjectivity is produced requires charting the intensities that form, deform and dissolve as enunciations on planes of expression. These intensities do not culminate in some final 'sense-making'. Rather, their formation as incomplete is essential to their functioning in capitalism. In forming incompletely, or partially, these bundlings of intensities bespeak a totality, or totalisation, as the next stage in ones development or progression. But this totality never arrives and, as we might expect in a system organised against quietism, we are induced to work harder for that new intensity that promises a new finality (which, again, never arrives). The incomplete bundlings or partial objects (POs) function as/at the core of this schizoanalysis because they show how the teacher is being turned toward testing and away from discipline (is opening to regimes of standardised testing). POs form in bodies as (productive) markers of lack. Rather than lack marking absence, as in Freud, for Deleuze and Guattari it manifests presence and is produced. 'Lack is created,' Deleuze and Guattari wrote, 'planned, and organized in and through social production' (Deleuze and Guattari 1983, p. 28). Lack 'creates empty spaces or vacuoles, and propagates itself in accordance with the organisation of an already existing organization of production' (Deleuze and Guattari 1983, p. 28). Lack, then, functions not as a marker of a desire that can be and will be satisfied sometime soon, but as a specific form of desire crucial to the reproduction of capitalism. This lack functions against, or in terms of, (social) fantasies of wholeness. The desire for openness to testing marks a new social fantasy of a smoothly functioning educational whole. While this is never realised, the creation of POs within specific spatio-temporalities (this classroom, this teacher, this student, this present) marks a proliferation of desire-productions leading in all directions.

All the desiring-productions that are misconceived and misperceived as lack point to some individual who lacks. If something is missing, it is not the object of desire. 'It is, rather, the *subject* that is missing in desire, or desire that lacks a fixed subject; there is no fixed subject unless there is repression' (Deleuze and Guattari 1983, p. 26). Schizoanalysis, then, can be conducted as a mapping of POs, not to fix them or to denote coherent totalities that satisfy the fantasy of completion at the individual, group or social levels, but rather to identify the myriad of desires indicated by multiple POs that produce teacher subjectivities within high stakes testing regimes.

Voice/pathways act as assemblages of enunciation that mobilise POs in specific ways. For Guattari, collective apparatuses of subjectification common to contemporary Western societies were produced via three 'interlacing' series of individualising and collectivising 'voices/pathways' (Guattari 2013, p. 3). Voices/pathways of power, knowledge and self-reference *require* POs to produce subjectivity. Guattari's articulation of voices/pathways to understand and map the production of subjectivity is essentially about creating a model of how POs function in productive ways at the level of the group, or processual, subject that itself constitutes and is constituted by power and knowledge.

Guattari's three voice/pathways of *power, knowledge,* and *self-reference* 'don't stop mixing together in a strange ballet' (Guattari 2013, p. 3). Mapping this ballet is the task of a schizoanalytic 'speculative cartography', a cartography predicated on neither a naïve universalism nor an appeal to a transcendent effectiveness of method (Guattari 2013, p. 5). As this paper is about those processes of subjectification that operate through high-stakes testing and the related data and recording machines, however, we turn to schizoanalytic cartography as a tool to clarify those problems of machinic subjectivity within neoliberalising ideologies and assemblages.

The voices/pathways of *power, knowledge* and *self-reference* are crucial for a schizoanalysis of a teacher opened to testing by NAPLAN in revealing a 'new "machine addiction" of subjectivity' (Guattari 2013, p. 1). This machine addiction is typified by the 'invasive grip of "computer-assisted" data banks' and driven by a paradoxical opening and closing–'an apparent democratisation of data of the access to data, to knowledge, associated with a segregative closing down of the means of their elaboration' (Guattari 2013, p. 1). Education has always been made up of multiple machines, 'machines driving other machines, machines being driven by other machines, with all the necessary couplings and connections' (Deleuze and Guattari 1983, p. 1). The coupling of the 'new' machine of NAPLAN to the classroom machine requires a mapping of the POs that are reordered to function in changed voices/pathways of a teacher opening to regimes of standardised testing.

Voice/Pathways

In the following section, we use the responses of a single teacher to exemplify schizoanalytic cartography. We do this cautiously, recognising Guattari's warning to avoid 'an analysis centred on a verbal material, based on a transferential micropolitics of black holes and on the semiological interpretation of affects and behaviours' (Guattari 2011, p. 170). In other words, we attempt no therapy, but rather find these answers to questions about the impact of NAPLAN for this teacher illustrative of the ways that datafied desire-production attests to the 'simultaneous accelerations and blockages, comparative speeds, differences in deterritorialisation creating relative fields of reterritorialisation' (Deleuze and Guattari 2005, p. 4). We use Guattari's conceptualisation of subjectivity that 'remains massively controlled by apparatuses of power and knowledge which place technical, scientific and artistic innovations at the service of the most retrograde figures of the sociality' (Guattari 2013, p. 15). If POs are the markers of lack, then voice/pathways are the expressions of their de- and reterritorialisation within assemblages of enunciation (collective) and sense-making (individuating).

Voices/pathways of *power* 'circumscribe and circumvent human groups from the outside' (Guattari 2013, p. 3). This can be affected in multiple ways, such as through direct coercion, panoptic surveillance or by the various mechanisms that make the soul a site of governance. Voices/pathways of *knowledge* are subjective (and subjectifying) articulations of 'techno-scientific and economic pragmatics' that put into memory hierarchies of knowledge and modes of thought (Guattari 2013, p. 3). Voices/pathways of *self-reference* refer to Guattari's 'group-subject', or that processual subjectivity that self-constitutes though constructing its own coordinates, creating its own processes of territorialisation and stratifications. Regularities of subjectivities, or the tendency for group and individual-group subjectivities to be stable and repetitive occurrences, are affected through practices and processes of self-reference that include 'the rhythms of lived experience, obsessive refrains, identificatory emblems, transitional objects, fetishes of all sorts' that affirm various acts of enunciation and capacitation of bodies (Guattari 2013, p. 4).

It is important to stress that the three voices/pathways interrelate and overlap. Mechanisms of governance, control and surveillance reconfigure in the subjectivity of a teacher engaging with high-stakes testing machines. These function through the tests and the visibility of data itself *and* through the ways in which the NAPLAN test machine interacts with pre-existing disciplinary apparatuses of power. These mechanisms enfold concerns over specific legitimations of knowledge, of technical knowledges such as test-construction, validity and the production of literacies and numeracies as testable constructs, with economic concerns of productive workers, citizens and productive knowledges. These inform and are internalised as self-referential terrains, as individuals respond to these voices and pathways of power and knowledge to produce themselves through the existential materials at hand.

Utopian1

'Utopian1' is the self-selected pseudonym of a participant in a 2012 survey asking teachers in Western Australia and South Australia for their perceptions of the impact of NAPLAN on their schools and classrooms. He identified as a 47-year-old contract teacher working in a South Australian public high school. He had sixteen years' teaching experience, and had been teaching at his current school for one year. He identified that the school in which he worked served a high socioeconomic community. We focus on his responses to five questions (Table 1).

This schizoanalysis of Utopian1's responses to NAPLAN identifies multiple affects forming in and as the voice/pathways of power, knowledge and self-reflection. In experiencing these affects, Utopian1 is induced to look outside the classroom, consistent with Deleuze's control society, where spaces of enclosure are 'opened' to 'the virtual, the power of metamorphosis, becoming' through databases that open teaching to exteriorities (Lazzarato 2006, p. 175). The effect of control is to employ digital technology to synthesise broadly communicable messages (that is, those that apply to all classrooms) in order for the 'capture, control and regulation of the action at a distance of one mind on another' which 'takes place through the modulation of flows of desires and beliefs and through the forces (memory and attention) that make these flows circulate in the cooperation between brains' (Lazzarato 2006, p. 185). Utopian1 names a variety of bodily affects (fear, anxiety and even paranoia) associated with the desiring-productions of socially induced lacks or fantasies. Utopian1's responses are strewn with markers of POs that name a variety of configurations within which lack is produced, naming virtual teachers, parents and students as POs that manifest lack. The students, though, are both parts of the strategic environment (who will participate in teaching to the test) and markers of a configuration

Table 1. Utopian1 on testing.

Question	Response
Positives of NAPLAN	Waste of the three weeks that are spent drilling. Fear of being singled out for a talk with the boss if class results are low. Distrust of the way the results are used. Some training for NAPLAN is actually useful for education but most is driven by a need to ensure that I have a contract next year.
Negatives of NAPLAN	Divisive feeling. Waste of potential teaching time. Thought there is some overlap with the benefits of teaching for the test, such as critical reading, test analysis, lots of test practice reducing fear, and so on.
Relationship with parents	Always nasty wait to see if some loony parent asks 'why is my child doing so badly? Why have I not taught them better? …' I am often tempted to tell such parents 'because your child is at their natural level'. Then ask them what sort of grades they received. Anathema in this school which is very middle class. Very sensitive 'adminospere' types running the show.
Relationship with staff/principal	As above the pressure is to perform. This is especially true if, like me, you are a contract teacher and paradoxically harder to achieve. In consequence one budgets more time than is useful to what is intended to be an informative test. The concomitant of this is that the other curriculum areas are denied. I have a mixed feeling about this since there are benefits for teaching to the test for the students despite the fact that its purpose is mainly used by various government officials to manipulate funding.
Does NAPLAN improve learning?	Partially. What informs q 8 is that I seek to distort the NAPLAN results for personal and professional advantage. As I suspect most teachers in my position do. Schools with weaker socio eco rankings must systematically aim to 'prepare' students or face perceived and real disadvantages. Having said that, I am aware that the skills required to do well in the test are productive and part of a balanced curriculum so worthy of time. The problem is that I will distort the degree of attention at the expense of other equally productive parts of a healthy classroom. I suspect that if the results were not linked to some sort of ranking, not directly linked to school incomes and public perceptions, it would reduce to the level of an interesting and potentially productive set of results, indicating general moves in student ability and learning.

Figure 1. The mutated three sphere/four sphere of U1.

that produces nostalgia for an era when teaching time was not sacrificed to preparation for the test.

The schizoanalytic model here presented (Figure 1) was fashioned after the universe Dante describes in his 'Divine Comedy'. While this diagram may appear to represent a Venn diagram, it envisions Utopian1's voice pathways as representing a non-Euclidean three-sphere cosmology where the observer is part of the diagrammatic peering into multiple spheres.[2] Unlike Dante's, which has two, Utopian1's is comprised of three sets of spheres. Again, unlike Dante's universe, in which the divine sphere is the determining one (gives movement to the whole system), in Utopian1's universe the three spheres all determine the other in the final instance. Thus, while the sub-spheres manifest series of effects and affects, each is driven by a different *Primum Mobile* as its outer determining sphere (named here as Power, Knowledge and Self-Reference). Utopian1 stands at the edge and centre of the three sets of spheres, with each comprised of different sub-spheres of POs. The formation of hierarchies, surveillance, discipline and competition, for example, is Power in action and expression. Points in each of the sub-spheres correspond to those in the other spheres. The POs in this schizoanalysis generally manifest points and vectors forming psychoses and neuroses (and lines of flight). Consider, for example, the production of opening to regimes of standardised testing, as neurosis and psychosis, through the sphere of POs of 'discipline' in the Power set of spheres corresponding with points in sub-spheres of 'through the data' (Self-reference) and 'the economic realities of contract teaching' (Knowledge). In this map the functions of 'discipline' in the voice-pathway Power opposes the modulatory 'through the data' and reinforces it. In the same way, 'the economic realities of contract teaching' corresponds with both 'discipline' and 'through the data'. A potential line of flight is the psychotic collapse of the Power and Knowledge spheres such that obsessive, and potentially manipulative, 'fabrication' is practised exclusively 'through the data'. A diminution in the intensity of Power and Knowledge opens a space of pure self-reference formed by the machines and technologies of testing and reporting. But this is a machinic surface increasingly constituted through modulatory regimes of standardised testing.

Voice/Pathways of Power

Utopian1 feels under pressure to compete, within a system that produces data that judge performance. The power of surveillance is present. He fears being 'singled out for a talk with the boss if class results are low' and his anxiety is exacerbated by his precarious labour. He knows that the assessment of his teaching is being carried out at a distance. He cannot control what occurs outside the classroom and he worries about a lack of effectiveness. He budgets more time that he would prefer on teaching to the test because he recognises the importance of his students' test scores for him. He is also aware that parents will have access to the scores of their children and, comparative statistics about cohorts of similar and dissimilar students. Utopian1 does not respond to complaints from parents because he feels no moral responsibility for the scores (they come from outside). He knows that the game has changed, his job is to produce results in ways that do not resonate with his past notions of 'teaching', and that is why he manipulates the data.

   Utopian1 functions in a hierarchical system in which he requires authorisation from superiors, while using authorisation as a resource in the classroom. He can be singled out by his boss; his school is governed by 'very sensitive "adminosphere" types'; he is also concerned that 'various government officials ... manipulate funding'; and that those in power rank schools and link results to school incomes. In short, he functions in an environment governed by an administrative hierarchy that he needs to satisfy. He is induced to feel concern about how those authority figures will view his results and use them to determine his future employment. His status depends on his test scores and, as a result, he turns his mind to what those who receive the results from those tests are thinking. But this then turns him to the student in a different way as he seeks to 'prepare' his students. He is aware that 'preparing' his students is not all he might do, or what he has done before, he fears the disciplinary effects if he does not prepare his students.

Voice/Pathways of Knowledge

Utopian1's status as a contract teacher is particularly important for the way he opens himself to high stakes testing. He prepares students for NAPLAN, despite feeling this may not always be in the best interests of the students, due to his need to ensure he had a contract for the following year. The economic pathway of precarious labour is a more common feature in school workforces and this promotes a performative ethic in his work that dances with his professional ethics. There are other techno-scientific resonances, for example the recognition that literacy and numeracy are central in the construction of teaching and learning, and his belief in the technical rationality of the tests themselves – if only the voice/pathways of power played out differently. Utopian1 knows that teachers fulfil certain habitual functions such as: preparing students for the world, adopting certain faces and comportments and manifesting professional values and ethics. The performative pressures manifest in the creation of new dislocations, and the intensification of old rivalries and oppositions, such as suspicions concerning authorities, parents and others who cannot legitimately claim professional knowledge. Clearly power and knowledge are related. Thus Utopian1 performs within multiple registers, such as the grammar of working in a middle class school, speaks certain truths, and that these assemblages of enunciation are affected through various internalisations of test data and testing processes.

Voice/Pathways of Self-reference

Utopian1's self-reflection is produced through how he folds his 'self' back into the machine to produce his own co-ordinates. One strategy that is evidenced is that of fabrication and/or manipulation of the data 'for personal and professional advantage'. In a competitive system,

Utopian1 manifests a care for the data above traditionally professional ethics such as care for individual student, moral conduct and probity. This is influenced heavily by his position as a contract teacher, and also by his understanding that he is engaged in a competitive data exercise, paradoxically he is 'for' the profession by being 'against' other teachers. The paradox of how his subjectivity engages with data must not be underestimated. On one hand he manipulates NAPLAN data to his advantage; on the other hand he worries that the performativity associated with data is a corrupting force. The scrutiny from outside that Utopian1 experiences is not his alone. He knows that the same outside is affecting all classrooms in all schools. His class's results will be synthesised with those of other classes in his school and the results for his school as a whole will be 'directly linked to school incomes and public perceptions'. He works in a school 'that is very middle-class', though, which requires a particular appropriation of test results when questioned by parents and administrators.

The Negative Task ...

If NAPLAN's effect on teacher subjectivities can be summed up in a single sentence, then, for us, it is that the classroom becomes a space of exteriority that affects self-reference, and subjectivity, in new ways. While some of this 'new' can be explained as an intensification of pre-existing forces and machinic flows, there is also the sense of a breaking down of old professionalisms and ethics. As datafication operates as a machine of capture, it also has the potential to release flows of desiring-production often locked within the interiorised space of the classroom. In this short paper, however, we have attended to the negative task of schizoanalysis in arguing that the promise of tests like NAPLAN rests upon the promise as a multitude of part objects to deliver wholeness. What remains to be written is the positive tasks of discovering desiring-production independent of representation and considering how we might escape, where that escape does not rest in trying to resurrect some imagined pure past (Deleuze and Guattari 1983).

What Utopian1 shows is that to capture responses to powerful, axiomatic machines requires practices of metamodelling . As Guattari remarks, the purpose of schizoanalysis is to understand 'how is it that you got where you are. "What is your model to you?"' (Guattari 1996, p. 133). For Utopian1, the global testing machine, and its local specificities, invites new responses and augments traditional responses always within the multiplicities of bodies connecting to other bodies.

Thus, Utopian1's story is one among many, but is really made up of multiple connections. Of course, what we cannot know is how these schizzes, part objects and mobile flows connect with bodies in enclosed spaces like classrooms, staffrooms and offices. Whereas standardised testing seeks to produce common responses among teachers (ostensibly in the cause of improved human achievement predicated upon a produced desire that improved data is a moral outcome), for Utopian1 this couples with multiple assemblages of enunciation that concern, often in normalising ways, what it means to teach, to become-teacher within a system that is calling forth a 'new' normal that is as much contextual (the turn to precarious labour, the relationships with parents) as it is personal (the response to authority). If we return to Guattari's provisional definition of schizoanalysis as outlined by Thompson and Savat (2015) as 'the analysis of the incidence of assemblages of enunciation among semiotic and subjective productions within a given, problematic context', then the case of Utopian1 is interesting because it is largely semiotic and subjective redundancies that are enunciated. This exemplifies what Guattari calls the carving out of 'existential territories' from the available semiotic materials and social connections in order to combat alienation (Watson 2008, p. 2). While testing may not precede, or independently cause, these forces at work in the professional subjectivity of Utopian1, it serves to demonstrate the 'process of self-organisation or singularisation' at work within these territories.

While testing data intensifies control and promotes anxiety and lack, paradoxically it de-individualises, and in doing this, new modes of becoming, interacting and producing education may be effected and affected. The potential for new becomings that reconfigure disciplinarity as teachings-yet-to-come is released. How effective this is as a deterritorialisation of the pedagogic event remains to be seen. After all, we should never believe that smooth space alone 'will suffice to save us' (Deleuze and Guattari 2005, p. 500).

Notes

1. The Australian National Assessment Program – Literacy and Numeracy (NAPLAN) is a series of standardised tests in literacy and numeracy that all school children in years three, five, seven and nine are required to sit each year. School results are published online on the 'My School' website, which enables comparisons between statistically similar schools. More contextual information about NAPLAN and 'My School' can be found in Lingard and Sellar (2013) and Thompson (2013).

2. While we are not able to go into more detail, an extended discussion is available in Peterson's 'Dante and the 3-Sphere' (1979).

References

Buchanan, Ian (2005) 'Space in the Age of Non-Place', in Ian Buchanan and Gregg Lambert, *Deleuze and Space*, Edinburgh: University of Edinburgh Press, pp. 16–35.

Buchanan, Ian and Gregg Lambert (2005) 'Introduction: Deleuze and Space', in Ian Buchanan and Gregg Lambert, *Deleuze and Space*, Toronto: Univeristy of Toronto Press, pp. 1–15.

Deleuze, Gilles (1995) 'Postscript on Control Societies', in Gilles Deleuze, *Negotiations*, New York: Columbia University Press, pp. 177–82.

Deleuze, Gilles and Félix Guattari (1983) *Anti-Oedipus: Capitalism and Schizophrenia*, Minneapolis, MN: University of Minnesota Press.

Deleuze, Gilles and Félix Guattari (2005) *A Thousand Plateaus: Capitalism and Schizophrenia*, Minneapolis, MN: The University of Minnesota Press.

Guattari, Félix (1984a) 'Towards a Micro-Politics of Desire', in Félix Guattari, *Molecular Revolution: Psychiatry and Politics*, London: Penguin Books, pp. 82–107.

Guattari, Félix (1984b) 'The Micro-Politics of Fascism', in Félix Guattari, *Molecular Revolution: Psychiatry and Revolution*, London: Penguin, pp. 217–32.

Guattari, Félix (1996) 'Institutional Practice and Politics', in Gary Genosko, *A Guattari Reader: Pierre-Félix Guattari*, Oxford: Blackwell Publishers Ltd, pp. 121–39.

Guattari, Félix (2011) *The Machinic Unconscious: Essays in Schizoanalysis*, Los Angeles, CA: Semiotext(e).

Guattari, Félix (2013) *Schizoanalytic Cartographies*, London: Bloomsbury.

Lazzarato, Maurizio (2006) 'The Concepts of Life and Living in the Societies of Control', in Martin Fuglsang and Bent Meier Sorensen, *Deleuze and the Social*, Edinburgh: Edinburgh University Press, pp. 171–90.

Lingard, Bob and Sam Sellar (2013) '"Catalyst Data": Perverse Systemic Effects of Audit and Accountability in Australian Schooling', *Journal of Education Policy*, 28: 5, pp. 634–56.

Lingard, Bob, Wayne Martino and Goli Rezai-Rashti (2013) 'Testing Regimes, Accountabilities and Education Policy: Commensurate Global and National Developments', *Journal of Education Policy*, 28: 5, pp. 539–56.

Peterson, Mark (1979) 'Dante and the 3-Sphere', *American Journal of Physics*, 47: 12, pp. 1031–5.

Thompson, Greg (2013) 'NAPLAN, MySchool and Accountability: Teacher Perceptions of the Effects of Testing', *The International Education Journal: Comparative Perspectives*, 12: 2, pp. 62–84.

Thompson, Greg and David Savat (2015) 'Introduction (Working Title)', *Deleuze Studies*, 9: 3, pp. x–xx.

Watson, Janelle (2008) 'Schizoanalysis and Metamodelling', *The Fibreculture Journal*, 12, pp. 1–15.

A Strange Craving to be Motivated: Schizoanalysis, Human Capital and Education

Sam Sellar   The University of Queensland

Introduction

This paper takes Deleuze's remarks on education in control societies as a starting point to survey recent developments in human capital theories, large-scale educational assessments and education policies that target motivation as a site for measurement and intervention. Motivation is just one of a constellation of related subjective dispositions (e.g. aspiration, engagement and persistence) that are now monitored and modulated through large-scale educational assessments in an effort to improve investments in human capital. The paper provides a brief mapping of the territorialities of human capital through analysis of developments in education policy since the 1960s, focusing on market decodings of desire, the axiomatisation of desire through the quantification of productive capacities, and State interventions to reterritorialise desire for the self-appreciation of one's economic value. Through this discussion, the paper aims to show how schizoanalysis, understood as meta-modelling (Guattari 2013), might be taken up as a methodological strategy in education policy studies to enable a reading of how economic and psychological models contribute to the production of human capital as a subjective form (Feher 2009).[1]

In the final sentences of *Postscript on Control Societies*, Deleuze (1995: 182) observes that 'Many young people have a strange craving to be "motivated," they're always asking for special courses and continuing education'. Deleuze was writing about control societies at the beginning of a new post-Cold War era for education policy, during which the rise

Deleuze Studies 9.3 (2015): 424–436
DOI: 10.3366/dls.2015.0196
© Edinburgh University Press
www.euppublishing.com/journal/dls

of neoliberal globalisation and the pervasive influence of human capital theory would reframe the aims of education and bring them into ever closer alignment with the needs of 'the economy'. Describing the general shift from discipline to control reflected in the breakdown and reworking of institutions such as prisons, schools, hospitals and factories, Deleuze's observations concerning young people and education in the 1990s were prescient and reflected the educational zeitgeist, which was manifest in the publication in 1996 of two influential policy documents by the Organisation for Economic Cooperation Development (OECD). The first of these documents, *The Knowledge-Based Economy* (OECD 1996a), positioned learning as a key driver of economic productivity and growth. The second, *Lifelong Learning For All* (OECD 1996b), emphasised the importance of individual motivation and willingness to pursue continuous education and assessment, which Deleuze (1995, p. 182) insightfully foresaw as 'the beginning of something new' in education. The OECD underlined the value of human capital for post-Fordist modes of production and, reflecting the rise of new modes of governance through data (Ozga 2009), argued that 'human capital indicators ... are central measures for the knowledge-based economy' (OECD 1996a: 43).

The brief survey of human capital theory provided here will touch on the work of Chicago School economists in the 1960s and 1970s, before discussing its development in the OECD's education work since the 1990s. During this time the OECD has become a more influential policy actor globally through the introduction of large-scale educational assessments such as the Programme for International Student Assessment (PISA) and its Indicators of Education Systems (INES) programme. Since the early 2000s, interest has grown, across the fields of economics, psychology and statistics, in the conceptualisation, classification and measurement of so-called 'noncognitive skills' as a valuable dimension of human capital. This development is reflected in the OECD's (2002) modelling of 'wider' human capital. Noncognitive skills refer to personality characteristics or subjective dispositions that are not measured by cognitive tests, but which contribute to academic success and economic productivity (Levin 2013). For example, the measurement and comparison of motivation among student populations through large-scale educational assessments has helped to constitute and differentiate groups who share the subjective dispositions of the ideal human capitalist subject (desire for more and more education) and groups who are found to be lacking in motivation and are thus deemed to require remedial intervention.

Governments now intervene to stimulate motivation among groups who appear caught in a mismatch between their desires and interests; both their supposed personal interests in self-investment through education and social interests in education as a driver of economic productivity and a means to reduce social welfare costs to the State. These interests are invoked by the neoliberal 'politics of aspiration', in which '[t]he aspiration to "better oneself" in material and commodified terms is presented as a natural sense of order or something that reflects the innate desires of human beings' (Raco 2009: 439). Those who lack aspiration are cast as 'pathological' capitalist subjects (Terranova 2013) who constitute a newly emergent education policy problem for which two solutions are generally proposed. The first is a market–governmental project to produce new representative territorialities of desire in order that they be invested in 'bettering oneself', while the second can be characterised as a critical sociological project that contests these reterritorialisations but struggles with how to actively work with desire beyond these territories. A schizoanalytical approach can help to recast the terms of this problem in order that we might move beyond current modulations of human capitalist subjectivity and critical eddies that can become an impasse of melancholic longing for lost or as yet unimagined alternatives to capital.

Schizoanalysis: Decoding, Axiomatics and Reterritorialisation

Deleuze and Guattari (1983) identify three inseparable tasks of schizoanalysis: destroying Oedipus or the representational territorialities of desire, discovering the desiring-machines operating outside of representation and reaching the investment of unconscious desire in the social field, as distinct from preconscious investments of interest. In his later work, Guattari (2013: 17) characterised schizoanalysis as a meta-model 'for reading *other modelling systems*'. This paper begins to map modelling systems in education that contribute to the production and modulation of human capitalist subjectivity. It does not perform a schizoanalysis *per se*, but rather aims to generate cartographical resources that could support schizoanalytic work in education in its task of 'successively undoing the representative territorialities and reterritorialisations through which a subject passes in his [sic] individual history' (Deleuze and Guattari 1983: 318). Here the focus is on human capital's existential territories (for example, motivation).

Three concepts are central to the mapping undertaken here: decoding, axiomatics and reterritorialisation. Holland (1996: 241) argues that, for

Deleuze and Guattari, the concept of decoding describes 'the historical replacement of meaning by abstract calculation as the basis of social order'. He continues:

> [D]ecoding is linked to axiomatisation, the process central to capitalism whereby streams of quantified factors of production (such as raw materials, skills and knowledges) are conjoined in order to extract differential surplus; decoding both supports and results from axiomatisation, transforming meaningful qualities into calculable quantities. (Holland 1996: 241)

This is a process that Espeland and Stevens (1998) have described as the social practice of commensuration; a process that has become a central mechanism for modulating multiplicity in control societies (Lazzarato 2006) and through which capitalism now monitors 'its own practices on a continuous basis' (Thrift 2005: 1). For Deleuze and Guattari (1983: 154), capitalism is a social formation or machine that is distinguished by its 'generalised decoding of flows' and an 'axiomatic of abstract quantities that keeps moving further and further in the direction of the deterritorialisation of the socius' (33). However, through the State, the nation and the family, '[c]apitalism institutes or restores all sorts of residual and artificial, imaginary, or symbolic territorialities, thereby attempting, as best it can, to recode, to rechannel persons who have been defined in terms of abstract quantities' (34). The desire that capitalism frees through decoding and deterritorialisation becomes captured in the capitalist axiomatic or reterritorialised by the State and the family.

Coding and decoding 'operate on symbolic representations and involve investments of mental energy' (Holland 1996: 242), in this case economic and psychological models of human capital and statistical entities, while deterritorialisation and reterritorialisation 'operate on physical bodies and involve material investments of energy', here the motivations of those who invest in self-appreciation or are subject to discursive and programmatic interventions aimed at the reterritorialisation of desire. The modelling of human capital, and analytical practices in the fields of economics, psychology and statistics, facilitates a decoding of productive capacity into abstract, measurable quantities. At the same time, State education policies and programmes function to reterritorialise the material energies of the individual learner–worker and to recode the purposes of education.

Michel Feher (2009: 26) has shown that 'the rise of human capital as a dominant subjective form is a defining feature of neoliberalism'. The concept of human capital has expanded from its basic definition as an individual's productive capacity, open to enhancement through education and training, to include any and all subjective dispositions that can be correlated with increased personal value, productivity and economic growth. The following section of the paper provides a brief survey of the emergence of human capital as a subjective form, beginning with the work of the Chicago School economists in the 1960s and concluding with the recent financialisation of human capital. This approach takes up the proposition of Deleuze and Guattari (1983: 318) that, in its tasks of undoing representative territorialities and discovering desiring-machines, schizoanalysis 'must go back by way of old lands, study their nature, their density; we must seek to discover how the machinic indices are grouped on each of these lands that permit going beyond them'.

The Expansion of Human Capital Theory

The concept of human capital has a long history extending back, as Deleuze and Guattari (1983: 270) note, to the work of Adam Smith and David Ricardo, which identified the nature of wealth 'as an abstract or deterritorialised subjective essence, or the activity of production in general'. Feher (2009: 25) observes that the basic concept of human capital is narrow in scope:

> The notion of human capital, initially, did not seem all that ambitious. It referred to the set of skills that an individual can acquire thanks to investments in his or her education or training, and its primary purpose was to measure the rates of return that investments in education produce or, to put it simply, the impact on future incomes that can be expected from schooling and other forms of training.

During the 1960s and 1970s, the work of Chicago School economists, such as Jacob Mincer, Theodore W. Schultz and Gary Becker, greatly popularised the concept, extending its purview and application in a range of fields including education. It was at this point in the evolution of human capital theory that ambitions for the concept began to grow.

At the beginning of the 1970s there was debate about whether collapsing distinctions between the individual and the value of their productive capacity offended the moral conception of human being. For example, Thurow (1970: 16) argued:

> A sharp distinction must be drawn between the 'value' of a man [sic] and the value of a man's earnings. A man's human capital indicates the present value of his future productive capacities. It does not indicate his worth as a human being.

Thurow's protest can be read as resistance to a process of decoding humanist values that began, as Deleuze and Guattari (1983: 300) argue, following Marx, with Ricardo's discovery of subjective abstract labour. This decoding would lead to the discovery of 'the interplay of machines and their agents underneath all the specific determinations that still linked desire or labor to a given person, to a given object in the framework of representation'.

The increasing elision of distinctions between humanist values and labour values can be seen in the arguments of Theodore W. Schultz (1971), whose work was influential in popularising human capital approaches in education. Schultz acknowledged that 'to treat human beings as wealth that can be augmented by investment runs counter to deeply held values' and was 'offensive to some' (p. 26). However, he argued that resistance to the expansion of human capital models beyond knowledge and skills gained through education and training was misplaced and constituted a limit on liberal freedoms: 'By investing in themselves, people can enlarge the range of choice available to them. It is one way free men [sic] can enhance their welfare' (p. 26). This argument can be seen as an important antecedent to the neoliberal responsibilisation of the self (Rose 1999).

Drawing on Feher (2009), the expansion of human capital through the work of Schultz, Becker and others can be seen as remaining within the coordinates of traditional liberal utilitarianism. It was only with the rise of neoliberal globalisation and the financialisation of capital that human capital emerged as a new subjective form. The shift in corporate governance strategies, away from maximising return on investments and toward increasing stock value, can also be applied to human capital: 'insofar as our condition is that of human capital in a neoliberal environment, our main purpose is not so much to profit from our accumulated potential as to constantly value or appreciate ourselves – or at least prevent our own depreciation' (Feher 2009: 27).

The emergence of human capital as a subjective form, and the associated logic of continual self-appreciation, has implications for how the value of human capital is measured. These implications are currently being felt in a range of areas, from economic statistics to education policy, where there are current projects to develop broader indicators of self-valuation, defined in terms of happiness or subjective well-being. This development constitutes what we might see as a key juncture in the decoding of flows and the augmentation of the capitalist axiomatic through statistical practices and the abstraction of subjective dispositions as exchange-value (Deleuze and Guattari 1983: 335). It is here that we shift to the education policy work of the OECD in the mid-1990s, which stands as an important precursor to recent developments in the measurement of human capital.

Expanding the Measurement of Human Capital

Significant changes occurred in the global education policy landscape during the 1990s. The OECD released its policy positions on knowledge-based economies and lifelong learning in 1996 and, in 1998, it published the first annual *Education at a Glance* report drawing on its INES programme. In 1997, the OECD established PISA to measure human capital flows at the end of compulsory schooling. PISA has become the most influential international assessment of educational outcomes with significant impact on education policy debates around the world. In each of the five triennial assessments, beginning with the first assessment in 2000, data have been published on student engagement and motivation (for example, OECD 2013), signalling efforts to quantify aspects of human capital that extend beyond the primary focus on reading, mathematical and science literacy.[2]

Early work to show the effects of personality traits on earnings was undertaken by Jencks (1972). More recently, Bowles et al. (2001) have argued that human capital indicators such as cognitive performance, years of schooling and socioeconomic factors explain only around half of the variance in individual earnings. These authors argue that an 'irreducibly heterogeneous' set of 'incentive-enhancing preferences' (Bowles et al. 2001: 158), including self-efficacy, shame and the inclination to discount present costs for future benefits, can be modelled as part of human capital. These preferences are frequently grouped under the category of 'noncognitive' skills. Noncognitive skills are already being measured in large-scale educational assessments such as PISA and interest in this work is growing significantly (Levin 2013, with the OECD currently working to develop this aspect of its assessments (Sellar and Lingard 201E).

The OECD (2002: 124) has argued for widening the definition and measurement of human capital to include broader sets of qualities beyond cognitive skills: '[T]here is more to human capital than the readily measurable – and very important – literacy, numeracy and workplace skills'. The concept of wider human capital was introduced and defined in terms of '[c]haracteristics that allow a person to build, manage and deploy basic human capital' (OECD 2002: 124). This broader definition of human capital includes the ability to acquire new skills, 'the ability to blend working and personal objectives' and any further '[p]ersonal characteristics ... which make people more attractive as employees, because they are more likely to deploy their skills productively' (OECD 2002: 124). It is noted that 'motivational characteristics are likely to be central' to the value of wider human capital (OECD 2002: 124). However, making these qualities commensurable also opens them to governmental intervention: 'A question arises of how and if education might seek to encourage desired motivational characteristics, in addition to cognitive skills' (OECD 2002: 124). Subjective dispositions such as motivation are thus becoming bound to the capitalist axiomatic and are acquiring an exchange-value through new calculative technologies. At the same time, the question of how to actively modulate desire to constitute economically productive modes of subjectivity is also raised.

Intensified Motivation and Aspirational Deficits

The motivations of human capital are intensified by decodings of productive capacities through statistical calculations and speculations that effectively make subjective qualities a form of financialised capital. For example, in April 2012 the Upstart investment platform was launched by a small group of ex-Google executives. Upstart enables you to invest directly in the potential future earnings of individuals. 'Upstarts' build a profile to market themselves to prospective backers, who make investments in return for a share of their income over a given period. An index that draws on a variety of data is used to calculate predicted income over the period of investment and thus the potential value of each Upstart's human capital stock. More recently, and following a similar model, US brokerage firm Fantex announced its intentions to sell stocks in the financial performance of athletes.

Such direct investment in people's potential value involves, as Guattari (2013: 10) argues, 'techniques of economic semiotization ... which imply a general virtualization of capacities for human initiative and a predictive calculus bearing on the domains of innovation – sort of writing cheques on the future – that allow the imperium of the market economies to expand indefinitely'. Upstarts list themselves as a public share offering and represent themselves as ideal human capitalist subjects whose productive capacity can be abstracted and valorised in monetary terms and who trade on their motivation to self-appreciate through education and entrepreneurial activity.

However, while the Upstarts provide an exemplary illustration of the 'strange craving to be motivated' observed by Deleuze more than two decades ago, data generated from large-scale assessments and other databases show motivations for education to be unevenly distributed across populations. From a pro-market perspective, this difference is attributed to capital's mixed signals in relation to motivation (Lindsey 2013). Growing income disparity is seen to be a good motivator because it brings the risks and benefits of growing inequality into sharp relief, leading to those on the bottom aspiring to reach the top; however, an overall rise in living standards takes the edge off this motivating incentive. Interventions to stimulate motivation are thus posited as a solution for the market–governmental project to reterritorialise desire: '[T]he future of human capitalism may well hinge on ... motivating the middling and lower ranks of society. ... what ultimately will matter is the strength of purely internal, personal motivations' (Lindsay 2013: 115).

This argument has been reflected in the higher education policies of many OECD nations that have set targets over the past decade to expand their higher education systems. In countries such as England and Australia, this policy objective has been framed in terms of raising aspirations for higher education among people from low socioeconomic status backgrounds. Raising aspiration has been presented as a form of governmental intervention to increase social mobility for individuals and families while simultaneously bolstering national investment in human capital, productivity and economic growth. These programmes have also been championed by progressive academics and activists working in universities who are concerned to widen access to higher education, exemplifying new modes of market-embedded morality by bringing together equity and economic arguments for widening education provision (Shamir 2008).

Desire that is not axiomatised as quantifiable exchange-value has become pathologised. Following Stiegler (2010), we can ask whether market decoding and the financialisation of (human) capital contribute to this motivational deficit. Stiegler suggests that the short-term drives produced by speculative financial capitalism, and valued in new human capital models and metrics, in conjunction with the attentional and libidinal economies of advertising, are leading to the collapse of social systems of longer-term desires, leading to a 'total exhaustion of libidinal energy and of capacities for investment, anticipation and will' (p. 116). This creates new problems for the State as it seeks to increase investments in human capital through education. The State must develop strategies for reterritorialising desire for continuing education and new modes of knowledge and service work. Human capital as a subjective form is thus actively produced through apparatuses of subjectification that combine coercive power (e.g. extensions to compulsory schooling) and new sources of information (e.g. rankings, comparisons and predicted income) that function to spur motivation from within. The two parts of the market–governmental project work together in the continual process of deterritorialisation and reterritorialisation.

Conclusion

> The more the capitalist machine deterritorializes, decoding and axiomatizing flows in order to extract surplus value from them, the more its ancillary apparatuses, such as government bureaucracies and the forces of law and order, do their utmost to reterritorialize, absorbing in the process a larger and larger share of surplus value. (Deleuze and Guattari 1983: 35)

Recent developments in human capital theory, large-scale educational assessments and education policy provide an illustrative example of market decoding and authoritarian reterritorialisations of libidinal energies. Human capital theory can be seen as accelerating the abstraction of the subjective essence of labour identified by Ricardo and analysed by Marx. This process is coupled with an augmentation of the capitalist axiomatic through the development of new models for quantifying the value of subjective dispositions. The formation and functioning of the OECD has contributed to this axiomatisation in important ways. New valorisations of human capital segment populations into groups based on the exchange-value of their subjective dispositions and create conditions in which pathological subjects can be targeted as a site of governmental intervention, with the objective of linking individual self-appreciation and social mobility to national economic growth.

The market–governmental response to the relatively new policy problem of low aspiration for education focuses on individuals and aims to make clear the gap between their desire and their potential exchange-value as human capital. As Lindsey (2013) implies, growing social inequality can be seen, from this perspective, as a useful governance mechanism to 'sharpen' desire for education and social mobility. Inequality thus provides an anxiety-inducing backdrop to the State remediation of pathological human capital through noo-political strategies to increase motivation by controlling attention and modulating the relation between subjectivity and time (Lazzarato 2006). The critical sociological response instead focuses on challenging the economisation of education and the normalisation of human capitalist subjectivity. However, while this approach advocates reimagining the purposes and processes of education outside of its function to increase personal exchange-value for some, and necessarily at the expense of others, it often remains trapped in strategies of passive resistance to capitalist deterritorialisation and State authority, rather than discovering and actively engaging with desiring-machines.

Schizoanalysis conceives of desire as a productive force that constitutes subjects from multiplicity. Importantly, Deleuze and Guattari see the process of decoding, which frees desiring-production from its representational territories, as a positive development within their historical materialist and schizoanalytic analysis of capitalism. Thus, schizoanalysis pursues a dissolution of the isolated individual subjectivity produced within disciplinary societies and thus finds points of resonance with the deterritorialisation effected by capitalism in control societies. The market–governmental response to the decoding of desire in the social field is to compensate for what cannot be captured in the capitalist axiomatic by reterritorialising desiring-production into individual subjectivation (self as capital). The critical sociological response is to reject the decoding of humanist values and to propagate models of individual subjectivity based on resistance (self as moral agent). In contrast to both strategies, Deleuze and Guattari advocate for new modes of collective subjectivity (group-subjects) and see possibilities for schizoanalysis to appropriate aspects of deterritorialising modelling systems and put them to work in new creative configurations in order to produce new processes of subjectification.

The mapping of changing existential territories of human capital undertaken in this paper implies a different problematisation of the changed conditions of desire for education and employment that Deleuze had already observed in the early 1990s. However, this problematisation is likely to appear heretical both to the market–governmental perspective, which detects the limits of capital that must be continually displaced, through reterritorialising compensations that sustain collective desire in the promises of the market and the project of self-appreciation, and by the critical sociological perspective, which generally sees market decoding as a force to be resisted. Schizoanalysis, in its positive tasks, shifts the terms of the analysis by approaching decoding as a positive force and by seeking further deterritorialisation of the socius by working with desiring-production that cannot be easily bound to the capitalist axiomatic or reterritorialised onto existing market values or reimagined universal social values. This implies open and experimental engagements with technologies of calculation and abstraction and a retreat from paternalist critical strategies that act in the name of others' interests. The mapping initiated in this paper is aimed at resourcing schizoanalytical work along these lines.

Notes

1. Contemporary education policy studies draw primarily on the disciplines of sociology, political science and economics. Deleuze and Guattari were ambivalent about the capacity of these human sciences to creatively resist opinion through the creation of scientific functions. As Stengers (2005: 154) observes, Deleuze and Guattari 'wondered whether all the human sciences ... however sophisticatedly presented or statistically verified ... would constitute just scientific opinion'. It is worth considering whether and how the mobilisation of schizoanalytic approaches in education policy studies might increase capacities to creatively resist consensual social scientific perceptions by reorienting thought toward conceptual and aesthetic poles.
2. While space does not allow for a developed analysis of the OECD from a Deleuzo-Guattarian perspective, there are clear paths to pursue here. The OECD was established in 1961 to supersede the Organisation for European Economic Cooperation (OEEC), which was established in 1948 to facilitate the post-war reconstruction of Europe under the Marshall Plan. The OECD has thus been closely associated with the axiomatisation of capital, particularly during what Deleuze and Guattari (1987: 462) observed as an intense period of 'the creation of new axioms after the Second World War: the Marshall Plan, forms of assistance and lending, transformations in the monetary system'. The OECD has since become an influential organisational actor in what Guattari characterised as the age of planetary computerisation, performing a global governance function through the cognitive and normative effects of its statistical work and economic assessments (Woodward 2009). These mechanisms can be seen as part of contemporary apparatuses of subjectification, particularly 'voices/pathways of *knowledge* articulated to techno-scientific and economic pragmatics from inside subjectivity' (Guattari 2013: 3).

References

Bowles, Samuel, Herbert Gintis and Melissa Osborne (2001) 'The Determinants of Earnings: A Behavioral Approach', *Journal of Economic Literature*, 39: 4, pp. 1137–76.

Deleuze, Gilles (1995) *Negotiations, 1972–1990*, trans. Martin Joughin, New York: Columbia University Press.

Deleuze, Gilles and Felix Guattari (1983) *Anti-Oedipus: Capitalism and Schizophrenia*, trans. Robert Hurley, Mark Seem and Helen R. Lane, Minneapolis, MN: University of Minnesota Press.

Deleuze, Gilles and Felix Guattari (1987) *A Thousand Plateaus: Capitalism and Schizophrenia*, trans. Brian Massumi, Minneapolis, MN: University of Minnesota Press.

Espeland, Wendy N. and Mitchell L. Stevens (1998) 'Commensuration as a Social Process', *Annual Review of Sociology*, 24, pp. 313–43.

Feher, Michel (2009) 'Self-Appreciation; or, The Aspirations of Human Capital', *Public Culture*, 21: 1, pp. 21–41.

Guattari, Felix (2013) *Schizoanalytic Cartographies*, trans. Andrew Goffey, London and New York: Bloomsbury.

Holland, Eugene (1996) 'Schizoanalysis and Baudelaire: Some Illustrations of Decoding at Work', in Paul Patton (ed.), *Deleuze: A Critical Reader*, Oxford and Cambridge, MA: Blackwell Publishers, pp. 240–56.

Jencks, Christopher (1972) *Inequality: A Reassessment of the Effect of Family and Schooling in America*, New York: Basic Books.

Lazzarato, Maurizio (2006) 'The Concepts of Life and the Living in the Societies of Control', in Martin Fuglsang and Bent Meier Sorenson (eds), *Deleuze and the Social*, Edinburgh: Edinburgh University Press, pp. 171–90.

Levin, Henry M. (2013) 'The Utility and Need for Incorporating Noncognitive Skills into Large-scale Educational Assessments', in Matthias von Davier, Eugene Gonzalez, Irwin Kirsch and Kentaro Yamamoto (eds), *The Role of International Large-scale Assessments: Perspectives From Technology, Economy, and Educational Research*, Dordrecht: Springer, pp. 67–86.

Lindsay, Brink (2013) *Human Capitalism: How Economic Growth has Made us Smarter – and More Unequal*, Princeton and Oxford: Princeton University Press.

Organisation for Economic Cooperation Development (1996a) *The Knowledge-Based Economy*, Paris: OECD Publishing.

Organisation for Economic Cooperation Development (1996b) *Lifelong Learning for All*, Paris: OECD Publishing.

Organisation for Economic Cooperation Development (2002) *Educational Policy Analysis*, Paris: OECD Publishing.

Organisation for Economic Cooperation Development (2013) *PISA 2012 Results: Ready to Learn (vol. III): Students' Engagement, Drive and Self-Beliefs*, Paris: OECD Publishing.

Ozga, Jenny (2009) 'Governing Education Through Data in England: From Regulation to Self-evaluation', *Journal of Education Policy*, 24: 2, pp. 149–62.

Raco, Mike (2009) 'From Expectations to Aspirations: State Modernisation, Urban Policy, and the Existential Politics of Welfare in the UK', *Political Geography*, 28: 7, pp. 436–44.

Rose, Nikolas (1999) *Powers of Freedom: Reframing Political Thought*, Cambridge: Cambridge University Press.

Schultz, Theodore W. (1971) *Investment in Human Capital: The Role of Education and of Research*, New York: Free Press.

Sellar, Sam and Bob Lingard (2014) 'The OECD and the Expansion of PISA: New Modes of Global Governance in Education', *British Educational Research Journal*, 40: 6, pp. 917–36.

Shamir, Ronen (2008) The age of responsibilization: on market-embedded morality. *Economy and Society*, 37: 1, pp. 1–19.

Stengers, Isabelle (2005) 'Deleuze and Guattari's last enigmatic message', *Angelaki*, 10: 2, pp. 151–67.

Stiegler, Bernard (2010) *For a New Critique of Political Economy*, Cambridge: Polity Press.

Terranova, Tiziana (2013) Ordinary Psychopathologies of Cognitive Capitalism, in Arne de Boever and Warren Neidich (eds), The Psychopathologies of Cognitive Capitalism: Part One, Berlin: Archive Books, pp. 45–68.

Thrift, Nigel (2005) *Knowing Capitalism*, London: Sage.

Thurow, Lester C. (1970) *Investment in Human Capital*, Belmont, CA: Wadsworth.

Woodward, Richard (2009) *The Organisation for Economic Cooperation and Development*, London: Routledge.

Fucking Teachers

P. Taylor Webb   University of British Columbia

Schizoanalysis is the variable analysis of the *n* sexes
in a subject, beyond the anthropomorphic representation that society
imposes on this subject, and with which it represents its own sexuality.
The schizoanalytic slogan of the desiring-revolution will be first of all: to
each its own sexes.

Deleuze and Guattari 1983: 296

Ball (2003: 221) noted that teachers exhibit 'a kind of *values
schizophrenia*' within the performative cultures of schooling. These
exhibitions occur when teachers enact pedagogical fabrications to meet
measurable outputs desired by policy, whilst simultaneously attempting
to maintain educational commitments that lie outside the 'capitalist
axiomatic' of schooling (Deleuze and Guattari 1983: 184).[1] As one
teacher put it:

> If I don't believe in what I'm teaching, then I will subvert it. I will change
> it. When the doors are open they will see something different than when the
> doors are closed. So if I don't believe in what I'm teaching, or what I'm told to
> teach, then I won't do it. I'm putting on – I'm doing two sets of lesson plans.
> Kind of like keeping two sets of books – you have the set of books for the
> auditors and you have the set of books that you're really doing your stuff.
> (Webb 2009: 112)

The resonances between teaching schizophrenia and the capitalism are
not lost on this teacher; and, like some of their accounting counterparts, teachers claim no fidelity between a fabrication and its pedagogical
meaning (Webb 2009). Fabrications, then, are used as a 'tactics of trans-
parency [that] produce a resistance of opacity' (Ball 2001: 211). The
doubled and performative spaces of pedagogy – authenticity/fabrication,

Deleuze Studies 9.3 (2015): 437–451
DOI: 10.3366/dls.2015.0197
© Edinburgh University Press
www.euppublishing.com/journal/dls

transparency/opacity, and shortly, compliance/resistance – led Ball (2003: 224) to conclude that, '[p]erformativity is promiscuous'.

The promiscuity of fabrications foregrounds, but simultaneously alters, enduring eroticisms about a feminised teaching body (Grumet 1988). These eroticisms are consummated between a teaching body that is constituted largely of women (NCES 2014)[2] and education policy that is masculinist (Blackmore 1993), heterosexual (Martino 2012) and neo-liberal (Ball 1997). Fabrications, then, enact liminal, consensual and phantasmic sexualities to the 'societies of control' in education (Deleuze 1992) – networks designed to hold teachers accountable to predetermined outcomes (for example, standards and high-stakes testing). Within, I use the pragmatic of *schizoanalysis* to explain how pedagogical fabrications are *n* sexualities performed as 'revolutionary movements' to the Oedipal fetishes of education policy (Deleuze 1995: 24). Here, teaching bodies produce *n* sexes when fabrications function as 'both resistance *and* capitulation' to the capitalist eroticisms of schooling (Ball 2003: 225).

I am aware that my attempt to cast pedagogical fabrications as forms of sexual activity will likely be met with scepticism – if met at all – due to the taboo of teachers and sexuality in schools. Further, I imagine a discussion about teachers enacting 'the *n* sexes of a subject' to be nearly incomprehensible due to the overwhelming Oedipal representations in education.[3] Hence, one purpose for my title is performative in nature – to call forth sexual repressions operating in education, perhaps evoked with terms like *offensive, inappropriate, vulgar* or *wrong* when reading the title. Throughout the essay, I use the title to illustrate four sexual repressions involved in a teaching schizoanalysis. It is not social graces that repress the *n* sexes in education, but, as I will discuss, it is panic regarding sex and its many forms in the schoolhouse.

I. Schizoanalysis

The truth is that sexuality is everywhere ...

Deleuze and Guattari 1983: 293

Schizoanalysis is based on the idea that '... everything is sexual or sex-influenced (*sexué*) ....' (Deleuze and Guattari 1983: 180). The significance of this idea is that sex and sexuality are ways to understand everyday social, political and cultural activity. More specifically, schizoanalysis is a critique of sex and sexuality derived from Oedipus, especially from the 'Mommy-Daddy-Me' triad. Thus, schizoanalysis can be used to examine social and political activity as forms of sexuality, but as alternative forms to Oedipal conceptions of sexuality. Schizoanalysis includes nonhuman sexualities (sexuality with what, rather than whom) to introduce a new set of pragmatics for revolutionary action.

As critique *and* pragmatic, schizoanalysis accounts for capitalism to identify how Oedipal sexualities and capitalism produce and reproduce each other. Foucault (2000: 207) noted:

> The art of government ... [is] concerned with answering the question of how to introduce economy – that is to say, the correct manner of managing individuals, goods, and wealth within the family (which a good father is expected to do in relation to his wife, children and servants) ... how to introduce the meticulous attention of the father towards his family into the management of the state.

The schoolhouse remains a crucial instrument in the practice of government (Apple 1995) – as a disciplinary machine (Foucault 1977) to the 'coded figures' they are today within the policies of neo-liberal accountability and high-stakes testing (Deleuze 1992: 6).

The relationships between Oedipus, governance and capitalism are multiplied through the production of desires. The production of desire accounts for how revolutionary action often betrays itself (Buchanan 2008: 116). This occurs when change attempts become enamoured with power. This betrayal, then, is '... the fascism in us all, in our heads and in our everyday behavior, the fascism that causes us to love power, to desire the very thing that dominates and exploits us' (Foucault 1983: xiii). Schizoanalysis was not developed to sensationalise illness but to emphasise both the production and precarity of desires that undermine revolutionary action.

Three tasks mobilise schizoanalysis (one negative, two positive). I quickly introduce these tasks, and elaborate on each later. The first task is designed to eliminate all things Oedipal, including ideas like the ego, super-ego and guilt. Deleuze and Guattari (1983: 311) called to arms: 'Destroy, destroy. The task of schizoanalysis goes by way of destruction – a whole scouring of the unconscious, a complete curettage. Destroy Oedipus, the illusion of the ego, the puppet of the superego, guilt, the law, castration.' While the most straightforward, the first task is perhaps the most difficult in educational settings given the omnipresence of Oedipus in education (indeed, being explicitly taught).

The second task:

> consists of discovering in a subject the nature, the formation, or the functioning of *his* desiring-machines, independently of any interpretations. What do you put into these machines, what is the output, how does it work, what are your nonhuman sexes? (Deleuze and Guattari 1983: 322)

Desire is produced socially and is not an inner drive of subjectivity. The second task of schizoanalysis, then, attempts to understand how different desires are produced through different desiring-machines. For example, marketing and advertisement are machines that produce desires. Likewise, education policy is a machine that produces desires about economy and becoming 'human capital', but also ideas about democracy. Importantly, the second task of schizoanalysis is designed to better understand how desires operate, for instance paradoxically, rather than what they mean.

I discuss nonhuman sexuality in relation to what is nonhuman in human sexuality, rather than from animality or vegetality. I use pedagogical fabrications to illustrate nonhuman sexuality in schools, and in ways similar to 'the way a bureaucrat fondles his records, a judge administers justice, a businessman causes money to circulate; the way the bourgeoisie fucks the proletariat ...' (Deleuze and Guattari 1983: 293). My focus is the extent to which nonhuman sexuality is performed (and why) rather than simply being (or only) a practice that can be performed with heterogeneous partners. In this sense, I decode sex in the neo-liberal schoolhouse by arguing that pedagogical fabrications are alluring and enacted sexualities designed to thwart the capitalist axiomatics of schooling.

The final (second positive) task is designed to reach:

> the investments of unconscious desire of the social field, insofar as they are differentiated from the preconscious investments of interest, and insofar as they are not merely capable of counteracting them, but also of coexisting with them in opposite modes (Deleuze and Guattari 1983: 350).

The ability to counteract *and* coexist with the investments of unconscious and preconscious desire introduce the bifurcations of a schizoanalytic approach: '... like keeping two sets of books ...' (example above).

II. The Oedipal

The Oedipal refers to a variety of processes and relationships involved with sex, sexuality and subjectivity. The Oedipal enunciates subjects by interiorising an 'I' in a triadic relationship of Mommy-Daddy-Me (hereafter MDM). Within these relations, a Law of the Father is developed which conditions the other points of the triangle. Deleuze (2004: 187) stated that the phallus 'founds sexuality *in its entirety* as system or structure, and in accordance to which the places occupied variously by men and women are distributed, as also the series of images and realities'. MDM, then, is a phallocentric model that privileges the masculine sex and through which the feminine sex is subordinated as lack or absence.

Importantly, MDM relies on incestuous desires (often incestuous rape) to account for sex and sexuality. This is achieved by producing ideas of the 'paternal' and 'maternal' as bases of heterosexual desire and affect. MDM is an anthropomorphic model that limits sexuality 'in the narrow cells of the types "couple", "family" and "person", "objects"' (Deleuze and Guattari 1983: 293). The anthropomorphism of MDM obscures the *n* sexualities between human and nonhuman entities. By treating sexuality as activities based in social, economic and political fields, Deleuze and Guattari broaden the scope with what human sexuality can be performed.

To be an 'I' requires internalising all the points of the MDM triangle, even partially. Partial objects (for example, breast, penis, scent and colour) are used to form conceptions of mothers and fathers, and subsequently to develop an Oedipal 'I'. MDM accounts for subjectivity through the use of partial objects – from partial objects. In other words, the assumption of an unified 'I', or whole object, derived from partial objects is questioned by schizoanalysis. Deleuze and Guattari (1983: 46) noted:

> Partial objects are not representations of parental figures or of the basic patterns of family relations; they are parts of desiring-machines, having to do with a process and with relations of production that are both irreducible and prior to anything that may be made to conform to the Oedipal figure.

Hence, any 'I' developed within MDM is done through repression of the dominant Oedipal machine. Instead, partial objects are 'explosions, rotations, vibrations' (44) and 'do not refer in the least to an organism that would function phantasmatically as a lost unity or a totality to come' (324).

Because the MDM roles shift, my analysis demonstrates how teachers manifest multiple roles at different times depending on the desiring-machines that operate upon them. Daughters become mommies; sons become fathers; daughters become fathers; sons become mothers.

My analysis uses the shifts in subjectivity to map the complexity of the teacher in relation to the desiring-machines in which they find themselves.

III. Teaching Schizophrenia: An Oedipal Reading

The sexual conflicts embodied within teaching schizophrenia are similar to other sexual politics that attempt to destabilise the subjugated gendered arrangements in which they are practised. Irigaray (1985: 76) articulated the political possibilities of subordinated arrangements when she stated:

> There is, in an initial phase, perhaps only one 'path,' the one historically assigned to the feminine: that of mimicry. One must assume the feminine role deliberately. Which means already to convert a form of subordination into an affirmation, and thus to begin to thwart it.

Teaching schizophrenia affirms, but rewrites, educational eroticisms and violence based on Oedipally arranged subjects (that is, mommies and women; daddies and men). For instance, Oedipal eroticisms and violence produce analyses that describe sordid educational affairs that 'constitute mental rape, destructive to a woman's ego. [They] are acts of domination, as despicable as the molestation of the daughter by the father' (Rich 1985: 26).[4]

Given my direction, there is risk in not acknowledging an Oedipal reading of teaching schizophrenia as incestuous rape, mental or otherwise. The literature is full of Oedipal vignettes to understand such educational violence. But, I suggest, the continued subjugation of teachers ('daughters') by policy regimes ('fathers') begs a new set of strategies that can be performed within another politic. I contend that the Oedipal politics in education have failed, and particularly *for* teachers. Instead, schizoanalysis illustrates a micro-, street-level, or guerrilla politic that is, in fact, practised everyday in the performing schoolhouse.

Pausing from the Oedipal, Guattari (1996: 206) contrasted schizoanalysis to psychoanalysis. He stated:

> Psychoanalysis transforms and deforms the unconscious by forcing it to pass through the grid of its system of inscription and representation. For psychoanalysis, the unconscious is always already there, genetically programmed, structured, and finalized on objectives of conformity to social norms. For schizoanalysis, it's a question of constructing an unconscious

... with machines, struggles, and arrangements of every nature. There's no question here of transfer, interpretation, or delegation of power to a specialist.

While Oedipus underscores the sexual violence of neo-liberal education policy, it does so in ways that reify familial subjects, replete with gender representations and heterosexual inscriptions. From the Oedipal, then, the article's title enunciates violent sexual acts about how to treat the 'mothers' and 'daughters' of education policy, with an emphasis on the repressions surrounding such power. But there is more.

When fabrications challenge the capitalist axiomatics of schooling, they carry the risk of being considered a 'cheater' (Aviv 2014) in the ethically-flattened, capitalist-oriented, and Oedipally-arranged spaces of education. Oedipal denouncements of cheaters (the example in the opening) treat teaching schizophrenia as an individual pathology. So-called cheaters ostensibly function as 'cockblocks' to the Oedipal desire to lay down with educational alterity (that is, educational mothers: 'achievement', 'learning' and 'success'). The resistance *and* acquiescence to neo-liberal policy is 'value-added' evidence of the bifurcations, contradictions and neuroses of the unfaithful teacher.

Oedipal readings of neo-liberal education policy miss (or ignore) that resistance *and* acquiescence indicate that teachers are working in opposite modes and experimenting with schizoanalysis. Oedipal readings of neo-liberal education policy also miss (or ignore) the sexual mimicry performed by fabrications. Teachers are slut-shamed when fabricating pedagogy and 'cheat' their expected monogamous fidelities to Oedipal schooling. *Bitter Milk* indeed (Grumet 1988). For the relatively few who adopt masculine roles in the psychotic milieus of neo-liberal education policy, the risks in circulating fabrications are levied in ways that emphasise the historical contempt of males in teaching. Masculine teachers are not slut-shamed like their female counterparts, but are, instead, symbolically castrated (again) and humiliated about their bygone educational inabilities by their removed phalluses.[5] Oedipus accentuates male ineffectiveness and humiliation by chiding cheaters for their delay in the murder of neo-liberal policy, of Father.

Cleverly, Oedipal readings of teaching schizophrenia invite the very capitalist axiomatics that produce it to cure this pedagogical 'psychosis'. Cries of cheaters, then, are the coquettish pleas for policy-fathers to maintain the Oedipal and capitalist machines of schooling. Psychoanalysis coaxes teachers to repair Oedipal repressions of gender, sex and sexuality, while insisting that teachers treat 'their' psychoses in a game that has been rigged from the start. An Oedipal politics of schooling simply perpetuates the

> ... perverse apparatus of repression and education, the red-hot irons, and the atrocious procedures have only this meaning: to breed man, to mark him in his flesh, to render him capable of alliance, to form him within the debtor-creditor relation, which on both sides turns out to be a matter of memory – a memory straining to the future (Deleuze and Guattari 1983: 190).

IV. Teaching Schizophrenia: An Anti-Oedipal Reading

Panic maintains the Oedipal arrangements in education while simultaneously delegating responsibility to managerialist approaches to education. Deleuze and Guattari (1983: 64) noted how Oedipal arrangements of teaching are maintained:

> When we learn the instructor, the teacher, is daddy, and the colonel too, and also the mother – *when all the agents of stoical production and anti production are in this way reduced to the figures of familial reproduction* – we can understand why the panicked libido no longer risks abandoning Oedipus, and internalizes it.

Education policy ensures the paternal safety against change, let alone revolution, even if it masquerades as a lever for transformation. And yet, teachers take risks everyday by circulating fabrications within the schoolhouse. Something other than psychosis is happening within the circulation of fabrications: educational desires are being capitulated to, but also, fucked-with or resisted.

Within a schizoanalytic reading, the article's title operates as a colloquial verb that describes sexualities that convert educational subordination into pedagogical affirmation. Teachers are sexually–politically active. This is a deeply frightening thought for many. A schizoanalysis of fabrications signals that something else is going on rather than the coy propositions of daughters–mothers, failed attempts at daddy's murder, or the nonsensical rantings of a genetically 'degenerate' individual. Instead, fabrications produce additional sexes of teaching subjects and signal a politics embodied by resistance, capitulation *and* forms of pleasure to the capitalist axiomatics of schooling. Within a micropolitics of fabrication, you can *stick it to the man* while cashing your check.

A pedagogical schizoanalysis thwarts the sexual positioning bequeathed by the capitalistic axiomatics of schooling by circulating fabrications back into the managerialist machine. The fake-orgasm has a resemblance to the kinds of pedagogical affirmations I am thinking about; but really, there is nothing fake about fabrications as much pleasure is consumed – and much action generated – when circulating fabrications back into the capitalist axiomatics of schooling (for instance, a fabricated test score). Teaching schizophrenia produces a kind of feedback loop within educational managerialism that stylises moments of educational pornography for public viewing (that is, school rankings). The skilled teaching schizophrenic will produce any number of fabrications to combat the audit cultures of schooling, and in turn, produce the *n* sexes of the teaching subject. But, like any politic, there are risks when engaged in a micropolitics of fabrication ...

V. Neo-liberal Education Policy as Dildo

> [Psychoanalysis] never gets through to anyone's desiring machines,
> because it's *stuck* in oedipal figure or structures; it never
> gets through to the social investment of the libido, because
> it's *stuck* in its domestic investments.

> Deleuze 1995: 20, my emphasis

Stuck. Stuck in Oedipus. Stuck on mommies and daddies. Stuck with anthropomorphic representations of sex and sexuality. Stuck being *Human, All Too Human* (Nietzsche 2011).

The sexual–political activity generated from fabrications becomes stuck and masturbatory when not used in opposite modes to the preconscious interests of policy. Here, neo-liberal education policy is a dildo. This educational sex toy is a nonhuman substitution for Daddy, but only affirms policy's phallus because it does not alter, replace or kill the Father. Moreover, this pedagogical masturbation intensifies and prolongs Oedipal penetration – an educational masochism that endures *and* enjoys the pains of neo-liberal policy.

However, fabrications may disparage penetration, and instead, prefer the haptic masturbatory pleasures of this educational sex toy. While still stuck, fabrications circumvent ideas of penetration associated with the phallus. As haptic pleasures, masturbatory fabrications co-opt the phallus, perhaps as penis-envy, in ways that obscure who is fucking who. In other words, masturbatory fabrications obscure who is penetrated and obscures whose penis is being enacted.

Now, the article's title invokes a third register that disparages the Oedipal teaching body by operating as an adjective with negative connotations. Repressed contempt for this body is released when the unconscious desires of teachers are treated as sexual neuroses or perversions, unearthed through psychoanalysis (rather than understood as democratic activity). This contempt is heightened when fabrications do not follow the Oedipal script of incestuous penetration, or penetration at all. Of course, political engagements in the schoolhouse are already contemptible (Webb 2009), but contempt for the schizo-body is aroused when fabrications are stuck on personal pleasure rather than revolutionary movements.

VI. Desiring-Machines and Educational Delirium

Sex, sexuality, and reproduction are central actors in high-tech
myth systems structuring our imaginations of
personal and social possibility.

Haraway 1991: 169

The 'n sexes in a subject' is a phrase that is a bit more understandable once sex and sexuality are construed as produced in desiring-machines. The phrase is also better understood when sex and sexuality are not just confined to something between humans, indeed, as Deleuze and Guattari (1983: 294) noted 'desiring machines are the nonhuman sex'. Within the schizoid moments of the edu-economic machine, teaching bodies use any number of nonhuman things to sex: the bulletin board is a flirtatious window into the classroom, student discipline titillates colleagues, and the pornography of test scores (Webb 2009). Here, imaginations of personal, social, sexual and political possibility begin to surface through the phrase 'the n sexes in a subject'.

The production of interests and desires from desiring machines is crucial to understanding teaching schizophrenia as a collective condition of the pedagogical body. The production of interests and desires is also important to usurp understandings of teaching schizophrenia as a psychotic condition of individuals – even if this is what it feels like at the end of the day. For instance, I have discussed fabrications as the n sexes of teachers in relation to the desiring machines of neo-liberal education policy (and accountability machines in particular). However, teachers are connected to many desiring machines – Oedipal machines, identity machines, gender machines and knowledge machines. It is within these different machines that teachers work, and more importantly where educational desires are produced.

Guattari discussed how desires are produced: 'We distinguish between two ways the social field's invested: preconsciously invested by interests and unconsciously invested by desire' (Deleuze 1995: 18). For instance, governmental investments into the teaching body are interests designed for labour-market production and gross domestic output. Preconscious investments often appear in the guise of ameliorating a deficient teaching body (Ingersoll 2005), where governments train teachers to be accountable, efficient, knowledgeable, and so on. In other words, preconscious investments into teaching bodies are reciprocating forms of support for the capitalist axiomatics of schooling and its Oedipal arrangements.

There is no shortage of unconscious desires invested into schooling by teachers. These desires may be related to a number of socially preferred sensibilities, for example, criticality, equality, caring, fairness, and so on. However, some unconscious desires are discriminatory, that is racist and sexist (Webb 2001). As noted, preconscious investments into schooling are also sexist, heteronormative, neo-liberal and racist (Leonardo 2009). Hence, teachers write and are written by preconscious interests and unconscious desires about their work. Preconscious interests and unconscious desires illustrate how teaching schizophrenia is a cacophony of divergent voices within the teaching body.

Guattari argued that '[t]he way interests are invested can be truly revolutionary, while at the same time leaving in place unconscious investments of desire that aren't revolutionary, that may even be fascistic' (Deleuze 1995: 18–19). Fascistic describes how unconscious desires operate as obsessive (masturbatory) neuroses and psychoses. Further, fascistic describes forces that prevent desire from destroying Oedipal arrangements of subjectivity (hence, circumscribing any kind of educational revolution). Fascistic characterises the desires for the very things that dominate and exploit teachers rather than seeking psychic investments that revolutionise education.

Without recourse to the three tasks of schizoanalysis, pedagogical fabrications can erode teachers' commitments, judgements and desires, if not replace them altogether. Guattari argued likewise, '... there can't be any revolution that serves the interests of oppressed classes until desire itself takes on a revolutionary orientation that actually brings into play unconscious formations' (Deleuze 1995: 19). Fabrications, then, are moments that signal opportunities to engage in the three tasks of schizoanalysis and to develop formations of revolutionary unconscious desires.

VII. Teaching Schizophrenia for Revolutionary Movements

Oedipus betrays teachers. It betrays teachers by limiting sexuality to relations of human reproduction. Oedipus entices the teaching body to sell out their unconscious desires, and pathologises and criminalises them when they do. Oedipus also betrays education. It betrays education through schooling's reproduction of its capitalist axiomatics. Oedipus seduces democratic education to abandon its unconscious desires and, then, repackages and sells them back in the form of the Father. Trapped within these two spaces of reproduction, teaching schizophrenia can devolve into practices of self-pleasure sustained through the very fabrications used in attempts to thwart neo-liberal policy.

Schizoanalysis is a way through these betrayals. The negative task of schizoanalysis seeks to eliminate Oedipal references and constructions within education. Its task is *not* to work through the repressions of neo-liberal governments – our mommy and daddy guilts – but rather, to note how interests and desires are produced and how teachers and schooling promulgate their production. Schizoanalysis provides the teaching body opportunity to examine their constitution qua teacher rather than coming to know oneself Oedipally (and hence, pathologically). Bifo (2008: 30) explained:

> Schizoanalysis ... is intended as a creation of new foci of attention able to induce a bifurcation, a path deviation, a rupture of the closed circuit of obsessive repetition and able to open a new horizon of possibilities for vision and for experience.

Fabrications mark a moment when interests and desires rupture. Fabrications, then, denote moments to develop possibilities for new experiences (and, new experiences for others). Importantly, fabrications provide opportunities to understand the production of desire and to understand the ways it functions within different desiring-machines. Referring to the example in the introduction, what desires are produced when teaching behind a closed door? What is the output of these desires? What are the nonhuman sexualities expressed in these desires? How do these desires counteract the capitalist and Oedipal axiomatics of schooling?

Schizoanalysis is *not* an exercise to align divergent interests and desires. In fact, pedagogical fabrications most poignantly counteract many preconscious interests of policy, but often without much awareness of how unconscious desire is involved in the production and circulation of fabrications. Thus, fabrications, in and of themselves, do not signal an end to Oedipus or the capitalist axiomatics of schooling; but instead, fabrications enact a guerrilla politics that 'alert us to the importance of a rupture or glitch, a break in a dominant regime that itself holds the possibility of something new' (O'Sullivan 2008: 96). Without asking teachers to 'cure' the psychotic capitalist axiomatics of schooling, schizoanalysis provides teachers ways to coexist with them in opposite modes. Nevertheless, schizoanalysis helps identify precise moments of policy neuroses and, with it, the neuroses between policy and teachers. Once teachers coexist in opposite modes with neo-liberal education policy, schizoanalysis enunciates a fourth register of the article's title. Here, the equivocating gerund in the title functions as an adjective to signal a valourised and emphasised politics. Of course, such valourisation is dependent on practising the *n* sexes of a teaching body, and in ways that eliminate Oedipus in education.

Acknowledgements

I acknowledge and thank the anonymous reviewers for their helpful comments. I also thank Paul S. Loeb for his suggestion. I take full responsibility for the result.

Notes

1. I use the phrase 'capitalist axiomatics' in relation to several educational constructs, including 'neo-liberal education policy', 'managerialism' and the 'audit culture'. While related to educational capitalism, I recognise that all these phrases signify different ideas.
2. In the United States.
3. My hyperbole is not intended to dismiss the important literature concerning transsexuality and education. However, I will not discuss the 'the *n* sexes of a subject' in terms of this literature because of my emphasis on nonhuman sexuality.
4. This description is based on incidents between students and instructors in higher education. In contrast, my focus is on the relationships between kindergarten-grade-12 (K-12) schooling, teachers, and education policy.
5. An exegesis of castration and schizoanalysis is beyond the scope of this paper. Nevertheless, Deleuze and Guattari do not treat castration as loss. Instead, castration is 'not the gaping wound ... but the myriad little connections, disjunctions, and conjunctions' (Deleuze and Guattari 1983: 315).

References

Apple, Michael (1995) *Education and Power*, London: Routledge.
Aviv, Rachel (2014) 'Wrong Answer', in *The New Yorker*, 21 July, available at http://www.newyorker.com/magazine/2014/07/21/wrong-answer (accessed 5 April 2015).

Ball, Stephen J. (1997) 'Policy Sociology and Critical Social Research: A Personal Review of Recent Education Policy and Policy Research', *British Educational Research Journal*, 23: 2, pp. 257–74.

Ball, Stephen J. (2001) 'Performativities and Fabrication in the Education Economy: Towards the Performative Society', in Denis Gleeson and Christopher T. Husbands (eds), *The Performing School: Managing, Teaching, and Learning in a Performance Culture*, New York: Routledge, pp. 210–26.

Ball, Stephen J. (2003) 'The Teacher's Soul and the Terrors of Performativity', *Journal of Education Policy*, 18: 2, pp. 215–28.

Bifo (2008) 'Alterity and Desire', in Simon O'Sullivan and Stephen Zepke (eds), *Deleuze, Guattari and the Production of the New*, New York: Continuum, pp. 22–32.

Blackmore, Jill (1993) 'In the Shadow of Men: The Historical Construction of Educational Administration as a Masculinist Enterprise', in Jill Blackmore and Jane Kenway (eds), *Gender Matters in Educational Administration and Policy: A Feminist Introduction*, London: Falmer.

Buchanan, Ian (2008) *Deleuze and Guattari's Anti-Oedipus: A Reader's Guide*, London: Continuum International Publishing Group.

Deleuze, Gilles (1992) 'Postscript on the Societies of Control', October, 59, pp. 3–7.

Deleuze, Gilles (1995) *Negotiations: 1972–1990*, New York: Columbia University Press.

Deleuze Gilles (2004) *Desert Islands and Other Texts: 1953–1974*, New York: Semiotext(e).

Deleuze, Gilles and Félix Guattari (1983) *Anti-Oedipus: Capitalism and Schizophrenia*, trans. Robert Hurley, Mark Seem and Helen R. Lane, Minneapolis, MN: University of Minnesota Press.

Foucault, Michel (1977) *Discipline and Punish: The Birth of the Prison*, trans. Alan Sheridan, New York: Random House, Inc.

Foucault, Michel (1983) 'Preface', in Gilles Deleuze and Félix Guattari, *Anti-Oedipus: Capitalism and Schizophrenia*, Minneapolis, MN: University of Minnesota Press, pp. xi–xiv.

Foucault, Michel (2000) 'Governmentality', in Paul Rabinow (ed.), *Michel Foucault: Power. The Essential Works of Foucault 1954–1984*, vol. 3, New York: The New Press, pp. 201–22.

Grumet, Madeleine R. (1988) *Bitter Milk: Women and Teaching*, Amherst, MA: University of Massachusetts.

Guattari, Félix (1996) 'A Liberation of Desire', in Gary Genesko (ed.), *The Guattari Reader*, Cambridge, MA: Blackwell Publishers, pp. 204–14.

Haraway, Donna (1991) 'A Cyborg Manifesto: Science, Technology, and Socialist-Feminism in the Late Twentieth Century', in *Simians, Cyborgs and Women: The Reinvention of Nature*, New York: Routledge, pp. 149–81.

Ingersoll, Richard (2005) 'The Problem of Underqualified Teachers: A Sociological Perspective', *Sociology of Education*, 78: 2, pp. 175–8.

Irigaray, Luce (1985) *This Sex Which is Not One*, trans. Catherine Porter and Carolyn Burke, New York: Cornell University Press.

Leonardo, Zeus (2009) *Race, Whiteness, and Education*, New York: Routledge.

Martino, Wayne (2012) 'Queering Masculinities as a Basis for Gender Democratization: Toward Embracing a Transgender Imaginary', in Christopher J. Greig and Wayne J. Martino (eds), *Canadian Men and Masculinities: Historical and Contemporary Perspectives*, Toronto: Canadian Scholars' Press Inc.

NCES (2014) 'Digest of Education Statistics 2013, Table 209.10. Number and Percentage Distribution of Teachers in Public and Private Elementary and Secondary Schools, by Selected Teacher Characteristics: Selected Years, 1987–8

Through 2011–12', available at http://nces.ed.gov/fastfacts/display.asp?id=28 (accessed 5 April 2015).

Nietzsche, Friedrich (2011) *Human, All Too Human*, available at http://www.gutenberg.org/files/38145/38145-h/38145-h.htm (accessed 5 April 2015).

O'Sullivan, Simon (2008) 'The Production of the New and the Care of the Self', in Simon O'Sullivan and Stephen Zepke (eds), *Deleuze, Guattari and the Production of the New*, New York: Continuum, pp. 91–103.

Rich, Adrienne (1985) 'Taking Women Students Seriously', in Margo Culley and Cantherine Portuges (eds), *Gendered Subjects: The Dynamics of Feminist Teaching*, London: Routledge, pp. 21–8.

Webb, P. Taylor (2001) 'Reflection and Reflective Teaching: Ways to Improve Pedagogy or Ways to Remain Racist?', *Race, Ethnicity and Education*, 4: 3, pp. 245–52.

Webb, P. Taylor (2009) *Teacher Assemblage*, Rotterdam: SensePublishers.

Notes on Contributors

Ian Buchanan is Professor of Cultural Studies at the University of Wollongong, Australia. He is the founding editor of *Deleuze Studies* and the author of *Dictionary of Critical Theory*.

Ian Cook is a Senior Lecturer at Murdoch University, Australia. His current areas of research involve applying Deleuzian philosophy to the following: the various manifestations of cyberspace (in particular, to different forms of gaming), political ideas, regimes and education.

Elizabeth de Freitas' research focuses on philosophical and socio-cultural studies of education research methods and mathematics teaching and learning. She is co-author of *Mathematics and the Body: Material Entanglements in the Classroom* (Cambridge University Press, 2014) and author of over 40 chapters and articles on a range of educational topics.

Tim Flanagan is a sessional lecturer at the University of Notre Dame, Australia. He received his PhD (Philosophy) from the University of Dundee before teaching variously at the University of Wolverhampton and the University of Greenwich. His research is oriented by the history of philosophy as figured in Deleuze.

jan jagodzinski is a Professor of Art and Media Education in the Department of Secondary Education, University of Alberta, Canada. Please visit his university website for a list of his interests and book publications: http://www.secondaryed.ualberta.ca/people/academicstaff/janjagodzinski. aspx

Jessica Ringrose is Professor of Sociology of Gender and Education, at the Institute of Education, University of London. Her work develops feminist poststructural, psychosocial, 'intersectional', and new materialist approaches to understanding subjectivity, affectivity and assembled power relations. Recent research explores teens' networked sexual cultures and the use of social media, and her new collaborative AHRC funded project is Documenting Digital Feminist Activism:

Deleuze Studies 9.3 (2015): 452–454
DOI: 10.3366/dls.2015.0198
© Edinburgh University Press
www.euppublishing.com/journal/dls

Mapping Feminist Responses to New Media Misogyny and Rape Culture. Her books and reports include: *A Qualitative Study of Children, Young People and 'Sexting'* (London: NSPCC, 2012); *Postfeminist Education?: Girls and the Sexual Politics of Schooling* (Routledge, 2013); *Deleuze and Research Methodologies* (EUP, 2013); and *Children, Sexuality and 'Sexualisation'* (Palgrave, 2015).

Francis Russell is a PhD candidate in cultural and literary studies at Curtin University, Australia, where he tutors in the Department of Art and the School of Media, Culture and Creative Arts. He has published articles on continental theory and contemporary art, and co-edits the contemporary art journal, *Cactaceae*. His doctoral research involves an investigation into continental theory and contemporary notions of resistance.

David Savat is situated at the University of Western Australia. He has a background in political theory and much of his research focuses on the social and political impact of digital media, including around issues of surveillance and political action. He is the Executive Editor of the journal *Deleuze Studies*, and has previously co-edited, with Mark Poster, *Deleuze and New Technology* (Edinburgh University Press, 2009). Most recently he published a major monograph, *Uncoding the Digital: Subjectivity and Action in the Control Society* (Palgrave Macmillan, 2013).

Sam Sellar is a Postdoctoral Research Fellow in the School of Education at the University of Queensland, Australia. Sam draws on social theory and philosophy to study education policy and pedagogies. He is currently involved in projects investigating international and national large-scale educational assessments, data infrastructure in education systems, new accountabilities in schooling and young people's orientations toward their futures. He is co-author (with Lingard, Martino and Rezai-Rashti) of the recently published book *Globalizing Educational Accountabilities* (Taylor & Francis, 2015) and associate editor of two journals: *Critical Studies in Education* and *Discourse: Studies in the Cultural Politics of Education*.

Greg Thompson is a Senior Lecturer at Murdoch University, Australia. He is an Australian Research Council Fellow, is Series Editor of *Local/Global Issues in Education* (Routledge) and an Associate Editor of *Discourse: Studies in the Cultural Politics of Education*. His recent books are *National Testing* (Routledge, 2015) and *Who is the Good High School Student?* (Cambria Press, 2011).

P. Taylor Webb is an Associate Professor in the Department of Educational Studies at the University of British Columbia, Canada. He teaches and researches education policy in relation to issues of governmentality, including bio- and micro-politics.

Printed and bound by CPI Group (UK) Ltd, Croydon, CR0 4YY

14/03/2025

01833346-0012